Arab Christians and the Qur'an from the Origins of Islam to the Medieval Period

History of Christian-Muslim Relations

Editorial Board

Jon Hoover (*University of Nottingham*)
Sandra Toenies Keating (*Providence College*)
Tarif Khalidi (*American University of Beirut*)
Suleiman Mourad (*Smith College*)
Gabriel Said Reynolds (*University of Notre Dame*)
Mark Swanson (*Lutheran School of Theology at Chicago*)
David Thomas (*University of Birmingham*)

VOLUME 35

Christians and Muslims have been involved in exchanges over matters of faith and morality since the founding of Islam. Attitudes between the faiths today are deeply coloured by the legacy of past encounters, and often preserve centuries-old negative views.

The History of Christian-Muslim Relations, Texts and Studies presents the surviving record of past encounters in a variety of forms: authoritative, text editions and annotated translations, studies of authors and their works and collections of essays on particular themes and historical periods. It illustrates the development in mutual perceptions as these are contained in surviving Christian and Muslim writings, and makes available the arguments and rhetorical strategies that, for good or for ill, have left their mark on attitudes today. The series casts light on a history marked by intellectual creativity and occasional breakthroughs in communication, although, on the whole beset by misunderstanding and misrepresentation. By making this history better known, the series seeks to contribute to improved recognition between Christians and Muslims in the future.

A number of volumes of the *History of Christian-Muslim Relations* series are published within the subseries *Christian-Muslim Relations. A Bibliographical History*.

The titles published in this series are listed at *brill.com/hcmr*

Arab Christians and the Qur'an from the Origins of Islam to the Medieval Period

Edited by

Mark Beaumont

BRILL

LEIDEN | BOSTON

Cover illustration: translation by Mark Beaumont of Qur'an 4:171.

Library of Congress Cataloging-in-Publication Data

Names: Woodbrooke-Mingana Symposium on Arab Christianity and Islam (7th : 2013 : Birmingham, England) | Beaumont, Ivor Mark, editor.
Title: Arab Christians and the Qur'an from the origins of Islam to the medieval period / edited by Mark Beaumont.
Description: Leiden ; Boston : Brill, 2018. | "These essays originated in the seventh Woodbrooke-Mingana Symposium on Arab Christianity held in Birmingham, UK, in 2013"—ECIP data view. | Includes bibliographical references and index.
Identifiers: LCCN 2018001097 | ISBN 9789004360747 (E-book) | ISBN 9789004360693 (hardback : alk. paper)
Subjects: LCSH: Qur'an —Christian interpretations—History—Congresses. | Christians—Middle East—History—Congresses.
Classification: LCC BP130.45 .W66 2013 | DDC 261.2/7089927—dc23
LC record available at https://lccn.loc.gov/2018001097

Typeface for the Latin, Greek, and Cyrillic scripts: "Brill". See and download: brill.com/brill-typeface.

ISSN 1570-7350
ISBN 978-90-04-36069-3 (hardback)
ISBN 978-90-04-36074-7 (e-book)

Contents

Notes on Contributors VII
Introduction IX

1 The Qur'an in Christian Arabic Literature: A Cursory Overview 1
Sidney H. Griffith

2 Qur'ānic Textual Archaeology. Rebuilding the Story of the Destruction of Sodom and Gomorra 20
Juan Pedro Monferrer-Sala

3 Manipulation of the Qur'an in the Epistolary Exchange between al-Hāshimī and al-Kindī 50
Sandra T. Keating

4 'Abd al-Masīḥ al-Kindī on the Qur'an 66
Emilio Platti

5 'Ammār al-Baṣrī: Ninth Century Christian Theology and Qur'anic Presuppositions 83
Mark Beaumont

6 'They Find Him Written with them.' The Impact of Q 7:157 on Muslim Interaction with Arab Christianity 106
Gordon Nickel

7 With the Qur'an in Mind 131
David Thomas

8 Early Islamic Perspectives of the Apostle Paul as a Narrative Framework for Taḥrīf 150
Michael F. Kuhn

9 Būluṣ ibn Rajā' on the History and Integrity of the Qur'an: Copto-Islamic Controversy in Fatimid Cairo 174
David Bertaina

Bibliography 197
Index 213

Notes on Contributors

Mark Beaumont

(PhD, Open University, 2003) is Research Associate at London School of Theology, United Kingdom. His most recent monograph, edited with Maha El-Kaisy Friemuth, is *al-Radd al-jamīl*—A Fitting Refutation of the Divinity of Jesus from the Evidence of the Gospel, *Attributed to Abū Ḥāmid al-Ghazālī*, (Leiden: Brill, 2016).

David Bertaina

(PhD, Catholic University of America, 2007) is Associate Professor in the History Department at the University of Illinois at Springfield, USA. His teaching expertise is on Late Antiquity and the Medieval Middle East and his research focuses on the history of Christian-Muslim encounters.

Sidney H. Griffith

(PhD, Catholic University of America, 1978) is Ordinary Professor Emeritus in the Department of Semitic and Egyptian Languages and Literatures, in the School of Arts and Sciences, at the Catholic University of America, Washington, DC, USA. His areas of scholarly interest are Syriac Patristics, Christian Arabic Literature, and the history of Christian/Muslim relations, especially within the World of Islam and in the Early Islamic period. Recent publications include, *The Church in the Shadow of the Mosque: Christians and Muslims in the World of Islam* (Princeton, NJ: Princeton University Press, 2007); *The Bible in Arabic: The Scriptures of the "People of the Book" in the Language of Islam* (Princeton, NJ: Princeton University Press, 2013).

Sandra T. Keating

(PhD Catholic University of America, 2001) is Associate Professor of Theology at Providence College in Rhode Island, USA. She has published *Defending the 'People of Truth' in the Early Islamic Period: The Christian Apologies of Abu Ra'itah* (Leiden: Brill, 2006).

Michael F. Kuhn

(PhD, Middlesex University, 2017) is Assistant Professor at The Arab Baptist Theological Seminary, Mansourieh, Lebanon.

Juan Pedro Monferrer-Sala
(PhD, University of Granada, 1996) is Full Professor of Arabic Studies at the University of Cordova, Spain. His most recent publications include "An Egyptian Arabic witness of the apocryphal epistle to the Laodiceans", *JCS* 18 (2016), pp. 57–83.

Gordon Nickel
(PhD, University of Calgary, Canada, 2004) directs the Centre for Islamic Studies at South Asia Institute of Advanced Christian Studies in Bangalore, India. He is the author of *Narratives of Tampering in the Earliest Commentaries on the Qur'an* (Leiden: Brill, 2011).

Emilio Giuseppe Platti
(PhD, Katholieke Universiteit (KU), Leuven, 1980) is Professor Emeritus at Katholieke Universiteit (KU), Leuven, Belgium. He is a Member of the Institut Dominican d'études Orientales in Cairo, Egypt. His publications include *Yahyâ Ibn 'Adî. Théologien chrétien et philosophe arabe*, Leuven, 1983, and *Islam, Friend or Foe?* (Louvain Monographs, 37), Louvain, 2008.

David Thomas
(PhD, Lancaster University, 1983) is Professor of Christianity and Islam at Birmingham University. Among his recent publications are *The Polemical Works of 'Alī al-Ṭabarī* (Leiden: Brill, 2016) and *Christian-Muslim Relations. A Bibliographical History, vols 1–11* (Leiden: Brill, 2009–17).

Introduction

When Arab armies swept through the Middle East in the 640's, they not only conquered largely Christian populations but also brought with them new scriptures they believed had been revealed by God, which claimed to have a message for Christians. The ensuing relationship between the Muslim rulers and their Christian subjects was influenced by the teaching of the Qur'an concerning Jesus who was only a messenger and not the Son of God as Christians believed. Jesus' death by crucifixion and subsequent resurrection from death were cast into doubt by the Qur'an. Muslims interpreted the Qur'an to say that the scriptures of the Christians were corrupt. How did Christians respond to these criticisms of their convictions? They were at least able to maintain their faith and practice after annual payments of a head tax. As time passed, conversions to Islam became more frequent not only to avoid taxation, but to gain opportunities for advancement in society. The purpose of Christian apologetic writing about Islam in the early centuries of the Islamic Era was both to enable Christians to defend their faith in the face of Muslim critique, and to stem the flow of Christians becoming Muslims. The contributions in this collection of essays are focused on the time frame between the arrival of Islam and the end of the Abbasid period in the late thirteenth century when Christians had become a minority in the Middle East.

The focus of these chapters reflects the importance of the topic of Christian attitudes to the Qur'an from the coming of Islam to the largely Christian Middle East. When Christians began to interpret the Qur'an they found many references to Biblical characters and themes. However, the overall message conveyed by the Scriptures of the Muslims seemed to demand a reinterpretation of those Biblical messages. The study of Arab Christian responses to the Qur'an has been developing over recent years. The publication of Clare Wilde's history of Christian attitudes to the Qur'an in 2014 gives a panoramic view of the topic.[1] The examination of detailed aspects of that history made in the following chapters will enhance the study of the relationship between Christians and Muslims in the formative centuries after the arrival of Islam.

The relationship of Christians in the Arab world to the scriptures of the Muslim majority was the topic of the seventh Woodbrooke-Mingana Symposium on Arab Christianity and Islam held from 16–20 September 2013 at Woodbrooke Quaker Study Centre, Selly Oak, Birmingham. The Symposium has been organised on a four yearly cycle by Professor David Thomas, of

---

1 Wilde, C., *Approaches to the Qur'ān in early Christian Arabic texts*, Palo Alto, 2014.

Birmingham University. On behalf of the participants in the series of Symposia, I would like to offer our grateful thanks to him for his leadership in the promotion of the study of Arab Christianity and Islam. The first volume in the series edited by David entitled *The History of Christian-Muslim Relations* was published by Brill in 2003 and this contained the collected papers from the fourth Woodbrooke-Mingana Symposium held on 12–16 September 2001. It is indeed a fitting tribute to David's commitment to publication that this volume appears in the same series after more than thirty other books making available research into the relationship between Arab Christians and Muslims.

The collected papers presented here are prefaced by a guest contribution from Sidney Griffith who has been a regular participant in the Mingana Symposia, but who was unable to be present at the 2013 event. We are grateful for his analysis of Arab Christian attitudes to the Qur'an that he has presented here entitled, 'The Qur'an in Christian Arabic Literature: A Cursory Overview.' Griffith argues that when Christian Arabic writers in the early Islamic period quoted from or alluded to the Qur'an in their works, or even sometimes built their apologetic or polemical arguments on proof-texts drawn from the Qur'an, they were deflecting challenges to Christian thought and practice, and commending the credibility of Christian doctrines in terms that would carry weight within the Arabic-speaking, Islamic milieu in which Christians and Muslims lived together. Due to its role as the first Arabic book, the Qur'an's diction and idiom, even its distinctly religious vocabulary, entered the common parlance not only of Muslims, but the spoken and written Arabic of Jews, Christians, and Muslims alike. Christian Arab authors made use of proof-texts from the Qur'an to enlist the authority of the Islamic scripture in their apologetic efforts to commend the veracity of Christian doctrines, albeit that these same doctrines were in most instances at variance with the Qur'an's own teaching, and that there was a vast difference between the Christian and Muslim readings of the same texts.

In the first of the collected papers from the seventh Mingana Symposium, Juan-Pedro Monferrer-Sala examines how the Qur'an comments on biblical personalities and stories that Christians had already interpreted for generations before the arrival of the message brought by the Prophet Muhammad. Christian and Jewish versions of biblical stories in Arabic likely formed part of the narrative context in which the Qur'an emerged. He compares the story of the destruction of Sodom and Gomorrah in the text of Genesis, in Rabbinic commentary, and in the Qur'an, and seeks to examine certain compositional and organisational aspects of the text to see how the story was received into the Qur'an. He argues that a wholly-narrative text lacking in additional elements, clearly amassed various discursive accretions over time. These were of three kinds: narrative, homiletic and paraenetic, their essential function being to enable people to learn lessons from the past. He identifies a pre-Qur'anic Arabic version which was subsequently adapted, disseminated and glossed to suit the requirements of the Qur'anic text that included not only the pre-Qur'anic text, but also additional elements of the story (narrative, homiletic, and paraenetic), some of which must already have been in circulation prior to the arrival of Islam.

The composition of the Qur'an became a topic of concern for Arab Christians in the early period of Muslim rule. Muslims claimed that the Qur'an came down intact from heaven via the angel Gabriel and that Muhammad had been faithful and faultless in the recitation of the message. Christian questioning of the reliability of these claims was most clearly expressed in the correspondence of al-Kindī with al-Hāshimī which Sandra Keating argues was written in the second half of the 820's. She believes that the author of al-Kindī's *Risāla* was a Syrian Orthodox (Jacobite) Christian, associated with the court of al-Ma'mūn, and in conversation with a Muslim, al-Hāshimī, who had invited him to Islam. She points out that al-Kindī had extremely detailed knowledge of the Qur'an and its early canonization, and that he indicates that some of what was once common knowledge of the collection and canonization of the 'official' *muṣḥaf* of the Qur'an had been lost because it was suppressed. Keating regards al-Kindī's *Risāla* as a non-official witness to the redaction of the Qur'an, as well as its early collection, in a carefully ordered account. While the accuracy of this account might be questioned, there is no doubt that al-Kindī is not interested in supporting the 'official version' of the origins of the Qur'an. This alone makes the *Risāla* a valuable text for understanding the early process of the reception of the Qur'an. Her particular focus is to show how the author turns the charge of *taḥrīf* against the Muslims, arguing that it is the Qur'an that was manipulated during its collection, and that the text the Muslims possess is not completely reliable.

Emilio Platti's contribution to the study of the al-Hāshimī-al-Kindī correspondence is a detailed study of the second part of al-Kindī's work concerning the authenticity of Qur'an. He agrees with Keating that 'Abdallāh al-Hāshimī and al-Kindī were themselves high ranking dignitaries at al-Ma'mūn's court, as suggested by al-Kindī's report of a speech given by the caliph to those who attended his counsel. Platti is more concerned than Keating to analyse the Muslim sources cited by the author relating to the collection of the Qur'an. He notes firstly, the argument of al-Kindī that the text of the Qur'an contains borrowed stories and religious material from two sources, the Torah and the Gospel. Secondly, according to al-Kindī, people were reading the Qur'an in so many different ways that the Caliph 'Uthmān decided to intervene and to ask some people to collect all available Qur'anic material. Platti shows that al-Kindī's information about the collection of the Qur'an is in accord with some Islamic traditions which are older than the Islamic material edited by Bukhārī (d. 870), Ṭabarī (d. 923) and Ibn Abī Dāwūd (d. 929). Platti is convinced that this early material found in al-Kindī's *Risāla* should be included in any future research on the collection of the Qur'an.

Mark Beaumont provides a close reading of the apologetic writing of ʿAmmār al-Baṣrī, a theologian from the East Syrian church who was active in the first half of the ninth century, to evaluate ʿAmmār's approach to the Qur'an. ʿAmmār defends the truth of Christianity by arguing that the first Christian disciples spread the faith not by human means but by reliance on divine signs that, according to the Qur'an, could not be copied. When Muhammad brought signs from God they were in continuity with earlier signs, such as the gospel that Jesus brought. Therefore, Muslims must accept that Christianity was accompanied by these signs to which the Qur'an testifies. However, the message of the Qur'an is not actually in continuity with the message that Jesus brought in the Christian Gospels. Since Muslims allege that Christians must have corrupted the pure teaching of Jesus, ʿAmmār mounts a defence of the authenticity of the Gospels by expressing astonishment that the disciples would have invented such a distasteful religion that centred on the worship of a crucified man, or such a narrow minded religion that prohibited re-marriage after divorce. The accusation of corruption is rather turned against Muslims who have to account for the way the Qur'an has altered the teaching of the Gospels. This is a theology of engagement that demonstrates attention to Muslim concerns that relies on carefully reasoned argument, and models for future generations of Christians, even to our own times, a respectful apologetic stance that does not refrain from asking Muslims the most difficult questions about the Qur'an.

Gordon Nickel follows up the theme of the Muslim accusation that Christians corrupted their scriptures. He studies the passages in the Qur'an that relate explicitly to Christians and their scriptures, both Old and New Testaments. He engages in a critical review of the interpretation of these texts in Qur'an commentary that expects the Christian scriptures to predict the coming of the Prophet Muhammad. He notes that there is a persistent tradition in Muslim thought and practice to search for verses in the Bible that can be claimed as prophecies of Islam's messenger. On the other hand, often at the same time and sometimes from the same writers, a Muslim accusation of biblical falsification has been based on the perception that no prophecies of Islam's messenger are to be found in the Bible.

David Thomas asks two related questions: How seriously did Christians take Islam in the early centuries of the Islamic era, and how seriously did they take the Qur'an? In a survey of key Muslim writers, he notes that in the mid eighth century, John of Damascus does not seem to think he needs to explain himself at length, nor to produce arguments to establish that Islam is a 'deceptive superstition' or that Muhammad is 'false'. He appears confident that his views are historically and logically sound and that Muslim opponents have no basis for claiming any validity in their beliefs. A more positive attitude to Islam and the Qur'an is seen by Thomas in the late eighth century writing of Timothy I, Patriarch of the East Syrian church. In his answers to questions posed by the Muslim Caliph al-Mahdī, Timothy gives no impression of feeling under threat or of being pressed intellectually to find an answer that was not immediately forthcoming. He seems to be aware that al-Mahdī is not equipped with the intellectual equipment either to follow what he says or to produce challenging responses. The most detailed interpretation of the Qur'an among Arabic-speaking Christians comes from about 1200 by the monk Paul of Antioch, who was made Melkite Bishop of Sidon. He holds that the Qur'an is limited in scope. It is partial because it is intended specifically for the *jāhilī* Arabs and no-one else, and it is temporary because as its teachings are progressively understood so their value is reduced through the process of recognising the far fuller truths they point to in the books of the Bible. The Qur'an is effectively a provisional version of the Bible, simplified down to give only glimpses of the full truth for minds that were particularly resistant. Arabic-speaking Christians in the early centuries of the Islamic era persisted in their attitude that they were superior to their counterparts. Thomas argues that this will have served an obvious psychological purpose, and helped them in part to continue believing that they were still part of God's purpose even in the face of his apparent abandonment of them. But it also made it difficult for them to approach Muslims with respect and a measure of regard.

Mike Kuhn studies the way that the Apostle Paul came to be regarded by Muslims as the chief corrupter of the pure gospel brought by Jesus. He points out that early Muslim apologists were content to argue that the Christians had misunderstood their Scriptures by corrupting their meaning. By the eleventh century, the view championed by Ibn Ḥazm and 'Abd al-Jabbār that Paul had led the first followers of Jesus astray, emerged to dominate subsequent Muslim attitudes to the corruption of the Christian scriptures. Kuhn notes three substantial sources of the Pauline narrative in early Islam. Each of these narratives is characterized by its objectives or narrative purposes. Firstly, Paul corrupted the laws or practices of the true religion. Secondly, Paul corrupted the doctrine of *tawḥīd*. Finally, Paul corrupted the preceding Scriptures. These three narratives of the Apostle Paul became integral to the developed Muslim doctrine of *taḥrīf*.

David Bertaina studies how an Egyptian Muslim convert to Christianity in the tenth to eleventh centuries wrote about the Qur'an. Paul (Būluṣ) ibn Rajā' (c. 950/60–c. 1020) produced a critique of Islam and the Qur'an, entitled *Clarity in Truth*, that was well-known in Fatimid Egypt. Bertaina shows that Ibn Rajā' reads parts of the Qur'an to agree with the Bible and states that the Qur'an regards the Bible as an authority. He considers many verses in the Arabic text beautiful. But on the other hand, Bertaina highlights how Ibn Rajā' finds the Qur'an problematic because of the lack of a consensus over its interpretation, the problematic means of its disclosure, its divergent readings in the seven schools, omissions from earlier versions of the text, its arbitrary canonization process, various word and phrase inconsistencies and repetitions, and outright contradictions. As a result, Ibn Rajā' holds the Qur'an to be a defective message. Bertaina argues that Ibn Rajā''s *Clarity in Truth* demonstrates that passages from the Qur'an shaped Coptic Christian identity and their views of Islam, and that Ibn Rajā's use of the Qur'an also reveals how Copts reinterpreted its passages to endorse their confessional identity.

CHAPTER 1

The Qur'an in Christian Arabic Literature: A Cursory Overview

Sidney H. Griffith

Prolegomena

When in the course of the eighth century the Christian communities at home in the newly proclaimed World of Islam adopted Arabic as a vehicle of ecclesiastical thought and expression, and even began to translate their scriptures into Arabic, the Qur'an itself also found its way into Christian discourse. While there is some evidence that Greek-speaking Christians in Palestine around the year 700 were already familiar with verses from the Qur'an,[1] the Arabic scripture is first mentioned by name in a Christian text in an apologetic work written in Syriac that was in all probability originally composed not long after the year 720.[2] In it a monk apologist for Christianity speaks to his Muslim interlocutor of the 'Qur'an, which Muhammad taught you.'[3] It would have been just about at this same time that St. John of Damascus (d.c. 749) brought up the Qur'an in the *De Haeresibus* section of his summary presentation of Christian faith, the *Fount of Knowledge*, composed in Greek. There, as the last of the heresies he was to discuss (no. 100), St. John spoke very disparagingly of the heresy that he described as 'the still-prevailing deceptive superstition of the Ishmaelites, the fore-runner of the Antichrist,' and he went on to say that Muhammad 'spread rumours that a scripture (*γρφην*) was

1 See S.H. Griffith, 'Anastasios of Sinai, the *Hodegos* and the Muslims', *Greek Orthodox Theological Review* 32, 1987, pp. 341–58.

2 See S.H. Griffith, 'Disputing with Muslims in Syriac: The Case of the Monk of Bêt Ḥālê with a Muslim Emir', *Hugoye* 3, 2000, http://syrcom.cua.edu/Hugoye/Vol3No1/HV3N1/Griffith.html. See also R.G. Hoyland, *Seeing Islam as Others Saw It: A Survey and Evaluation of Christian, Jewish and Zoroastrian Writings on Early Islam*, Princeton, 1997, pp. 465–72. See now the full text published and translated into English in D.G.K. Taylor, 'The Disputation between a Muslim and a Monk of Bēt Ḥālē: Syriac Text and Annotated English Translation', in S.H. Griffith and S. Grebenstein, eds, *Christsein in der islamischen Welt: Festschrift für Martin Tamcke zum 60. Geburtstag*, Wiesbaden, 2015, pp. 187–242.

3 Hoyland, *Seeing Islam as Others Saw It*, p. 471; Taylor, 'The Disputation between a Muslim and a Monk', pp. 206 and 229.

 | DOI 10.1163/9789004360747_002

brought down to him from heaven.'[4] Throughout the discussion, and in the course of his polemics against Islam, John of Damascus alludes to or quotes passages from the Qur'an, recognizably but usually not literally. Of the text itself he says, 'This Muhammad, as it has been mentioned, composed many idle tales, on each one of which he prefixed a title,'[5] and John goes on to mention some of the names of the *sūras*, again not accurately, but recognizably: the Woman, God's Camel, the Table, the Heifer. As Robert Hoyland has remarked, 'This composition exerted great influence upon the language, tone and content of subsequent Byzantine polemic against Islam.'[6] And it was a negative, even hostile tone. But even though he was himself in all probability an Arabic-speaking Aramean, writing in Greek within the World of Islam, the attitude displayed in John of Damascus' Greek text was not to be typical of the approach to Muhammad, the Qur'an and Islam of the Arabic-speaking Christians writing in Arabic in the same milieu some years later,[7] albeit as we shall see below a similar attitude is displayed in at least one anonymous Arabic text written by a Christian in the next century, a text that includes numerous quotations from the Qur'an, cited largely for polemical purposes.[8]

---

4 D.J. Sahas, John of Damascus on Islam: 'The Heresy of the Ishmaelites', Leiden, 1972, p. 133. See R. Le Coz, ed., Jean Damascène: Écrits sur Islam, Paris, 1992. See also S.H. Griffith, 'John of Damascus and the Church in Syria in the Umayyad Era: The Intellectual and Cultural Milieu of Orthodox Christians in the World of Islam', Hugoye 11, 2008, http://syrcom.cua.edu/Hugoye/Vol11No2/HV11N2/Griffith.html, Hoyland, Seeing Islam as Others Saw It, pp. 480–9.

5 Sahas, *John of Damascus on Islam*, p. 137.

6 Hoyland, *Seeing Islam as Others Saw It*, p. 488.

7 See M.N. Swanson, 'Beyond Prooftexting: Approaches to the Qur'ān in Some Early Arabic Christian Apologies', *The Muslim World* 88, 1998, pp. 297–319; S.H. Griffith, 'The Qur'ān in Arab Christian Texts: The Development of an Apologetic Argument: Abū Qurrah in the *Maǧlis* of al-Ma'mūn', *Parole de l'Orient* 24, 1999, pp. 203–33.

8 This is the fictional correspondence, composed in Arabic by a now unknown Christian, between a Muslim character, significantly named 'Abd Allāh ibn Ismā'īl al-Hāshimī and a Christian character named 'Abd al-Masīḥ ibn Isḥāq al-Kindī, in which the latter polemically disposes of the claims advanced in behalf of Islam, Muhammad and the Qur'an by the former. The text was translated into Latin under the auspices of Peter the Venerable in the twelfth century. See J.M. Sendino, 'Al-Kindi, Apologia del Christianismo', *Miscelanea Comillas* 11 and 12, 1949, pp. 339–460. An English translation is available in N.A. Newman, *Early Christian-Muslim Dialogue: A Collection of Documents from the First Three Islamic Centuries (632–900A.D, Translations with Commentary*, Hatfield, 1993, pp. 355–545. For discussion of the text see B. Landron, *Chrétiens et Musulmans en Irak: Attitudes Nestoriennes vis-à-vis de l'islam*, Paris, 1994, pp. 78–89; E. Platti, 'Des Arabes chrétiens et le Coran: Pérennité d'une polémique', in D. De Smet, G. de Callataÿ, and J.M.F. Van Reeth, eds, *Al-Kitāb: La sacralité du texte dans le monde de l'Islam*, Bruxelles, Louvain-la-Neuve, Leuven, 2004, pp. 333–45;

The Qur'an in Christian Arabic Texts

In Christian Arabic apologetic texts generally one finds some ambivalence about the Qur'an. On the one hand, some authors argue that it cannot possibly be a book of divine revelation, citing in evidence its composite, and, as they saw the matter, its all too human origins.[9] But on the other hand, its literary and religious power in the new cultural milieu, the sheer beauty of its language, especially in oral recitation,[10] proved impossible for them to resist. So given the progressive enculturation of Middle Eastern Christian communities into the Arabic-speaking World of Islam from the eighth century onward, most Christian writers in Arabic themselves commonly employed Qur'anic words and phrases in their own parlance.[11] Inevitably its language suffused their religious consciousness and they readily used Qur'anic terms to translate Christian concepts, such as referring to 'Christians' themselves as 'Nazarenes' (*al-naṣārā*), and the 'apostles' as 'messengers' (*al-rusul*), to mention only two among many such examples. Some writers even built their apologetic arguments in behalf of the truthfulness of Christianity on a certain interpretation of particular verses from the Islamic scripture. In short, while Christian apologists argued that the Qur'an is not a canonical scripture on the level of the Torah or the Gospel, they nevertheless also, and not infrequently, quoted from it more or less accurately both in testimonies to the truth of Christian teachings and as a source of felicitous Arabic expression. Alternatively, some Syriac and Christian writers in Arabic of the ninth century were also very much alive to what they perceived to be the original Christian inspiration of much of the Qur'an. They argued that the Qur'an's original Christian origins were obscured by the distortion and alteration of its text and the misappropriation of its meanings at the hands of those Muslim writers who would later thwart this early expression of a burgeoning Arab Christianity. We may briefly consider an example of each of these approaches to the Arabic Qur'an on the part of

P. Bruns, 'Briefwechsel min einem Muslim: Al-Kindis Apologie des Christentums (9. Jh.)', in S.H. Griffith and S. Grebenstein, *Christsein in der islamischen Welt*, pp. 269–81. See also the article by Sandra Keating in the present volume.

9 See in particular the al-Hāshimī/al-Kindī correspondence mentioned just above in footnote 8.

10 On this point see N. Kermani, *God is Beautiful: The Aesthetic Experience of the Quran*, Cambridge, 2015, (English trans. of *Gott ist schön*, Munich, 2007).

11 See S.H. Griffith, 'The Qur'an in Arab Christian Texts: The Development of an Apologetical Argument: Abū Qurah in the *Mağlis* of al-Ma'mūn', *Parole de l'Orient* 24, 1999, pp. 203–33.

Arabic-speaking Christian writers who lived and wrote in the World of Islam in the early Islamic period, up to 1300.

The Qur'an as a Font of Scriptural Proof-Texts

Within the context of its own inter-religious controversies, the Islamic scripture in several instances demands that its adversaries produce proof (*al-burhān*) for the position they are espousing in contrast to what the Qur'an proclaims. For example, in the controversy with Jews and Christians, the Qur'an says, 'They say, "No one will enter the Garden except those who are Jews or Nazarenes/ Christians (*al-naṣārā*)." Those are their wishes. Say, "Produce your proof (*burhānakum*) if you are telling the truth"' (Q 2:111). It seems that the proof envisioned in this verse is scriptural proof, for in other passages where the term 'proof' (*al-burhān*) is mentioned in the inter-religious context it is clear that the 'proof' is the Qur'an itself. For example, in the context of its critique of Christian doctrine, the Qur'an says in regard to itself, 'O People, proof (*burhān*) has come to you from your Lord; He has sent down a clear light [i.e. the Qur'an] to you' (Q 4:174). Similarly, in the context of the rejection of polytheism, the Qur'an speaks in reference to itself and to earlier scriptures when it advises Muhammad, 'Say, "Produce your proof (*burhānakum*). This is the scriptural recollection (*dhikr*) of those with me, and the scriptural recollection (*dhikr*) of those before me"' (Q 21:24).[12] Given this Qur'anic call for scriptural proof for the positions espoused by those whose teachings it criticizes; it is perhaps not surprising that some Christian Arabic writers actually sought some of their own proof texts in the Qur'an itself, or listed quotations from the Qur'an along

12 It is clear that the term *dhikr* in this passage refers to the recollection of scripture passages, perhaps liturgical pericopes recounting events in salvation history that are thought of as being recorded in the heavenly *kitāb*. See A. Neuwirth, 'Vom Rezitationstext über die Liturgie zum Kanon', in S. Wild, ed., *The Qur'ān as Text,* Leiden, 1996, pp. 69–105. One recent translator of the Qur'ān actually renders the term *dhikr* in this verse with the word 'scripture'. See M.A.S. Abdel Haleem, trans., *The Qur'an: A New Translation*, Oxford, 2004, Q 21:24, p. 204. In two other passages the Qur'an uses the phrase, *ahl al-dhikr* as a virtual synonym for *ahl al-kitāb*; see Q 16:43 and 21:7. It is interesting too to note in this connection that al-Ṭabarī listed *dhikr* as one of the names of the Qur'an, alongside the names: *qur'ān, furqān*, and *kitāb*. See D.A. Madigan, *The Qur'ān's Self-Image: Writing and Authority in Islam's Scripture*, Princeton, 2001, p. 130.

with quotations from the Bible among the proofs from scripture offered in support of the religious veracity of a position they were defending.[13]

One of the most interesting Arab Christian texts to cite the Qur'an in testimony to the truth of Christian doctrines is actually one of the earliest Christian Arabic texts we know.[14] It is anonymous and its first modern editor gave it the name it still carries in English, *On the Triune Nature of God*; it was composed in all likelihood in the third quarter of the eighth century.[15] The author quotes from the Qur'an explicitly and in his work he uses both the vocabulary and the thought patterns of the Qur'an. In an important way the vocabulary of the Qur'an had become his religious lexicon. This feature of the work is readily evident in the poetical introduction to the text, which by allusion and the choice of words and phrases echoes the diction and style of the Qur'an.[16] As Mark Swanson has rightly remarked, 'The text simply *is* profoundly Qur'anic.'[17] One can see it even in English translation, as in this brief passage from the opening prayer:

---

13 It is interesting to note in passing that some Arab Christian apologists named their treatises, *Kitāb al-burhān*. The ninth century, 'Nestorian' writer, ʿAmmār al-Baṣrī is a case in point and the editor of his text knew of seven other instances of Christian apologetic texts with this same name. See M. Hayek, *ʿAmmār al-Baṣrī: apologies et controverses*, Beirut, 1977, pp. 32–3.

14 There is another early Arab Christian text from the late eighth century or the very early ninth century, a fragmentary papyrus, in which the author quotes the Qur'an and names the *sūras* from which he quotes. But the text is too fragmentary to allow one to say much about the author's overall purposes. See G. Graf, 'Christliche-arabische Texte. Zwei Disputationen zwischen Muslimen und Christen', in F. Bilabel and A. Grohmann, eds, *Griechische, koptische und arabische Texte zur Religion und religiösen Literatur in Ägyptens Spätzeit*, Heidelberg, 1934, pp. 8–23.

15 See M.D. Gibson, *An Arabic Version of the Acts of the Apostles and the Seven Catholic Epistles, with a Treatise on the Triune Nature of God*, London, 1899, pp. 74–107 (Arabic); and 2–36 (English); M. Gallo, trans., *Palestinese anonimo: omelia arabo-cristiana dell'VIII secolo*, Rome, 1994. See also S.K. Samir, 'The Earliest Arab Apology for Christianity (c. 750)', in S.K. Samir and J. Nielsen, eds, *Christian Arabic Apologetics during the Abbasid Period (750–1258)*, Leiden, 1994, pp. 57–114. See now M.N. Swanson, 'An Apology for the Christian Faith', in S. Noble and A. Treiger, eds, *The Orthodox Church in the Arab World, 700–1700: An Anthology of Sources*, DeKalb, 2014, pp. 40–59, and 292–7.

16 See Samir, 'The Earliest Arab Apology', pp. 69–70; Swanson, 'Beyond Prooftexting', pp. 305–8.

17 Swanson, 'Beyond Prooftexting', p. 308.

We ask you, O God, by Your mercy and your power,
to put us among those who know your truth,
follow Your will, and avoid your wrath,
[who] praise Your beautiful names, (Q 7:180)
and speak of Your exalted similes. (cf. Q 30:27)
You are the compassionate One,
the merciful, the most compassionate;
You are seated on the throne, (Q 7:54)
You are higher than creatures,
You fill up all things.[18]

Shortly after this prayer, the author makes a statement that may well serve as an expression of his purpose in composing his work. Again, the attentive reader can hear the Qur'anic overtones clearly. The author says,

> We praise you, O God, and we adore you and we glorify you in your creative Word and your holy, life-giving Spirit, one God, and one Lord, and one Creator. We do not separate God from his Word and his Spirit. God showed his power and his light in the Law and the Prophets, and the Psalms and the Gospel, that God and his Word and his Spirit are one God and one Lord. We will show this, if God will, in those revealed scriptures, to anyone who wants insight, understands things, recognizes the truth, and opens his breast to believe in God and his scriptures.[19]

One notices straightaway the author's intention to make his case for Christian teaching from the scriptures; he names the Law (*al-Tawrah*), the Prophets (*al-Anbiyā'*), the Psalms (*al-Zubūr*), and the Gospel (*al-Injīl*), scriptures that he names as they are named in the Qur'an. Moreover, in emphasizing God, his Word, and his Spirit, the author recalls the Qur'an's own mention of these three names in the often quoted phrase, 'The Messiah, Jesus, Son of Mary, was nothing more than a messenger of God, His word that He imparted to Mary, and a spirit from Him' (Q 4:171). What is more, the author is willing to include explicit citations from the Qur'an among the scripture passages he quotes in testimony to the credibility of the Christian doctrine. On the one hand, addressing the Arabic-speaking, Christian readers who were his primary audience, the author speaks of what 'We find in the Law and the Prophets and the Psalms and the

18 Adapted from the text and translation in Samir, 'The Earliest Arab Apology', pp. 67–8.

19 Gibson, *An Arabic Version*, p. 3 (English), and 75 (Arabic). Here the English translation has been adapted from Gibson's version.

Gospel,' in support of the Christian doctrines of the Trinity and the Incarnation. On the other hand, several times he rhetorically addresses Muslims; he speaks of what 'You will find ... in the Qur'an,' and he goes on to cite a passage or a pastiche of quotations from several *sūras*, in support of the doctrines, in behalf of the veracity of which he has been quoting or alluding to scriptural evidence from passages and narratives from the Old or New Testaments.[20] For example, at one point in the argument, in search of testimonies to a certain plurality in the Godhead, the author turns to the scriptures for citations of passages in which God speaks in the first person plural. Having quoted a number of such passages, he goes on to say:

> You will find it also in the Qur'an that 'We created man in Misery' (Q 90:4), and 'We have opened the gates of heaven with water pouring down' (Q 54:11), and have said, 'And now you come unto us alone, as we created you at first' (Q 6:94). It also says, 'Believe in God, and in his Word; and also in the Holy Spirit' (Q 4:171). The Holy Spirit is even the one who brings it down (i.e. the Qur'an) as 'a mercy and a guidance from thy Lord' (Q 16:64, 102). But why should I prove it from this (i.e. the Qur'ān) and bring enlightenment, when we find in the Torah, the Prophets, the Psalms, and the Gospel, and you find it in the Qur'an, that God and His Word and His Spirit are one God and one Lord? You have said that you believe in God and His Word and the Holy Spirit, so do not reproach us, O men, that we believe in God and His Word and His Spirit: we worship God in His Word and His Spirit, one God and one Lord and one Creator. God has made it clear in all of the scriptures that this is the way it is in right guidance (*hudan*) and true religion (*dīn al-ḥaqq*).[21]

Evidently in this passage the Christian author is addressing himself directly, at least in part, to readers of the Qur'an as well as to the devotees of the Christian Bible. He speaks of what 'We find in the Torah, the Prophets, the Psalms, and the Gospel,' and of what 'You find ... in the Qur'an.' One also notices in this passage the prominence of the author's references to God, His Word, and His Spirit, and how they provide a continual evocation of Q 4:171. Like almost every Arab Christian apologetic writer after him, the author of *On the Triune Nature of God* takes this verse as Qur'anic testimony to the reality that the one God is

---

20 See Gibson, *An Arabic Version*, pp. 5–6 (English) and 77–8 (Arabic). See the passage quoted and discussed in Griffith, *The Church in the Shadow of the Mosque*, p. 55.

21 Adapted translation from Gibson, *An Arabic Version*, pp. 5–6 (English), and 77–8 (Arabic).

in fact possessed of Word and Spirit and that they are He, the Son of God and the Holy Spirit, as the Christians speak of them.

In a further passage, the author of *On the Triune Nature of God* takes advantage of another verse in the Qur'an to explain how it came about that by the action of the Holy Spirit, God's Word, the Son of God, became incarnate and was clothed, even veiled (*iḥtajaba*),[22] in Mary's human nature. 'Thus,' he says, 'God was veiled (*iḥtajaba*) in a man without sin.'[23] The 'veiling' language here once again evokes a particular passage in the Qur'an: 'God speaks with man only by way of revelation, or from behind a veil (*ḥijāb*), or He sends a messenger and he reveals by His permission what He wishes' (Q 42:51). The author of our treatise likens Jesus' humanity to the veil, from behind which the Qur'an says God might speak to man.[24]

On the Triune Nature of God is somewhat unique among Christian Arabic texts by reason of the manner of its obvious accommodation to the Qur'an and its citation of the Islamic scripture alongside biblical texts in testimony to the veracity of Christian doctrines. Yet the author obviously also maintains the distinction between the Bible and the Qur'an; when he cites the latter, one finds the introductory phrase, 'You will also find (it) in the Qur'an …,' or, 'It is also written in the Qur'an …,'[25] phrases that effectively distinguish the scriptures. It does not appear that the author accepts the Qur'an as a canonical scripture; throughout the treatise he adduces arguments from the Bible and Christian tradition expressly to refute the Qur'an's critique of Christian doctrine and practice.[26] Nevertheless it is also clear that for him the Arabic Qur'an does possess evidentiary potential and probative value for Christian apologetic purposes in the Islamic milieu. The text certainly presumes that its Christian readers are familiar with the Qur'an and it may even suggest that they positively esteem its language.

It is true that the treatise *On the Triune Nature of God* is unique among Christian Arabic texts in its forthright emulation of Qur'anic style and its obvious willingness to align testimonies from the Arabic Qur'an with those from the Jewish and Christian scriptures, albeit in a subsidiary position. Nevertheless, and in spite of the fact that there were also Christian Arabic texts

22 See Gibson, *An Arabic Version*, p. 11 (English), and p. 83 (Arabic).

23 Gibson, *An Arabic Version*, p. 13 (English), and p. 85 (Arabic).

24 This theme of Jesus' humanity as a 'veil', echoing the Qur'anic text, became quite popular in later 'Melkite' Arabic works of religious apology; see Swanson, 'Beyond Prooftexting', pp. 301–2.

25 See Gibson, *An Arabic Version*, pp. 5, 12, 33 (English), and 77, 84, 104 (Arabic).

26 See the remarks in Gallo, *Palestinese anonimo omelia*, p. 61, esp. n. 50.

that disparaged the Qur'an, including a reported 'Refutation of the Qur'an' by the 'Nestorian' Abū Nūḥ al-Anbārī (*fl.* 780's),[27] it remained the case in the early Islamic period that other Christian Arabic writers also frequently quoted from the Qur'an, sometimes inexactly, as if from memory, and echoed its words and phrases in their ordinary discourse.[28] The point is that by contrast with the attitudes of Christians living outside of the World of Islam, who produced Greek or Latin translations of the Arabic text,[29] many of whom despised Islam and demeaned it at every opportunity for almost a millennium,[30] Arabic-speaking Christians were for the most part willing, positively, and with a measure of respect, to engage the Qur'an religiously, albeit that their purpose was primarily the more clearly to express their own traditional Christian faith in Arabic, within the hermeneutical circle of the Qur'an's influence. For unquestionably the Qur'an had set the parameters in the Arabic-speaking world for the discussion of important religious doctrines, even Christian ones. Christian theologians often spoke in the same religious idiom in Arabic as did their contemporary Muslim counterparts, and Qur'anic terms became common in Christian discourse. In early Islamic times, and well up into the thirteenth century, a number of Arabophone Christian writers regularly cited passages from the Qur'an in defense of the veracity of the religious ideas they commended, and they quarreled with Muslim exegetes who interpreted the pertinent verses

27 See B. Landron, *Chrétiens et Musulmans en Irak: Attitudes Nestoriennes vis-à-vis de l'Islam*, Paris, 1994, p. 54; M.N. Swanson, 'Abū Nūḥ al-Anbārī', in D. Thomas and B. Roggema, eds, *Christian-Muslim relations: a bibliographical history volume I (600–900)*, Leiden, 2009, pp. 397–400.

28 For more on this topic, see Griffith, 'The Qur'ān in Arab Christian Texts', esp. pp. 214–23; S.H. Griffith, 'Answers for the Shaykh: A 'Melkite' Arabic Text from Sinai and the Doctrines of the Trinity and the Incarnation in 'Arab Orthodox' Apologetics', in E. Grypeou, M. Swanson and D. Thomas, eds, *The Encounter of Eastern Christianity with Early Islam*, Leiden, 2006, pp. 277–309, esp. 288–301.

29 Thomas Burman has shown that scholarly, western translators of the Qur'an often did their work philologically correctly, and very carefully strove to present the text in the light of the current modes of Islamic interpretation, albeit that they may have disdained Islam. See T. Burman, *Reading the Qur'ān in Latin Christendom, 1140–1560*, Philadelphia, 2007, esp. pp. 36–59.

30 See H. Bobzin, 'A Treasury of Heresies': Christian Polemics against the Koran', in S. Wild, ed., *The Qur'ān as Text*, Leiden, 1996, pp. 157–75; *idem*, 'Translations of the Qur'ān', in *Encyclopaedia of the Qur'ān, volume 5*, Leiden, 2006, pp. 340–58. See also Z. Elmarsafy, *The Enlightenment Qur'ān: The Politics of Translation and the Construction of Islam*, Oxford, 2009.

differently.[31] A notable case in point is the anonymous, but widely circulated, ninth century tract, 'The Disputation of the Monk Abraham of Tiberias in Jerusalem', in which the Christian author buttresses his arguments with numerous quotations from the Qur'an.[32]

Another notable instance of an important Christian Arabic writer's engagement with the Qur'an and with Muslim interpreters of the Qur'an appears in the third installment of Mar Elias of Nisibis' (975–1046) *Kitāb al-majālis*, in his account of his efforts in the *majlis* of the *wazīr* Abū l-Qāsim al-Ḥusayn al-Maghribī (981–1027) to argue from passages in the Qur'an that Christians should be considered true Monotheists; they are not to be thought of as guilty of assigning partners to the one God (*al-shirk*).[33] Mar Elias reports that the *wazīr* began the conversation by saying that he had at first been satisfied with Mar Elias' explanations of Christian Monotheism, but that having subsequently consulted the Qur'an and having found the passage that says, 'They have disbelieved who say, "God is third of three"' (Q 5:73), he realized that 'in many places' the Qur'an actually describes Christians 'in terms of *al-shirk*.'[34] To counter this charge, Mar Elias proceeds to quote and comment on ten verses from the Qur'an that seem to him clearly to distinguish Christians from the *mushrikūn*, and he goes on to argue on the basis of current Qur'anic exegetical principles against those Muslims who would allege that such passages in the Qur'an, seemingly favorable to Christian *tawḥīd*, are to be considered abrogated by later passages in the Arabic scripture. Rather, Mar Elias argues that exegetically speaking, abrogation actually does not apply to such verses, since they do not enjoin scriptural precepts (*al-farā'iḍ*) or legal commands, to which alone, he contends, abrogation could legally apply. Furthermore, he argues

31 See U. Pietruschka, 'Die Verwendung und Funktion von Koranzitaten in christlichen Apologien der frühen Abbasidenzeit (Mitte 8. Jahrhundert—Anfang 10. Jahrhundert)', in W. Beltz and J. Tubach, eds, *Religiöser Text und soziale Struktur*, Halle, 2001, pp. 271–88.

32 See G.B. Marcuzzo, ed. and trans., *Le Dialogue d'Abraham de Tibériade avec 'Abd al-Raḥmān al-Hāšimī à Jérusalem vers 820*, Rome, 1986; K. Szilágyi, 'Christian Learning about Islam in the Early Abbāsid Caliphate: The Muslim Sources of the *Disputation of the Monk Abraham of Tiberias*', in J. Scheiner and D. Janos, eds, *The Place to Go: Contexts of Learning in Baghdād, 750–1000 C.E.*, Princeton, 2014, pp. 267–342.

33 See Elias of Nisibis, '*Kitāb al-majālis*', in L. Cheikho, ed., *Trois traits de polémique et de théologie chrétiennes*, Beyrouth, 1923, pp. 26–71, chapter 3, pp. 42–7. On Mar Elias and his work see B. Landron, *Chrétiens et Musulmans en Irak: Attitudes Nestoriennes vis-à-vis de l'Islam*, Paris, 1994, esp. pp. 112–20; S.K. Samir, *Foi et culture en Irak au XIe siècle*, Aldershot, 1996; J.P. Monferrer Sala, 'Elias of Nisibis', in D. Thomas and A. Mallett, eds, *Christian-Muslim Relations: A Bibliographical History, vol.* 2 (900–1050), Leiden, 2010, pp. 727–41.

34 Elias of Nisibis, *Kitāb al-majālis*, in Cheikho, *Trois traités anciens*, p. 42.

that there are many other passages in the Qur'an, which can be seen clearly to entail the conclusion that Christians are indeed to be listed among the Monotheists (*muwaḥidūn*), and so on the basis of the Qur'an's own testimony, he argues, they cannot therefore rightly be said to be Polytheists (*mushrikūn*).[35]

Mar Elias buttressed the strength of his interpretations of the passages he quoted from the Qur'an in favor of viewing the Christians as true Monotheists by citing the favorable opinions of well known Muslim scholars and commentators on the Qur'an. First among them of course is Abū Ja'far Muḥammad al-Ṭabarī (839–923), along with the early authorities, Mujāhid ibn Jabr (642–722) and Qatādah ibn Di'āmah (d.735), and concluding with a reference to the work of the near contemporary, Ash'arī *mutakallim*, Abū Bakr Muḥammad ibn al-Ṭayyib al-Bāqillānī (930–1013). Obviously Mar Elias was well informed about the views of Muslim scholars on topics of interest to him, especially in the matter of the interpretation of passages from the Qur'an that he found useful for his apologetic purposes.

Perhaps the most well-known of the Christian Arabic writers' engagements with the Arabic Qur'an for apologetic purposes came in the twelfth century. The 'Melkite' bishop of Sidon, Paul of Antioch (*fl. c.* 1180–1200),[36] who was the author of a number of theological treatises in Arabic,[37] wrote a 'Letter to a Muslim Friend' in Sidon, in which he skillfully deploys selected passages from the Qur'an to build a defense of Christianity as the true religion and one which the Qur'an itself enjoins Muslims to respect. Paul's contention is that the Qur'an enfranchises Christianity and proves that its doctrines are not such as to be compared with the unbelief (*al-kufr*) of polytheists (*al-mushrikūn*).[38]

Using the literary form of a public letter, Paul presents a scenario according to which he has just returned from an extended visit to the cities of Constantinople, Rome and the land of the Franks, where, due to his status as a bishop, he says he had gained entrée to the company of both civil leaders and scholars. Paul reports that these people asked him about Muhammad and about the scripture he claimed God had sent down to him. Referring no doubt

35 See Elias of Nisibis, *Kitāb al-majālis*, in Cheikho, *Trois traités anciens*, pp. 42–7. So far there has been no modern scholarly study of this chapter in Mar Elias' work.

36 On the problem of dates, see S.K. Samir, 'Notes sur la 'lettre à un musulman de Sidon' de Paul d'Antioche', *Orientalia Lovaniensia Periodica* 24, 1993, pp. 179–95.

37 See P. Khoury, *Paul d'Antioche, évêque melkite de Sidon* (*XIIe.s.*), Beyrouth, 1964.

38 See S.H. Griffith, 'Paul of Antioch', in Noble and Treiger, *The Orthodox Church in the Arab World*, pp. 216–35, and 327–31. The article includes an introduction, an English translation of Paul's Letter, and an up-to-date bibliography. See now the article by David Thomas on Paul's use and abuse of the Qur'an in the present volume.

to the Greek translations of the Qur'an, Paul says that these Christian, non-Muslims whom he had met on his journey, told him that they had arranged to gain access to the Muslim scripture. So Paul reports that in response to his questions, almost as if he were a spokesman for the Muslims, these foreign Christians quoted passages from the Qur'an to prove that Islam itself was only for those who speak Arabic and that their scripture actually enjoins respect for Christians and commends the veracity of their doctrines and the rectitude of their religious practices. Paul, of course, cites the passages from the Arabic Qur'an, some sixty of them in all. He very artfully weaves the quotations, allusions and echoes of the Qur'an's text, often cited inexactly and bundled into catenae of quotations of phrases and half phrases, into a coherent defense of Christianity. At the end of the letter, Paul tells his Muslim friend that if the foreign readers of the Qur'an have gotten it right, as he has reported their scripture-based reasoning, then God will have 'reconciled opinions and put a stop to the quarrelling between His servants, the Christians (*al-naṣārā*) and the Muslims.'[39] If, however, there are problems, Paul says that his Muslim friend will explain the matter to him and that he, Paul, will transmit the objections to his foreign interlocutors, who had made him an intermediary (*safīran*).

The ingenuity of the letter as an apologetic tract is evident, including the ploy that Paul is but the intermediary for foreign readers of the Qur'an. And while the reading of the Islamic scripture is on the face of it a respectful one, it is also quite obviously a selective, not to say a 'Christianizing' reading.[40] In the end, Paul intended his reading to undercut the Qur'an's obvious critique of Christian faith and religious practice and contrariwise, positively to commend Christianity. It is no wonder that on the one hand, the text quickly gained popularity among Arabic-speaking Christians and on the other hand prompted Muslim scholars to write refutations of it. Already in the thirteenth century, the text was known in Cairo and the prominent Muslim legal scholar Shihāb al-Dīn Aḥmad ibn Idrīs al-Qarāfī (1228–1285) included a point by point refutation of the letter in his book *Proud Answers to Impudent Questions*.[41] Then in

39 Khoury, *Paul d'Antioche*, p. 83 (Arabic), and p. 187 (French).

40 See the comments of David Thomas, 'Paul of Antioch's *Letter to a Muslim Friend* and *The Letter from Cyprus*', in D. Thomas, *Syrian Christians under Islam: The First Thousand Years*, Leiden, 2001, pp. 203–21, esp. pp. 208–13.

41 Shihāb al-Dīn al-Qarāfī, *Al-ajwibat al-fākhirah ʿan al-asʾilat al-fājirah*, ed. B.Z. ʿAwa, Cairo, 1987. On Shihāb al-Dīn, see S.A. Jackson, *Islamic Law and the State: The Constitutional Jurisprudence of Shihāb al-Dīn al-Qarāfī*, Leiden, 1966. See now D.R. Sarrió Cucarella, *Muslim-Christian Polemics across the Mediterranean: The Splendid Replies of Shihāb al-Dīn al-Qarāfī (d.684/1285)*, Leiden, 2014.

Cyprus, sometime in the thirteenth century, now unknown Christian hands expanded Paul of Antioch's letter to a length some 'three or even four times as long'[42] as the original. This Cypriot letter, as we may call the expanded recension of Paul's original letter to his Muslim friend in Sidon, eventually came to the attention of two prominent Muslim scholars in Damascus in the early years of the fourteenth century, and they both wrote refutations of it, quoting long portions of the text in their refutations. They were Muḥammad ibn Abī Ṭālib al-Dimashqī (*fl. c.* 1320)[43] and Taqī al-Dīn Aḥmad ibn Taymiyyah (1263–1328).[44] Their works were to mark a turning-point in the history of Christian/Muslim relations; thereafter few original works of Christian theology were composed in Arabic.

Toward the beginning of his subsequently very influential book in refutation of the Cypriot letter, *The Sound Response to Those Who Have Changed the Religion of the Messiah,*[45] Ibn Taymiyyah commented on the letter's widespread influence among the Christians of his time, a circumstance that doubtless inspired his own work, at least in part. He wrote:

> A letter arrived from Cyprus in which there is an argument for the religion of Christians. In it the scholars of their religion as well as the eminent persons of their church, ancient and modern, plead their case with religious and intellectual arguments. ... That which they state in this book is the basic support on which their scholars depend, both in our time and in previous ages, although some of them may elaborate further than others depending on the situations. We have found them making use of this treatise before now. Their scholars hand it down among themselves, and old copies of it still exist.[46]

---

42 Thomas, 'Paul of Antioch's *Letter*', p. 215.

43 See the publication and discussion of both the Cypriot Letter and al-Dimashqī's refutation of it in R.Y. Ebied and D. Thomas, eds and trans, *Muslim-Christian Polemic during the Crusades: The Letter of the People of Cyprus and Ibn Abī Ṭālib al-Dimashqīs Response,* Leiden, 2005.

44 See T.F. Michel, *A Muslim Theologian's Response to Christianity: Ibn Taymiyya's al-Jawab al-Sahih,* Delmar, 1984.

45 A recent edition is Taqī al-Dīn Aḥmad ibn Taymiyyah, *Al-Jawāb al-ṣaḥīḥ liman baddala dīn al-masīḥ,* ed., M. Ismāʿīl, 2 vols, Cairo, 2003.

46 Quoted in the translation of T.F. Michel, *A Muslim Theologian's Response,* p. 93. See the full passage in Ibn Taymiyyah, *Al-jawāb al-ṣaḥīḥ,* vol. 1, pp. 22–3. In the part left out by Michel, Ibn Taymiyyah says, 'This makes it necessary for us to quote in response what each section of the text proposes, to explain the mistakes according to what is correct, so that intelligent people might profit from it and so that the measured speech and scripture that God

While in earlier Islamic times there were some Muslim responses to the apologetic tracts written by Arabic-speaking Christians, the rebuttals by major Muslim scholars of the thirteenth and fourteenth centuries to Paul of Antioch's Qur'an-based reasoning in support of the veracity of Christian faith and practice were at once traditional and unprecedented. They came at a time when the center of gravity of Muslim intellectual life had shifted from Baghdad to Cairo and Damascus, when the crusades were underway, and when the Christian populations in the World of Islam were beginning their long slide into demographic insignificance. In regard to the strength of the unusual Islamic response to an apology for Christianity, it was perhaps not irrelevant that Paul of Antioch's letter to his Muslim friend in Sidon, and its expansion into the Cypriot letter, was almost entirely based on a Christian reading of the Arabic Qur'an. With all the selectivity and sleight of hand in quotation that one can point out in the text, it nevertheless appealed to what seemed to be obvious interpretations, from a non-Muslim perspective, of the passages of the Qur'an that it quoted. Thereby, one might opine, the text gained an unprecedented purchase on the attention of Muslims and solicited the rebuttals that would long remain some of the most authoritative Islamic challenges to Christianity in the Arabic-speaking world, extending from the thirteenth and fourteenth centuries even into the twenty-first century.

The Qur'an as a Crypto-Christian Scripture

One of the most intriguing accounts from early Islamic times, claiming Christian origins for the Arabic Qur'an comes in an apologetic/polemical text that was composed in all probability in the ninth century and originally in Syriac. In due course it has been transmitted over the centuries in Syriac in both 'Jacobite' and 'Nestorian' recensions, and in both a short and a long Arabic recension. Modern scholars typically refer to this work as the legend of Sergius Baḥīrā and the story has long remained popular in eastern Christian circles.[47]

---

sent with His messengers might become clear. I will quote what they mention in their own words, section by section, and I will follow up each section with the corresponding answer basically systematically, fittingly conclusively', Ibid., p. 23.

47 The currently definitive edition, translation and discussion of the Syriac and Arabic recensions of the legend, surpassing all previous studies, is Barbara Roggema, *The Legend of Sergius Baḥīrā: Eastern Christian Apologetics and Apocalyptic in Response to Islam*, Leiden, 2009. See also K. Szilágyi, 'Muḥammad and the Monk: The Making of the Christian Baḥīrā Legend', *Jerusalem Studies in Arabic and Islam* 34, 2008, pp. 169–214.

In its origins, the legend builds on the account in the early Islamic biography of Muhammad according to which in his youth, while on a journey to Syria with his uncle Abū Ṭālib, the future prophet and his entourage encountered a Christian monk named Baḥīrā who, as the story goes, with the help of Christian texts in his possession, was able to recognize the sign of future prophet-hood on Muhammad's body.[48]

Utilizing this Islamic reminiscence of an event in Muhammad's early life as a frame-narrative for the legend, the now unknown Syriac author composed a narrative in which a fellow monk introduces the main character of the story as a monk of doubtful orthodoxy called Sergius Baḥīrā. The narrator then recounts Sergius Baḥīrā's story as he unfolds it. The text includes both an apocalypse of Baḥīrā,[49] in which the monk recapitulates themes from Syriac apocalyptic narratives written by Syriac-speaking Christians in earlier Islamic times,[50] and a section that the modern editor calls Baḥīrā's teachings, in which the monk catechizes Muhammad in Christian doctrine and practice in a manner he deemed suitable for the communication of Christianity to Bedouin Arabs.[51] It is in the section of the text recounting Baḥīrā's teachings, as they are presented in the Arabic recensions of the legend, that one finds the development of the idea that the Qur'an was originally a Christian composition, composed by Baḥīrā, and designed to suit the requirements for Muhammad to evangelize the Arabs.[52] All the recensions insist that Baḥīrā's tutelage of Muhammad in Christianity was in the end corrupted by others, most notably initially by the famous early Jewish convert to Islam, Kaʿb al-Aḥbār, thereby accenting an anti-Jewish dimension already prominent in the text. The legend of Sergius Baḥīrā or various parts of it or allusions to it circulated widely in Syriac and Arab Christian apologetic and polemical works in the Middle East from the ninth century onwards.[53] And perhaps the idea that found the widest

48 See 'A. Saʿd, ed., *Al-Sīrat an-nabawwiyyah l'ibn Hishām,* 4 vols, Beirut, 1975, vol. 1, pp. 165–6; A. Guillaume, trans., *The Life of Muhammad: A Translation of Ibn Ishāq's Sīrat Rasul Allah,* Karachi, 1978, pp. 79–81.

49 See Roggema, *The Legend,* pp. 61–93.

50 Most notably the Apocalypse of Pseudo-Methodius, and other apocalyptic texts of the seventh and eighth centuries. See F.J. Martinez, 'La Literatura Apocalíptica y las Primeras Reacciones Cristianas a la conquista islámica en Oriente', in G. Anes and Á. de Castrillón, eds, *Europa y el Islam,* Madrid, 2003, pp. 143–222.

51 See Roggema, *The Legend,* pp. 95–128.

52 See Roggema, *The Legend,* pp. 129–49. See also B. Roggema, 'A Christian Reading of the Qur'ān: The Legend of Sergius-Baḥīrā and Its Use of Qur'ān and Sīrā', in D. Thomas, ed., *Syrian Christians under Islam; the First Thousand Years,* Leiden, 2001, pp. 57–73.

53 See Roggema, *The Legend,* pp. 151–208.

circulation is that the Qur'an was originally a Christian composition and that the monk Sergius Baḥīrā, was its original author.

In the longer Arabic recension of the legend, the redactor of the story has ingeniously woven some forty verses from the Qur'an into the narrative in such a way as to show first 'that the Qur'an is authored by a Christian, and secondly, that Muslim polemic against Christian doctrine is not justified.'[54] In the telling, Sergius Baḥīrā speaks in the first person, and having described his meeting with Muhammad more or less according to the Islamic story in the *Sīrah*, the monk tells him to leave with his companions but to return later for personal instruction. Muhammad comes back alone three days later and his catechesis begins. The monk teaches him the basic doctrines of Christianity about God's Word and His Spirit and extracts a promise that when Muhammad and his people come to power they will protect the Christians and not extract taxes from them, neither *jizya* nor *kharāj*. The monk instructs Muhammad to claim he is a prophet in order to gain a hearing among his people and when he says, 'How will they believe me, while I do not possess a book?' Sergius Baḥīrā says, 'I will take it upon me to write for you what you need and to tell you about any given matter that they ask you about, be it reasonable or not.' And the monk begins at the beginning, with Q 1:1, the opening phrase of every *sūra* but one; he says:

> And I wrote for him: '*In the name of God, the Merciful, the Compassionate*'. With this I mean the Holy Unified Trinity: 'God' is the Father and the Eternal Light, and 'the Merciful' is the Son, who is merciful to the peoples and has purchased them with his holy blood, and 'the Compassionate' is the Holy Spirit whose compassion is bestowed amply on all and who dwells in all believers. And I taught him things that brought him close to the true faith.[55]

From here on, through his account of the rest of the forty some verses of the Qur'an that he quotes or paraphrases as he teaches Muhammad, Sergius Baḥīrā fairly consistently employs the formula, 'I wrote for him …, with this I mean …,' first reciting the verse, then either mentioning the Christian truth he meant to commend with the Qur'an's words, or countering an Islamic, anti-Christian interpretation of the Qur'an passage that was common in early Islamic times. Here, due to considerations of time and space, one must resist the temptation to recount what the monk says about the many verses he says

54 Roggema, *The Legend*, p. 148.

55 Roggema, *The Legend*, p. 459.

he wrote for Muhammad. Suffice it to mention one or two of the more interesting instances, sufficient to show how in this composition the author not only promotes the idea that in its origins the Qur'an was a Christian book, but also how he proposes to correct what he takes to be mistaken Muslim readings of the Arabic scripture, by supplying the original meaning. In the ensemble, the exercise becomes an apology for Christianity, based on proof-texts from the Qur'an interpreted from a Christian perspective.

In reference to the verse of the Qur'an that Muslims were already taking to mean that Jesus did not die on the cross, Sergius Baḥīrā says, 'I also wrote for him: "They did not kill him and they did not crucify him, but it was made to appear so to them" (Q 4:157). With this I mean that Christ did not die in the substance of his divine nature but rather in the substance of his human nature.'[56] In another instance, the monk says, 'I also wrote for him, "If you are in doubt about what has been revealed to you, then ask those to whom the scripture was given before you" (Q 10:94). With this I intended to prove that the Holy Gospel is truer than any of the scriptures, and cannot be impaired by those who want to discredit it, nor can any change (*taghyīr*) or corruption (*taḥrīf*) be correlated with it.'[57] In a passage in which he conflates several verses from the Qur'an, Sergius Baḥīrā takes responsibility for specifying Muhammad's role in the history of salvation, He says, 'And I wrote for him too: "Muhammad is the messenger of God (*rasūl Allāh*) (Q 48:29). He sent him with guidance and the true religion, that He may make it prevail over all religion, though the polytheists be averse" (Q 9:33 and 61:9). And I wrote for him: "Muhammad is no more than a messenger. Messengers have passed away before him" (Q 3:144), and: "God and His angels bless the prophet. O you who believe, bless him and salute him" (Q 33:56).'[58]

Along the way, the monk offers some explanation of his project to tutor Muhammad. He says, 'Innumerable things I wrote for him with which to try to make him incline toward the faith of truth and the confession of the coming of Christ to the world and also to make him denounce the Jews regarding what they allege against our Lord, the true Messiah.'[59] But the monk knows that much of what he wrote for Muhammad 'will be changed and subtracted from and added to many times, because after him people will follow him who will become inimical and hateful to us.'[60] In the end, Sergius Baḥīrā confesses

56 Roggema, *The Legend*, p. 463.

57 Roggema, *The Legend*, p. 469, slightly altered.

58 Roggema, *The Legend*, pp. 487–9.

59 Roggema, *The Legend*, p. 471.

60 Roggema, *The Legend*, p. 489.

that he had overreached and that he had sinned in what he had done with Muhammad. He said,

> I wanted his prophet-hood to be in the name of the Trinity, confessed to be one, the Father, the Son, and the Holy Spirit.... I wanted to confirm the kingdom of the Sons of Ishmael, in order that the promise of God to Abraham about Ishmael would be fulfilled.[61] That was all I intended, so I devised prophet-hood for him and I produced a scripture for him and I presented it as having come down to him as a revelation, so that the words of our Lord Christ in his Gospel, 'After me false prophets will come to you. Woe to the one who follows them' (Mt. 24:11) would be fulfilled.[62]

Even from the few quotations given here, one clearly sees how the author of the legend in its Arabic recension made use of selected quotations from the Qur'an. It is important to recognize that these relatively few quotations did not make up the entirety of the catechesis of Muhammad in the narrative. Rather, they are woven into the whole fabric of the story, telling how, the author claims, the monk of questionable ecclesiastical standing, Sergius Baḥīrā, invented both the Qur'an and Islam and taught Muhammad as a strategy for evangelizing the Bedouin Arabs, a strategy that, as the monk concedes, was ill conceived and ultimately failed. Obviously, the whole work is an attempt apologetically and polemically to discount Islam's religious claims in Arabophone Christian eyes and perhaps it was also an effort to forestall Christian conversions to Islam.

The Qur'an between Christians and Muslims

While it is clear from the preceding cursory overview of instances in which Christian Arabic writers in the early Islamic period quoted from or alluded to the Qur'an in their works, or even sometimes built their apologetic or polemical arguments on proof-texts drawn from the Qur'an, it does not appear that they were normally involved in a deep or disinterested study of the Islamic scripture or its interpreters for their own sakes. Rather, the Christian Arabic writers' interests were the practical ones of deflecting challenges to Christian thought and practice, and to commending the credibility of Christian doctrines in terms that would carry weight within the Arabic-speaking, Islamic

61 See Gen. 21:15–21, and 25:12–18.

62 Roggema, *The Legend*, p. 511.

milieu in which Christians and Muslims lived together. For this purpose Christian Arabic writers sometimes chose verses from the Qur'an for comment and interpretation, and sometimes they used Qur'anic vocabulary and turns of phrase in an effort the more effectively to articulate in Arabic and to defend Christian faith within the purview of Islam. Most often, even in the many instances in which the Qur'an verses were quoted accurately, there is a vast difference of course between the Christian and Muslim readings of the same texts. The Christian writers' interests were primarily rhetorical, not exegetical, and not confessional.

Due to its role as the first Arabic book, the Qur'an's rhetorical potential within the Arabic-speaking world extended far beyond its religious role as the Islamic scripture; it became the principal authority on the basis of which grammarians, lexicographers, and theoretical linguists consciously constructed the parameters within which the newly inter-communal language would be spoken, written, and understood. Inevitably then the Qur'an's diction and idiom, even its distinctly religious vocabulary, entered the common parlance not only of Muslims, but the spoken and written Arabic of Jews, Christians, and Muslims alike. So it is not surprising that given the Qur'an's hovering presence over the spoken and written Arabic word that Christian theologians and apologists who wrote in Arabic in early Islamic times would have made use of the probative potential of Qur'anic proof-texts in their public discourse, which would therefore be accessible to whomever, Jew, Christian, or Muslim, who understood Arabic.

It is clear that in most instances in which Christian Arabic authors made use of proof-texts from the Qur'an in the course of their reasoning their purpose was to enlist the authority of the Islamic scripture in their apologetic efforts to commend the veracity of Christian doctrines, albeit that these same doctrines were in most instances at variance with the Qur'an's own teaching. Similarly, Muslim apologists from the ninth century onward themselves regularly employed proof-texts from the Jewish and Christian scriptures, Islamically interpreted, to commend the veracity of points of Muslim faith at variance with Jewish or Christian readings of the same scriptural passages. There is no small irony to be observed in the practice of contemporary Christians and Muslims writing in Arabic who regularly quoted from one another's scriptures, the actual texts of which they mutually viewed askance and with suspicion, which they then interpreted from their own perspectives, to support views that were obviously at variance with the views espoused by those to whom the quoted or misquoted scriptures primarily belonged.

CHAPTER 2

Qur'ānic Textual Archaeology. Rebuilding the Story of the Destruction of Sodom and Gomorra

Juan Pedro Monferrer-Sala

The Qur'ānic Witnesses and Its Source Framework

The Story of the destruction of Sodom and Gomorrah forms part of the saga recounted in Gn 18–19. These two chapters, which narrate a whole day in the life of Abraham in which Lot also appears,[1] are a textual example of what might be termed the 'shared tradition' common to the three monotheistic religions.

In the Biblical textual tradition, Gn 19 was always seen as a largely autonomous story within the Abraham-Lot narrative cycle to which it belongs. Because of the events it narrates, the Story has always been received as an archetypal account of man's depravity.[2]

It unfolds in three narrative sections: a) the destruction of Sodom (19:1–11); b) the saving of Lot (19:12–29); and c) Lot's incest with his daughters (19:30–38). This structure also serves to highlight the three major narrative elements on which commentators were later to focus:[3] a) the judgement and destruction of Sodom as a city of sin; b) the sparing of Lot because of his kinship with Abraham; and c) Lot's final tragic downfall, brought about by his incestuous relations with his daughters.

This paper seeks to examine certain compositional and organisational aspects of the text in order to see how the Story was received into the Qur'ān. In textual terms, the first striking feature is that the Qur'ānic references to the Story are scattered to form a kind of mosaic made up of tessellae of varying origins, one of which is conspicuous by its absence: the omission—also found in

1 H. Haag, 'Abraham und Lot in Gen 18–19', in A. Caquot and M. Delcor, eds, *Mélanges bibliques et orientaux. Festschrift M. Henri Cazelles*, Kevelaer, 1981, pp. 173–179.

2 R.N. Whybray, 'Genesis', in by John Barton and John Muddiman, eds, *The Oxford Bible Commentary*, Oxford, 2007, pp. 52–53.

3 See on this issue E. Grypeou and H. Spurling, 'Abraham's Angels: Jewish and Christian Exegesis of Genesis 18–19', in E. Grypeou and H. Spurling, *The Exegetical Encounter between Jews and Christians in Late Antiquity*, Leiden–Boston, 2009, pp. 181–203.

 | DOI 10.1163/9789004360747_003

certain Christian authors[4]—of any reference to Lot's incest with his daughters, as described in Gn 19:30–38 and explicitly in apocryphal texts such as JubEt 16:8.[5]

This irregular mosaic comprises varying numbers of *āyāt* spread over nine *suwar* (a total of 69, ranging from a maximum of 20 in *sūra* 15 to a minimum of 2 in *sūra* 21), as indicated in the synoptic table below. For textual purposes, as we shall see, the most important of the nine is *sūra* 11, marked here with an asterisk.

The synoptic table has been drawn up with a view to reconstructing the Story by comparing references.[6]

Symbols and abbreviations

{x}	independent verses
x^{ad}	added verse(s)
x^{misc}	miscellaneous verses
x^{n}	neuter verse(s)
x^{unrel}	unrelated verse(s)

suwar →	7	11*	15	21	26	27	29	37	54
		70^{n}							
		74^{n}	58^{n}					133^{n}	
		76^{n}							
		77	61–64						
	80,81	78	67–71		165–166	54–55	28–29		
	{82}					{56}			
		79							
		80							
ā			59						
y			60						
ā →	83	81	65		170–172	57		134–135	34, 38
t			66						
			73						

4 See the present writer's forthcoming paper: 'The Lyre of Exegesis. Ibn al-Ṭayyib's analytical patterns of the account of the destruction of Sodom'.

5 *The Book of Jubilees*. Edited and translated by J.C. VanderKam, CSCO 510–511, scriptores aethiopici 87–88, 2 vols, Louvain, 1989, I, pp. 93–94 (Ethiopic), II, pp. 94–95 (English).

6 A map of the verses drawn only from similarities between the Qur'ān and Gn 19 is provided by D. Masson, *Le Coran et la révélation judéo-chrétienne. Études comparées*, 2 vols, Paris, 1958, I, pp. 370–371.

TABLE (*cont.*)

suwar →	7	11*	15	21	26	27	29	37	54
	84	82	74		173	58		136	34
		83							
			{76}						
			72^{misc}						35–37^{misc}
			75^{misc}	74–75^{unrel}	167–169^{misc}		30^{misc}	137–138^{misc}	39^{misc}
			77^{misc}						

The chronology of the Qur'ān's construction is an issue that has yet to be fully resolved. Further contributions may still be made to the methodological criteria used for chronological demarcation,[7] based partly—though not exclusively—on internal textual evidence.[8] The chronological classifications of the nine *suwar* of interest here, provided by Nöldeke and Hirschfeld using two different models, are as follows:

Nöldeke's classification[9]

Mecca 2	54	37	26	15	21	27
Mecca 3	11	29	7			

7 G. Böwering, 'Chronology and the Qur'ān', in Jane Dammen McAuliffe, ed., *Encyclopaedia of the Qur'ān*, 6 vols, Leiden—Boston—Köln, 2001–6, I, pp. 316–335, esp. 322–331; G. Böwering, 'Recent research on the construction of the Qur'ān', in G.S. Reynolds, ed., *The Qur'ān in Its Historical Context*, London—New York, 2008, pp. 71–73. On Bell's contribution see R. Firestone, 'The Qur'ān and the Bible: Some Modern Studies of Their Relationship', in J.C. Reeves, ed., *Bible and Qur'ān: Essays in Scriptural Intertextuality*, Leiden, 2003, pp. 11–16. See also H. Motzki, 'Alternative accounts of the Qur'ān's formation', in J.D. McAuliffe, ed., *The Cambridge Companion to the Qur'ān*, New York, 2006, pp. 63–65.

8 B. Sadeghi, 'The Chronology of the Qur'ān: A Stylometric Research Program, *Arabica* 58, 2011, pp. 210–299.

9 T. Nöldeke, *Geschichte des Qorans*, ed. Friedrich Schwally, Leipzig, 1909 (2nd ed., rep. Hildesheim, 1961), I, pp. 117–143 (Mecca 2) and 143–164 (Mecca 3).

Hirschfeld's chronological arrangement, based on passages rather than—like Nöldeke's—on *suwar*, assigns the texts making up the story to a category he terms 'the descriptive revelations', within the larger division of the 'Meccan revelations':[10]

IV Descriptive revelations	26	54	37	27	15	21	11	7	29

Bell's classification marked a step forward in textual criticism, examining in greater depth the minor units as classifying elements[11] and thus providing the basis for subsequent proposals by Blachère and Watt.[12] The work on intratextual analysis by Sinai and the quantitative method used by Schmid[13] are likely to shed new light on the issue of chronology. Reynolds challenges the assumption that the Qur'ān can only be understood when approached in chronological order, suggesting that—in terms of textual or literary criticism—this is no more than a groundless axiom.[14] To avoid entering this vexed debate, suffice it to state that all the passages to be examined here belong to the so-called 'Meccan revelations', and specifically to second and third periods.

This being so, the texts in question can be assigned, for chronological purposes, to the 'central body of revelation', i.e. after the first phase (Mecca 1) and before the final phase (Medina).[15] However, acceptance of this chronology in turn implies a diachronic compositional process inherent in thematic or

10 H. Hirschfeld, *New researches into the composition and exegesis of the Qoran*, London, 1902, p. 144.

11 R. Bell, *The Qur'ān: Translated, with a Critical Re-Arrangement of the Sūras*, 2 vols, Edinburgh, 1937.

12 W.M. Watt, 'The Dating of the Qur'ān: A Review of Richard Bell's Theories', *Journal of the Royal Asiatic Society*, April 1957, pp. 46–56. See also Watt, *Bell's Introduction to the Quran, completely revised and enlarged by W. Montgomery Watt*, Edinburgh, 1970, pp. 108–114, 127–135.

13 N. Sinai, 'The Qur'ān as a process", and N.K. Schmid, "Quantitative text analysis and its application to the Qur'ān: Some preliminary considerations', in A. Neuwirth, N. Sinai and M. Marx, eds, *The Qur'ān in Context: Historical and Literary Investigations into the Qur'ānic Milieu*, Leiden—Boston, 2010, pp. 407–439 and 441–460 respectively.

14 G.S. Reynolds, 'Le problème de la chronologie du Coran', *Arabica* 58, 2011, pp. 477–502.

15 On the Meccan *sūras*, A. Neuwirth, *Studien zur Komposition der mekkanischen Suren*, Berlin, 1996.

genre cycles[16] like the destruction of Sodom and Gomorrah.[17] The diversity of the passages comprising the Story thus stems from a twofold compositional process: a) chronological (textually diachronic rather than synchronic); and b) narrative, at oral and written level.

Account's Rebuilding

An essential requirement when reconstructing a story from a series of preserved narrative fragments is to determine beyond any shadow of doubt what might be termed the *lectio optima*, particularly when so many variants of a single reading are to be found. An acceptable process must be established, in other words, to distinguish between versions of the same text, with a view to identifying which reading of a given narrative segment is closest to the putative textual referent of the Qur'ānic text.

The *recentiores, non deteriores* principle, applied not to textual recension but to the adaptation or subsequent rewriting of a brief text such as that studied here, may provide further valuable assistance, as long as it remains subordinate, as a methodological criterion, to the *lectio optima*. Even so, caution should clearly be exercised when combining these two approaches to textual criticism.

A crucial issue to be resolved is the need to opt for one of two or more equally-acceptable readings. To overcome this problem, a dual approach has been applied by critics, sometimes with a fair degree of success: a) *difficilior lectio potior*; b) *utrum in alterum abiturum erat*. Both principles are well known: the first states that if one of two readings is more difficult to understand, it is likely to be the correct one; the second rests on the belief that a later text is more likely to have corrupted or simplified an earlier, more complex text. In any case, these alternative procedures must, again, be employed with considerable caution.

Bell offers the following explanation of how the Story entered the Qur'ān:[18]

16 Cf. N. Sinai, 'The Qur'ān as a process', in *The Qur'ān in Context*, pp. 408–416.

17 Although neither city is mentioned in the Qur'ān, they are accepted as being two of the 'overthrown cities' refered to in Q 9:71; 69:11.

18 R. Bell, *The Origin of Islam in Its Christian Environment*, Edinburgh, 1925 (rep. 1968), p. 108. Cf. H.P. Smith, *The Bible and Islam. The influence of the Old and New Testaments on the religion of Mohammed*, New York, 1897, p. 86.

> I think it probable also that he (Muḥammad) heard something about the destruction of Pharaoh, and of the overwhelming of the Cities of the Plain, from general Arab sources before he realised that the stories were in the Bible. But he soon taps some source of information as to definitely Biblical stories, and finds these a rich mine of material for his purpose. It confirms the supposition that his information came in answer to his own inquiries that the stories evidently reached him piecemeal with no indication of any connection amongst them or of the order in which they stood in the Bible

As occurs with other texts, the Qur'ānic materials of the Story reflect a varied compositional process which has little to do with the process of reception suggested by Bell. The approach adopted here to those materials coincides largely with the analytical method employed by Reynolds for a series of Qur'ānic texts,[19] though it places greater emphasis on reception and composition (the archaeology of the text) than on matters of dissemination (homiletic discourse), whilst fully recognising the importance of this latter compositional feature.

Text Preliminary Architecture

As indicated earlier, of the nine *suwar* containing references to the Story, number 11 (*ṣūrat Hūd*),[20] offers the most narratively-compact text with respect to the passage in Gn 19. The following equivalences are noted between the two texts:

Hebrew Masoretic Text		Qur'ān	
19:1	1 וַיָּבֹאוּ שְׁנֵי הַמַּלְאָכִים סְדֹמָה, בָּעֶרֶב, וְלוֹט, יֹשֵׁב בְּשַׁעַר-סְדֹם; וַיַּרְא-לוֹט וַיָּקָם לִקְרָאתָם, וַיִּשְׁתַּחוּ אַפַּיִם אָרְצָה.	11:77	وَلَمَّا جَاءَتْ رُسُلُنَا لُوطًا سِيءَ بِهِمْ وَضَاقَ بِهِمْ ذَرْعًا وَقَالَ هَٰذَا يَوْمٌ عَصِيبٌ

19 G.S. Reynolds, *The Qur'ān and Its Biblical Subtext*, Leiden–New York, 2010, pp. 23–36.

20 For the variants of Q 11:77–83: A. Jeffery, *Materials for the history of the text of the Qur'ān. The old codices*, Leiden, 1937, pp. 46–47, 136–137, 248, 291, 319.

TABLE (*cont.*)

Hebrew Masoretic Text		Qur'ān	
4 טֶרֶם, יִשְׁכָּבוּ, וְאַנְשֵׁי הָעִיר אַנְשֵׁי סְדֹם נָסַבּוּ עַל-הַבַּיִת, מִנַּעַר וְעַד-זָקֵן: כָּל-הָעָם, מִקָּצֶה. 5 וַיִּקְרְאוּ אֶל-לוֹט וַיֹּאמְרוּ לוֹ, אַיֵּה הָאֲנָשִׁים אֲשֶׁר-בָּאוּ אֵלֶיךָ הַלָּיְלָה; הוֹצִיאֵם אֵלֵינוּ, וְנֵדְעָה אֹתָם. 6 וַיֵּצֵא אֲלֵהֶם לוֹט, הַפֶּתְחָה; וְהַדֶּלֶת, סָגַר אַחֲרָיו. 7 וַיֹּאמַר: אַל-נָא אַחַי, תָּרֵעוּ. 8 הִנֵּה-נָא לִי שְׁתֵּי בָנוֹת, אֲשֶׁר לֹא-יָדְעוּ אִישׁ--אוֹצִיאָה-נָּא אֶתְהֶן אֲלֵיכֶם, וַעֲשׂוּ לָהֶן כַּטּוֹב בְּעֵינֵיכֶם; רַק לָאֲנָשִׁים הָאֵל, אַל-תַּעֲשׂוּ דָבָר, כִּי-עַל-כֵּן בָּאוּ, בְּצֵל קֹרָתִי.	19:4–8	وَجَاءَهُ قَوْمُهُ يُهْرَعُونَ إِلَيْهِ وَمِن قَبْلُ كَانُوا يَعْمَلُونَ السَّيِّئَاتِ قَالَ يَا قَوْمِ هَٰؤُلَاءِ بَنَاتِي هُنَّ أَطْهَرُ لَكُمْ فَاتَّقُوا اللَّهَ وَلَا تُخْزُونِ فِي ضَيْفِي أَلَيْسَ مِنكُمْ رَجُلٌ رَّشِيدٌ	11:78
—		قَالُوا لَقَدْ عَلِمْتَ مَا لَنَا فِي بَنَاتِكَ مِنْ حَقٍّ وَإِنَّكَ لَتَعْلَمُ مَا نُرِيدُ	11:79
—		قَالَ لَوْ أَنَّ لِي بِكُمْ قُوَّةً أَوْ آوِي إِلَىٰ رُكْنٍ شَدِيدٍ	11:80
12 וַיֹּאמְרוּ הָאֲנָשִׁים אֶל־לוֹט, עֹד מִי־לְךָ פֹה־חָתָן וּבָנֶיךָ וּבְנֹתֶיךָ וְכֹל אֲשֶׁר לְךָ בָּעִיר הוֹצֵא, מִן־הַמָּקוֹם. 15 וּכְמוֹ הַשַּׁחַר עָלָה וַיָּאִיצוּ הַמַּלְאָכִים בְּלוֹט לֵאמֹר קוּם קַח אֶת־אִשְׁתְּךָ וְאֶת־שְׁתֵּי בְנֹתֶיךָ הַנִּמְצָאֹת פֶּן־תִּסָּפֶה בַּעֲוֺן הָעִיר. 26 וַתַּבֵּט אִשְׁתּוֹ, מֵאַחֲרָיו; וַתְּהִי נְצִיב מֶלַח. 27 וַיַּשְׁכֵּם אַבְרָהָם בַּבֹּקֶר אֶל־הַמָּקוֹם אֲשֶׁר עָמַד שָׁם אֶת־פְּנֵי יְהוָה. 28 וַיַּשְׁקֵף עַל-פְּנֵי סְדֹם וַעֲמֹרָה וְעַל־כָּל-פְּנֵי אֶרֶץ הַכִּכָּר וַיַּרְא וְהִנֵּה עָלָה קִיטֹר הָאָרֶץ כְּקִיטֹר, הַכִּבְשָׁן.	19:12, 15,26, 27–28	قَالُوا يَا لُوطُ إِنَّا رُسُلُ رَبِّكَ لَن يَصِلُوا إِلَيْكَ فَأَسْرِ بِأَهْلِكَ بِقِطْعٍ مِّنَ اللَّيْلِ وَلَا يَلْتَفِتْ مِنكُمْ أَحَدٌ إِلَّا امْرَأَتَكَ إِنَّهُ مُصِيبُهَا مَا أَصَابَهُمْ إِنَّ مَوْعِدَهُمُ الصُّبْحُ أَلَيْسَ الصُّبْحُ بِقَرِيبٍ	11:81

Hebrew Masoretic Text		Qur'ān	
וַיְהִי בְּשַׁחֵת אֱלֹהִים אֶת־עָרֵי הַכִּכָּר וַיִּזְכֹּר אֱלֹהִים אֶת־אַבְרָהָם וַיְשַׁלַּח אֶת־לוֹט מִתּוֹךְ הַהֲפֵכָה בַּהֲפֹךְ אֶת־הֶעָרִים אֲשֶׁר־יָשַׁב בָּהֵן לוֹט.	19:29	فَلَمَّا جَاءَ أَمْرُنَا جَعَلْنَا عَالِيَهَا سَافِلَهَا وَأَمْطَرْنَا عَلَيْهَا حِجَارَةً مِّن سِجِّيلٍ مَّنضُودٍ	11:82
—		مُّسَوَّمَةً عِندَ رَبِّكَ وَمَا هِيَ مِنَ الظَّالِمِينَ بِبَعِيدٍ	11.83

The first point of interest is that the series Q 11:79–80,83 has no match either in Gn 19 or in the remaining *suwar*. The second is that Q 11:70,74,76, classified here as neutral verses, address the theme of Abraham's encounter with the three men, as narrated in Gn 18,[21] which serves—as it does in the Genesis saga—as the gateway to the text. Much was made of the encounter motif—one of the "star" stories in the Abrahamic cycle—in Rabbinical, Patristic and Ecclesiastical literature and by Christian commentators in general.[22] These three verses reflect different narrative strategies, as indicated below, with three precise discursive functions (rewriting, *reductio* and apostrophe), the first two narratological and the third clearly rhetorical:

a) Rewriting+*reductio* (Q 11:70): Rewriting of Gn 18:8 probably through TNeoph 18:8 והוון מתחמין היך אכלין והין שתין 'and they seemed to be eating and drinking'[23] (cf. καὶ ὀπτήσας ἐκόμισεν αὐτοῖς ὑπὸ τῇ δρυΐ κατακειμένοις, 'and they gave him to believe that they did eat')[24] and explicative *reductio* of 18:20–21.

21 On the identity of Abraham's visitors in Rabbinical literature and the Church Fathers, see E. Grypeou and H. Spurling, 'Abraham's Angels: Jewish and Christian Exegesis of Genesis 18–19', in E. Grypeou and H. Spurling, eds, *The Exegetical Encounter between Jews and Christians in Late Antiquity*, Leiden–Boston, 2009, pp. 181–203.

22 J.P. Monferrer-Sala, 'The Lyre of Exegesis. Ibn al-Ṭayyib's analytical patterns of the account of the destruction of Sodom', forthcoming.

23 Cf. Targum Onkelos 18:8: ואכלון, 'and they eat'.

24 F. Josephus AI I,11,2 §197, and n. c in p. 97, in Josephus, *Jewish Antiquities*, books I–IV. With an English translation by H. St. J. Thackeray, London–Cambridge, MA, 1930 (rep. 1961).

b) *Allusio* + *reductio* (Q 11:74): Allusion to the news that Sarah would bear a child (Gn 18:10) and evaluative *reductio* of Abraham's conversation with God in 18:13–32.[25]

c) Apostrophe (Q 11:76), referring to 18:22–32, which pronounces on the events narrated in Q 11:74–75.

As the synoptic table above shows, there is no exact match between the Qur'ānic and Biblical verses. While there is obviously a link between the two narratives in terms of general content, the Qur'ān version is at no point textually dependent on the Biblical text. We shall be returning to both later, when discussing other possible materials; suffice it to highlight here—as a highly-relevant narratological element—the *reductio* offered by the Qur'ān with respect to the Bible account. For example, Q 11:77 refers directly to Gn 19:1, but the extension *sīʾa bihim wa-ḍāqa bihim dharʿan* ('he was grieved for them, and he lacked strength to protect them') is an allusion to Gn 19:2–10, while *hadhā yawmun ʿaṣībun* ('this is a terrible day') alludes to the Story as a whole, as a conclusion to the destruction which is to unfold. The eight remaining *suwar* add a number of discursive elements allowing us to complete the redactional map of the Story, discussed below.

I

Q 11:77	Q 15:61–64
وَلَمَّا جَاءَتْ رُسُلُنَا لُوطًا سِيءَ بِهِمْ وَضَاقَ بِهِمْ ذَرْعًا وَقَالَ هَٰذَا يَوْمٌ عَصِيبٌ	فَلَمَّا جَاءَ آلَ لُوطٍ الْمُرْسَلُونَ ﴿61﴾ قَالَ إِنَّكُمْ قَوْمٌ مُنْكَرُونَ ﴿62﴾ قَالُوا بَلْ جِئْنَاكَ بِمَا كَانُوا فِيهِ يَمْتَرُونَ ﴿63﴾ وَأَتَيْنَاكَ بِالْحَقِّ وَإِنَّا لَصَادِقُونَ ﴿64﴾

Of the two *suwar*, which Nöldeke assigned to Mecca 2 (Q 15:61–64) and Mecca 3 (Q 11:77), the text of Q 11:77 provides a summary rewriting of Gn 19:1–9, while Q 15:61–64 offers an exhortative evaluation of the events narrated.

25 E. Noort, 'For the sake of righteousness. Abraham's negotiations with YHWH as prologue to the Sodom narrative: Genesis 18:16–33', in E. Noort, E.J.C. Tigchelaar, eds, *Sodom's Sin: Genesis 18–19 and its Interpretation*, Leiden–Boston, 2004, pp. 3–15.

We are dealing, therefore, with two different types of discourse: narrative in the first case, homiletic in the second. Interestingly, the homiletic discourse contains certain variants with respect to the narrative segment: e.g.:

Q 15:61–64		Q 11:77
āla Lūṭin	=	*Lūṭan*
al-mursalūna	=	*rusulnā*

In the first example, the homiletic segment indicates that the messengers were sent to Lot's family,[26] while in the narrative passage the encounter is with Lot, as narrated in Gn 19:1. An interesting feature of the second example is that instead of the passive participle *mursalūna*, the narrative text opts for *rusul*, the plural of *rasūl*, a technical term applied to Muḥammad. By contrast, *mursalūna* is never applied to Muḥammad. HMT refers to *hammalĕʾāḵîm* ('the two angels', cf. Gn 18:2 שְׁלֹשָׁה אֲנָשִׁים 'three men'). The Judaeo-Arabic version of the Pentateuch by Saʿadya (10th c.) gives *al-malakāni* (אלמלכאן),[27] a reading also offered by St. Makar Bib. 1[28] and Lagarde II, whilst Lagarde I opts for the plural *al-malāʾika*.[29] Christian authors speak of two angels the third figure appearing to Abraham being Jesus.[30]

The Qur'ān's use of *rusul*/*mursalūna* ('messengers') is evidently a piece of theological adaptation. Ibn Kathīr (14th c.) describes them as *al-rusul al-kirām*, a phrase which he glosses as follows: *wa-baʿatha (Allāh) rusulahu al-kirām wa-malāʾikatahu al-ʿiẓām* ('(God) sent his noble messengers, his archangels', identified by the *mufassirūn* as Gabriel (Jibrīl), Michael (Mīkāʾīl) and Isrāfīl, who

26 On Qur'anic Lūṭ as a messenger (*rasūl*) sent to his people, see F. Leemhuis, 'Lūṭ and his people in the Koran and its early commentaries', in E. Noort, E.J.C. Tigchelaar, eds, *Sodom's Sin*, pp. 97–113.

27 *Œuvres complètes de R. Saadia ben Iosef al-Fayyoûmî. Vol. I. Version arabe du Pentateuque*, ed. J. Derenbourg, Paris, 1893, p. 27.

28 Fol. 50a.

29 *Materialien zur Kritik und Geschichte des Pentateuchs*, ed. P. de Lagarde, 2 vols, Leipzig, 1867, II, p. 18, I, p. 122. On this issue, see E. Grypeou and H. Spurling, 'Abraham's Angels', in E. Grypeou and H. Spurling, eds, *The Exegetical Encounter*, pp. 181–203.

30 Eusebius, *Ecclesiastical History* I,9 (ed. G. Bardy, *Eusèbe de Césarée. Histoire ecclésiastique*, 3 vols, Paris, 1952, 1955, 1958); Sozomen, *Historia ecclesiastica* II,4 (ed. J. Bidez & G.C. Hansen, Sozomenus, *Kirchengeschichte*, Berlin, 1960); Cyril of Jerusalem, *Catecheses ad illuminandos* X,6 (ed. W.C. Reischl & J. Rupp, *Cyrilli Hierosolumorum archiepiscopi opera quae supersunt omnia*, 2 vols, Munich, 1848); Irenaeus, *Adversus haereses* III,6,1 (ed. A. Rousseau & L. Doutreleau, *Irénée de Lyon. Contre les heresies, livre 3*, Paris, 1974). Cf. Justin Martyr, Dialog. 19, 56, 60 (ed. E.J. Goodspeed, *Die ältesten Apologeten*, Göttingen, 1915).

appeared in the form of young men of fair countenance (*ʿalā hayʾat shubbān ḥisān al-wujūh*)[31] at dusk (*ʿinda ghurūb al-shams*),[32] a chronological element present in Gn 19:1 ("at even") but not found in the Qurʾān.

While the homiletic segment follows a linear structure, the condensed narrative segment is structured in three sections, thus retaining the narrative gradation found in Gn 19:1–9:

Gn 19:1–3	وَلَمَّا جَاءَتْ رُسُلُنَا لُوطًا
Gn 19:4–8	سِيءَ بِهِمْ وَضَاقَ بِهِمْ ذَرْعًا
Gn 19:9	وَقَالَ هَذَا يَوْمٌ عَصِيبٌ

II

Q 11:78	Q 7:80–81
وَجَاءَهُ قَوْمُهُ يُهْرَعُونَ إِلَيْهِ وَمِنْ قَبْلُ كَانُوا يَعْمَلُونَ السَّيِّئَاتِ قَالَ يَا قَوْمِ هَؤُلَاءِ بَنَاتِي هُنَّ أَطْهَرُ لَكُمْ فَاتَّقُوا اللَّهَ وَلَا تُخْزُونِ فِي ضَيْفِي أَلَيْسَ مِنْكُمْ رَجُلٌ رَشِيدٌ	وَلُوطًا إِذْ قَالَ لِقَوْمِهِ أَتَأْتُونَ الْفَاحِشَةَ مَا سَبَقَكُمْ بِهَا مِنْ أَحَدٍ مِنَ الْعَالَمِينَ ﴿80﴾ إِنَّكُمْ لَتَأْتُونَ الرِّجَالَ شَهْوَةً مِنْ دُونِ النِّسَاءِ بَلْ أَنْتُمْ قَوْمٌ مُسْرِفُونَ ﴿81﴾

31 Ibn Kathīr, *Tafsīr al-Qurʾān al-Karīm*, 4 vols, Cairo, 1994 (7th ed.), II, p. 434; cf. Ibn Kathīr, *Qiṣaṣ al-anbiyāʾ*, Cairo, 1918, p. 182–183; al-Thaʿlabī, *Qiṣaṣ al-anbiyāʾ al-musammā ʿarāʾis al-majālis*, Beirut, *s.d.*, p. 91; Ibn Muṭarrif al-Ṭarafī, *Qiṣaṣ al-anbiyāʾ*, ed. Roberto Tottoli, Berlin, 2003, p. 53. Al-Kisāʾī, *Qiṣaṣ al-anbiyāʾ*, ed. Isaac Eisenberg, 2 vols, Leiden, 1922–23, p. 146 gives Jibrīl wa-Mīkāʾīl wa-Isrāfīl wa-ʿAzrāʾīl ... *ʿalā ṣūrat al-bashar*. *Tanwīr al-miqbās min Tafsīr Ibn ʿAbbās*. Translated by M. Guezzou, ed. Yousef Meri, Amman, 2007, p. 236 gives 'Gabriel and the angels with him'.

32 Ibn Kathīr, *Qiṣaṣ al-anbiyāʾ*, Cairo, 1918, p. 183; cf. al-Ṭabarī, *Tafsīr. Jāmiʿ al-bayān ʿan taʾwīl āy al-Qurʾān*, ed. ʿAbd Allāh b. ʿAbd al-Muḥsin al-Turkī, Cairo, 2001, XII, p. 496; Ibn Kathīr, *Tafsīr*, II, p. 434, and al-Thaʿlabī, *Qiṣaṣ*, p. 91: *nuṣf al-nahār*.

Q 15:67–71
وَجَاءَ أَهْلُ الْمَدِينَةِ يَسْتَبْشِرُونَ ﴿67﴾ قَالَ إِنَّ هَؤُلَاءِ ضَيْفِي فَلَا تَفْضَحُونِ ﴿68﴾ وَاتَّقُوا اللَّهَ وَلَا تُخْزُونِ ﴿69﴾ قَالُوا أَوَلَمْ نَنْهَكَ عَنِ الْعَالَمِينَ ﴿70﴾ قَالَ هَؤُلَاءِ بَنَاتِي إِنْ كُنْتُمْ فَاعِلِينَ ﴿71﴾
Q 26:165–166
أَتَأْتُونَ الذُّكْرَانَ مِنَ الْعَالَمِينَ ﴿165﴾ وَتَذَرُونَ مَا خَلَقَ لَكُمْ رَبُّكُمْ مِنْ أَزْوَاجِكُمْ بَلْ أَنْتُمْ قَوْمٌ عَادُونَ ﴿166﴾
Q 27:54–55
وَلُوطًا إِذْ قَالَ لِقَوْمِهِ أَتَأْتُونَ الْفَاحِشَةَ وَأَنْتُمْ تُبْصِرُونَ ﴿54﴾ أَئِنَّكُمْ لَتَأْتُونَ الرِّجَالَ شَهْوَةً مِنْ دُونِ النِّسَاءِ بَلْ أَنْتُمْ قَوْمٌ تَجْهَلُونَ ﴿55﴾
Q 29:28–29
وَلُوطًا إِذْ قَالَ لِقَوْمِهِ إِنَّكُمْ لَتَأْتُونَ الْفَاحِشَةَ مَا سَبَقَكُمْ بِهَا مِنْ أَحَدٍ مِنَ الْعَالَمِينَ ﴿28﴾ أَئِنَّكُمْ لَتَأْتُونَ الرِّجَالَ وَتَقْطَعُونَ السَّبِيلَ وَتَأْتُونَ فِي نَادِيكُمُ الْمُنْكَرَ فَمَا كَانَ جَوَابَ قَوْمِهِ إِلَّا أَنْ قَالُوا ائْتِنَا بِعَذَابِ اللَّهِ إِنْ كُنْتَ مِنَ الصَّادِقِينَ ﴿29﴾

Q 11:78 again offers a rewriting of Gn 19:4–8, with an *additio* (*a-laysa minkum rajulun rashīdun*, 'is there not among you a right-minded man?')[33] which alludes to Abraham's conversation with God in Gn 18:23–32. This *additio* is a valuable piece of internal exegesis, in that it highlights the confrontation of the two concepts at the heart of the Story: good and evil, Lot versus the Sodomites. This is a narrative feature eschewed by Christian Arab chroniclers such as Eutychius of Alexandria.[34] Here, the term *rashīd*, as applied to Lot's behaviour, recalls the Hebrew *ṣaddîq* 'righteous' (צַדִּיק), as opposed to *rāshāh* 'impious' (רָשָׁע), the term applied to the Sodomites in Gn 18:23,25. The Hebrew *ṣaddîq* is a *terminus technicus* in Jewish literature, serving to express a person's right-mindedness (*rashīd*) with regard to observance of the Law.[35] The subject of God's conversation with Abraham was developed in Judaic writings: according to the Haggadah (Tanḥuma' *wayada'* 24, 70b), God revealed to Abraham his intention of destroying Sodom in order that Abraham would intercede on behalf of the city and its inhabitants.[36]

By contrast, Q 7:80–81 is strictly a paraphrased interpretation of Gn 19:5 *wĕ-nēdĕʿāh ʾōtām* 'that we may know him' (< יָדַע 'know a person carnally, of sexual intercourse'),[37] preferring the euphemistic approach also used in Q 26:165: *a-ta'tūna al-dhukrāna*, i.e. 'don't you come to the males …?' (cf. Q 27:55; 29:29)[38] to the rather more specific explication found in some apocryphal texts, including JubEt 16:5.[39] The Qur'ān, following the OT (Lev 18:22; 20:13; cf. Rom 1:26–27),[40] presents the homosexuality of the Sodomites as a sin

33 English Qur'anic texts are given according to Maulana Muhammad Ali's *Translation of the Holy Quran*, London, 1955, except where the translation is ours.

34 Eutychius of Alexandria, *Annals*, ed. L. Cheikho, Beirut – Paris – Leipzig, 1906, p. 22.

35 J.P. Monferrer-Sala, '*Marginalia semitica*. II: entre la tradición y la lingüística', *Aula Orientalis* 25, 2007, pp. 115–117. For the use of *ṣaddîq* in Qumrān scrolls see Robert Eisenman and Michael Wise, *The Dead Sea Scrolls Uncovered. The First Complete Translation and Interpretation of 50 Key Documents Withheld for Over 35 Years*, New York, 1993, p. 81.

36 Cf. A.I. Katsh, *Judaism in Islam. Biblical and Talmudic backgrounds of the Koran and its commentaries*, New York, 1980 (3rd ed.), p. 174, n. 2.

37 F. Brown, S.R. Driver and C.A. Briggs, *Hebrew and English Lexicon of the Old Testament*, Boston–New York, 1906, p. 394a.

38 Cf. *Visio Pauli* 39 (Latin text ed. by M.R. James, *Apocrypha anecdota*, Cambridge, 1893).

39 *The Book of Jubilees*, ed. & trans. J.C. VanderKam, I, pp. 93–94 (Ethiopic), II, pp. 94–95 (English).

40 Cf. J.B. De Young, 'The meaning of "nature" in Romans 1 and its implications for biblical proscriptions of homosexual behavior', *Journal of the Evangelical Theological Society* 31:4, 1988, pp. 429–441.

against divine law. Saʿadya's Judaeo-Arabic version renders *wĕ-nēdĕʿāh ʾōtām* as *ḥattā nuwāqiʿahum* ('that we may cohabit with them').[41] The same translation is offered by Lagarde II, whilst similar strategies are offered by Lagarde I (*li-nakūna maʿahumā*, 'that we may be with them')[42] and St. Makar Bib. 1 (*li-nuḍājiʿuhumā*, 'that we may lie with them').[43]

The rewriting given by Q 15:67–71 fully parallels that of Q 11:78, adding supplementary information to the text on which the two rewritings are based (Gn 19:4–8).

III

Q 15:67–71	Q 11:78
وَجَاءَ أَهْلُ الْمَدِينَةِ يَسْتَبْشِرُونَ ﴿67﴾	وَجَاءَهُ قَوْمُهُ يُهْرَعُونَ إِلَيْهِ وَمِن قَبْلُ كَانُوا يَعْمَلُونَ السَّيِّئَاتِ
قَالَ إِنَّ هَؤُلَاءِ ضَيْفِي فَلَا تَفْضَحُونِ ﴿68﴾ وَاتَّقُوا اللَّهَ وَلَا تُخْزُونِ ﴿69﴾ [...] قَالَ هَؤُلَاءِ بَنَاتِي إِن كُنتُمْ فَاعِلِينَ ﴿71﴾	قَالَ يَا قَوْمِ هَؤُلَاءِ بَنَاتِي هُنَّ أَطْهَرُ لَكُمْ فَاتَّقُوا اللَّهَ وَلَا تُخْزُونِ فِي ضَيْفِي
قَالُوا أَوَلَمْ نَنْهَكَ عَنِ الْعَالَمِينَ ﴿70﴾	—
—	أَلَيْسَ مِنكُمْ رَجُلٌ رَّشِيدٌ

Q 26:165–166, Q 27:54–55/Q 29:28–29 do not correspond to any specific passage of Gn 19; rather, they are expansions through which the author voices his evident opposition to the sexual practices of the Sodomites.

41 *Saadia, Pentateuque*, ed. J. Derenbourg, p. 27.

42 *Materialien*, ed. P. de Lagarde, II, p. 18, I, p. 122.

43 Fol. 50a.

IV

Q 11:81	Q 15:59–60
قَالُوا يَا لُوطُ إِنَّا رُسُلُ رَبِّكَ لَن يَصِلُوا إِلَيْكَ فَأَسْرِ بِأَهْلِكَ بِقِطْعٍ مِّنَ اللَّيْلِ وَلَا يَلْتَفِتْ مِنكُمْ أَحَدٌ إِلَّا امْرَأَتَكَ إِنَّهُ مُصِيبُهَا مَا أَصَابَهُمْ إِنَّ مَوْعِدَهُمُ الصُّبْحُ أَلَيْسَ الصُّبْحُ بِقَرِيبٍ	إِلَّا آلَ لُوطٍ إِنَّا لَمُنَجُّوهُمْ أَجْمَعِينَ ﴿59﴾ إِلَّا امْرَأَتَهُ قَدَّرْنَا إِنَّهَا لَمِنَ الْغَابِرِينَ ﴿60﴾
	Q 15:65–66
	فَأَسْرِ بِأَهْلِكَ بِقِطْعٍ مِّنَ اللَّيْلِ وَاتَّبِعْ أَدْبَارَهُمْ وَلَا يَلْتَفِتْ مِنكُمْ أَحَدٌ وَامْضُوا حَيْثُ تُؤْمَرُونَ ﴿65﴾ وَقَضَيْنَا إِلَيْهِ ذَٰلِكَ الْأَمْرَ أَنَّ دَابِرَ هَٰؤُلَاءِ مَقْطُوعٌ مُّصْبِحِينَ ﴿66﴾
	Q 15:73
	فَأَخَذَتْهُمُ الصَّيْحَةُ مُشْرِقِينَ
	Q 7:83
	فَأَنجَيْنَاهُ وَأَهْلَهُ إِلَّا امْرَأَتَهُ كَانَتْ مِنَ الْغَابِرِينَ
	Q 26:170–172
	فَنَجَّيْنَاهُ وَأَهْلَهُ أَجْمَعِينَ ﴿170﴾ إِلَّا عَجُوزًا فِي الْغَابِرِينَ ﴿171﴾ ثُمَّ دَمَّرْنَا الْآخَرِينَ ﴿172﴾

Q 27:57
فَأَنجَيْنَاهُ وَأَهْلَهُ إِلَّا امْرَأَتَهُ قَدَّرْنَاهَا مِنَ الْغَابِرِينَ
Q 37:134–135
إِذْ نَجَّيْنَاهُ وَأَهْلَهُ أَجْمَعِينَ ﴿134﴾ إِلَّا عَجُوزًا فِي الْغَابِرِينَ ﴿135﴾
Q 54:34
إِنَّا أَرْسَلْنَا عَلَيْهِمْ حَاصِبًا إِلَّا آلَ لُوطٍ نَّجَّيْنَاهُم بِسَحَرٍ
Q 54:38
وَلَقَدْ صَبَّحَهُم بُكْرَةً عَذَابٌ مُّسْتَقِرٌّ

Q 11:81 is, again, a summarised recasting of the events narrated in Gn 19:12–13, 15, 26. This *āya* has a range of equivalences. Q 15:59–60 and Q 15:65–66, which provide a *prophetia ex eventu*, serve to interpret a dual chronological allusion: night and dawn as references to the flight from, and destruction of, Sodom. Similar concern for the timing of the destruction is shown in Q 15:73 (cf. Gn 19:23). An interesting discursive feature is that Q 11:81 and Q 15:65–66 use the same segment: *fa-asri bi-ahlika biqiṭʿin mina l-layli* ('travel with your family in a part of the night'), suggesting that this is a *lectio optima* and is thus likely to be an original segment of the Qur'ānic Story.

A separate group formed by Q 7:83, 26:170–172, 27:57 and 37:134–135 focuses on one motif of the 'Story', narrated in Gn 19:26: the sparing of Lot and his family, except for his wife. In Q 54:34, the reference to the saving of Lot's family is accompanied by an allusion to the punishment visited upon the city (*ḥāṣiban*, i.e. 'a sandstorm',[44] cf. Q 11:82 *ḥijāratun min sijjīlin*, 'stones of clay')[45] and its timing, "at dawn" (*bi-saḥarin*). This latter strategy,[46] expressed by al-Thaʿlabī (11th c.) using the dual structure *saḥr-ṣubḥ* (*fa-lammā kāna al-saḥr … fa-lammā aṣbaḥū*),[47] is a *reductio* of Gn 19:23 הַשֶּׁמֶשׁ יָצָא עַל־הָאָרֶץ ("The sun was risen upon the earth"),[48] but harmonizes with Gn 19:15 *kĕmô hashshaḥar* (כְּמוֹ הַשַּׁחַר, 'at dawn'), as is evident in the cognates *saḥar*/*shaḥar* (cf. Peshīṭtā *shfar*), used here with a view to assimilating parallel chronological references.[49] A similar strategy is to be found in the Rabbinical literature, e.g. Pirqê Rabî ʾElîʿezer XXV:5: ביון שעלה עמוד השחר 'as the dawn of the morning rose'.[50]

The Qurʾān's treament of the timing of certain episodes reflects a number of exegetical and narrative strategies that merit attention. In both Arabic and Hebrew, *saḥar*/*shaḥar* denotes daybreak, i.e. the moment at which the darkness of the night starts to become light, before the sun rises (cf. Gn 19:23; Judg 19:25–26); this is the time of day mentioned in Q 11:81, which we can also take as the *lectio optima* because it is the *lectio longior* (cf. Q 15:65–66, 73; 54:38): *qiṭʿin min al-layli … al-ṣubḥu* ('in a part of the night … the morning')[51] rather than simply *saḥar*.

The punishment and its precise timing are the sole content of Q 54:38, where *ḥāṣiban* is glossed as *ʿadhābun mustaqirrun* ('a lasting chastiment') and *bi-saḥarin* as *bukratan* ('in the morning'); the DO *bukratan* is highlighted by the intensive verb form *ṣabbaḥa* with a view to stressing that first moment of the day, the clear light of dawn.

44 Cf. Ibn Kathīr, *Tafsīr*, IV, p. 267: *al-ḥijāra*.

45 For the interpretation of *sijjīl* as *ḥijāra min ṭīn*, see al-Ṭabarī, *Tafsīr*, XII, pp. 526–530 and al-Bayḍāwī, *Anwār al-tanzīl wa-asrār al-taʾwīl*, 5 vols, Beirut, *s.d.*, III, pp. 117.

46 So in *mufassirūn* like al-Ṭabarī, *Tafsīr*, XII, p. 519 (cf. 524) and al-Bayḍāwī, *Anwār*, III, pp. 116.

47 Al-Thaʿlabī, *Qiṣaṣ*, p. 92.

48 *Saadia, Pentateuque*, ed. J. Derenbourg, p. 28: *al-shams kharajat ʿalā al-arḍ* (אלשמס כרגת עלי אלארץ). Christian Arabic versions give: *fa-lammā ṭalaʿat al-shams ʿalā al-arḍ, wa-l-shams qad intasharat ʿalā al-arḍ* (*Materialien*, ed. P. de Lagarde, II, p. 19, and I, p. 124 respectively), *wa-ashraqat al-shams ʿalā al-arḍ* (St. Makar Bib. 1 fol. 51a).

49 On 'harmonization', see E. Tov, *Textual criticism of the Hebrew Bible*, Assen, 1992 (2nd rev. ed.), pp. 307–308; E.J. Epp and G.D. Fee, *Studies in the theory and method of New Testament textual criticism*, Grand rapids MI, 1992, pp. 175–178.

50 *Sefer Pirqê Rabî ʾElîʿezer*, Warsaw, 1870, p. 46.

51 Cf. Ibn Kathīr, *Qiṣaṣ al-anbiyāʾ*, p. 186: *fa-lammā khalaṣū min bilādihim wa-ṭalaʿat al-shams fa-kānat ʿinda shurūqihā* ('and when they left their city came the sun, it was sunrise'); cf. Cf. Ibn Kathīr, *Tafsīr*, II, p. 536. Ibn Kathīr, Tafsīr, IV, p. 267: *ākhir al-layl* 'end of the night'.

V

Q 11:82	Q 7:84
فَلَمَّا جَاءَ أَمْرُنَا جَعَلْنَا عَالِيَهَا سَافِلَهَا وَأَمْطَرْنَا عَلَيْهَا حِجَارَةً مِّن سِجِّيلٍ مَّنضُودٍ	وَأَمْطَرْنَا عَلَيْهِم مَّطَرًا فَانظُرْ كَيْفَ كَانَ عَاقِبَةُ الْمُجْرِمِينَ
	Q 15:74
	فَجَعَلْنَا عَالِيَهَا سَافِلَهَا وَأَمْطَرْنَا عَلَيْهِمْ حِجَارَةً مِّن سِجِّيلٍ
	Q 26:173
	وَأَمْطَرْنَا عَلَيْهِم مَّطَرًا فَسَاءَ مَطَرُ الْمُنذَرِينَ
	Q 27:58
	وَأَمْطَرْنَا عَلَيْهِم مَّطَرًا فَسَاءَ مَطَرُ الْمُنذَرِينَ
	Q 37:136
	ثُمَّ دَمَّرْنَا الْآخَرِينَ

Q 11:82 (= Q 15:74) equates to Gn 19:24–25, but opts for an *inversio narrationis*: where the biblical text first narrates the shower of fire and brimstone, and afterwards the cities' overturn, the Qur'ān reverses that order. Q 7:84, with its final exhortation, refers only to rain without specifying its content (*wa-amṭarnā ʿalayhim maṭaran*, 'and we sent rain upon them'), although the elided term is clearly that referred to in Q 11:82 (= Q 15:74): *ḥijāratan min sijjīlin*, which—as we shall see—has a very precise meaning. An identical *lectio* is offered by Q 11:82 and Q 15:74; this is particularly relevant to our purpose, since the repetition confirms that this is a *lectio optima*, whose basic narrative elements could be the *testimonia* of a putative pre-Qur'ānic version.

Q 26:173 (= 27:58) are *iterationes* of Q 7:84, varying only in the final exhortation, while Q 37:136 includes a vague allusion to Gn 19:25 (כָּל־יֹשְׁבֵי הֶעָרִים, 'all the inhabitants of the cities').

Where the Hebrew text of Gn 19:24 reads וַיהוָה הִמְטִיר עַל-סְדֹם וְעַל-עֲמֹרָה ('And the Lord caused it to rain upon Sodom and Gomorrah'),[52] Q 11:82 gives *fa-lammā jā'a amrunā* (...) *amṭarnā ʿalayhā* ('and when our order came (...) we caused it to rain upon her'). The Christian Arab versions offer *wa-amṭara Allāh ʿalā Sudūm wa-Ġāmūrrā al-kibrīt wa-l-nār* (Lagarde II), *wa-amṭara al-Rabb al-Ilāh ʿalā Sudūm wa-ʿĀmūrrā* (Lagarde I),[53] *wa-amṭara al-Rabb ʿalā Sādūm wa-Ġāmūr nāran wa-kibrītan*.[54] The causative *amṭarnā* ('we caused it to rain') is clearly a calque on the Hebrew hiphil הִמְטִיר ('caused it to rain', cf. LXX ἔβρεξεν), and adopts the internal-narrator technique, replacing the omniscient third-person narrator of Gn 19:24 with the first-person narrative characteristic of the Qur'ān.

The reading *amr* ('order') has no match in HMT nor in later Syriac and Arabic versions. But far from being a simple addition, it appears to hark back to an old tradition found in Patristic texts[55] and apocryphal literature dealing with the Story. JubEt 16:5, for example, gives: 'During this month the Lord executed the judgement of Sodom and Gomorrah'.[56] The term used for 'judgement' is ኵነኔ (*kʷənnāne*; cf. JubEt 16:6), which means 'judgment, sentence', as does the Arabic *amr*.[57]

Another interesting feature is the phrase *jaʿalnā ʿāliyahā sāfilan* ('we turned them upside down') used in Q 11:82; 15:74 to render the HMT הָפַךְ ('to overthrow, ruin' = Peshīṭtā ܗܦܰܟ).[58] The two Arabic versions edited by Lagarde opt for the causative *aqlaba*,[59] whereas St. Makar Bib. 1 gives *hadama* ('razed').[60] The Nestorian Ibn al-Ṭayyib uses *maṣdar inqilāb* ('overthrow') and Saʿadyah *qalaba*.[61] The root *qlb* is also used by al-Thaʿlabī to refer to Sodom's destruction.[62]

52 Ignatius, *ad Antiochenos* 2 (ed. F.X. Funk and F. Diekamp, *Patres apostolic*, Tübingen, 1913, ep. 9). Cf. Justin Martyr, Dialog., 56.

53 *Materialien*, ed. P. de Lagarde, II, p. 19, I, p. 124.

54 Fol. 51a.

55 Justin Martyr, Dialog., 128; Irenaeus, *Adversus haereses* IV,10,1; V,17,1.

56 *The Book of Jubilees*, ed. & trans. J.C. VanderKam, I, p. 93 (Ethiopic), II, p. 94 (English).

57 Cf. W. Leslau, *Comparative Dictionary of Geʿez (Classical Ethiopic)*, Wiesbaden, 1991, p. 287b.

58 R. Payne Smith, *Thesaurus syriacus*, 2 vols, Oxford, 1879, 1901, I, col. 1036.

59 *Materialien*, ed. P. de Lagarde, II, p. 19, I, p. 124.

60 Fol. 51a.

61 *Saadia, Pentateuque*, ed. J. Derenbourg, p. 29.

62 Al-Thaʿlabī, *Qiṣaṣ*, p. 92.

Both could have made use of the cognate *afaka* in form VIII ('to be turned upside down'), whence the plural active participle *mu'tafikāt* used to denote cities which were overturned by divine punishment.[63] The preference for *inqilāb*/*qalaba* reflects the fact that the Qur'ān here eschews the strategy adopted in Q 11:82 and 15:74 (*ja'alnā 'alayhā sāfilahā'*) in favour of the root *'fk* in form VIII *i'tafaka*[64] through the active participle, both in 9:70 (*mu'tafikāt*) and in 53:53 (*mu'tafika*).[65] Ibn al-Ṭayyib and Sa'adyah therefore rejected the cognates of the respective Syriac and Hebrew originals, thus moving further away from the Qur'ānic term. If Ibn al-Ṭayyib eschews the perfective verb form preferred by the Peshīṭtā (ܗܦܰܟ), it is not due to a wish to imitate the Qur'ān, but rather because with *inqilāb* Ibn al-Ṭayyib is directly rendering the emphatic feminine participle used in Gn 19:29: ܗܦܝܟܬܐ < הֲפֵכָה ('overthrow, reverse, ruin'). JubEt 16:7 adopts a similar strategy, giving the noun ገፍታኤ (*gəftāʾē*), i.e. 'subversion, overthrowing'.[66]

The use of *ḥijāratun min sijjīlin manḍūdin* ('stones of clay, one on another') to render גָּפְרִית וָאֵשׁ ('brimstone and fire') in Gn 19:24,[67] this is clearly an interpretation of the Hebrew *gāfrīt wā-'esh*, and *manḍūdin* is an evaluative addition to the causative *amṭarnā*: "we caused it to rain stones ... one on another", i.e. in large amounts. Use of the loanword *sijjīl* is wholly comprehensible if we assume that *sijjīl* (meaning 'writing material' in 21:104, and 'lumps of baked clay (used as missiles)' in 11:82, 15:74, and 105:4) and *sijjīn* ('clay tablet', 83:7–8) are variants of the same word[68] and we remember that "catapult missiles were jestingly known as Babylonian letters".[69] Tertullian speaks of *incendio*,

63 Al-Kisā'ī, *Qiṣaṣ al-anbiyā'*, ed. I. Eisenberg, p. 146. Cf. G.W. Freytag, *Lexicon arabico-latinum*, 4 vol., Halle, 1830–37, I, p. 44a-b.

64 On the unconvincing hypothesis of the relationship of *afaka* with Gə'ez *'afākiyā*, see M.R. Zammit, *A Comparative Lexical Study of Qur'ānic Arabic*, Leiden – Boston – Köln, 2002, p. 592. Cf. W. Leslau, *Comparative Dictionary of Ge'ez*, p. 9b.

65 Fr. Dietrich, *Arabisch-deutsches Handwörterbuch zum Koran und Thier und Mensch vor dem König der Genien*, Leipzig, 1894, p. 6b.

66 *The Book of Jubilees*, ed. & trans. J.C. VanderKam, I, p. 94 (Ethiopic), II, p. 95 (English). On *gəftāʾē*, see W. Leslau, *Comparative Dictionary of Ge'ez*, p. 184a. Cf. Marius Chaine, *Grammaire éthiopienne*, Beirut, 2002 (3rd. ed., rep. from 1907), p. 264b.

67 *Saadia, Pentateuque*, ed. J. Derenbourg, p. 29 translates *kibrītan wa-nāran* (כבריתא ונארא) "brimstone and fire".

68 So Ibn Kathīr, *Tafsīr*, II, p. 436.

69 F. Corriente, 'Some notes on the Qur'ānic *lisānun mubīn* and its loanwords', in J.P. Monferrer-Sala and A. Urbán, eds, *Sacred Text: Explorations in Lexicography*, Frankfurt am Main, 2009, p. 40.

i.e. 'conflagration' (*Adverus Judaeos* II,10)[70] and *igneo exussit*, i.e. 'tempest of fire' (*Adversus Marcionem* IV,29),[71] while Aphraates (*De fide* 12)[72] says that "the Sodomites were burned like straw and reed and stubble".

The phrase *jaʿalnā ʿāliyahā sāfilan* ('we turned them upside down') used in the Qur'ān to describe the destruction of Sodom is not without what might be termed "intratextual" interest. It corresponds to the Hebrew *yahafōk* (Syr. *hfak̲*), which in turn gave rise to a tradition regarding the destruction of the five cities of the Plain, which Rabbinical tradition explains by stating that "the angel stretched out his hand and overturned them" (אחד שלח מלאך את ידו והפכן):[73]

> ויהפוך את הערים האל רבי לוי בשם רבי שמואל בר נחמן חמשת הכרכים הללו היו יושבות על צור אחד שלח מלאך את ידו והפכן הה"ד (איוב כח)
>
> *And he overthrew those cities* (19:25). Rabbi Levi said in the name of R. Samuel b. Naḥman: These five cities were built on one rock, so the angel stretched out his hand and overturned them, as it is written, *He putteth forth his hand upon the flinty rock, he overturneth the mountains by the roots* (Job 18:9)

The Talmud Babli (BMeṣ 86b) tells us that Gabriel came to Abraham to inform him that he would overturn Sodom (גבריאל אזל למיהפכיה לסדום).[74] The iconographical task of overturning the earth (*taqallaba*) is well-known in Christian apocryphal literature, where it is also entrusted to the Archangel Gabriel, who will be sent by Christ as soon as the Antichrist is conquered and immediately before the Final Judgement:[75]

---

70 *Tertulliani Aduersus Iudaeos*, ed. H. Tränkle, Wiesbaden, 1964.

71 *Tertullian adversus Marcionem*, ed. E. Evans, Oxford, 1972.

72 G. Lenzi et al., *Afraate. Le esposizioni vol. I–II*, Brescia, 2012.

73 *Midrash Bereshit Rabba*, ed. J. Theodor and Ch. Albeck, *wayyera* 51,4; English translation: *The Midrash Rabbah. I. Genesis*, ed. H. Freedman and M. Simon, p. 446.

74 *Babylonian Talmud; Seder Nizikin*, ed. I. Epstein, trans. E.W. Kirzner et al. Tractate Baba Mezia, London, 1935, *ad locum*. See also Cf. L. Ginzberg, *The Legends of the Jews*, I, p. 255. Cf. Ibn Muṭarrif al-Ṭarafī, *Qiṣaṣ al-anbiyāʾ*, ed. R. Tottoli, p. 53.

75 On this text and its sources, see J.P. Monferrer-Sala, '"The Antichrist is coming ..." The making of an apocalyptic *topos* in Arabic (Ps.-Athanasius, Vat. ar. 158 / Par. Ar. 153/32)', in D. Bumazhnov et al. (eds.), *Bibel, Byzanz und christlicher Orient. Festschrift für Stephen Gerö zum 65. Geburtstag*, Louvain, 2011, pp. 674–675, and J.P. Monferrer-Sala, '"Texto", "subtexto" e "hipotexto" en el 'Apocalipsis del Pseudo Atanasio' copto-árabe', in Raif Georges Khoury, J.P. Monferrer-Sala and M.J. Viguera Molins, eds, *Legendaria Medievalia en honor de Concepción Castillo Castillo*, Córdoba, 2011, pp. 427–428.

ويظهر الرب يسوع المسيح له المجد علي مدينته مع ملايكته ويضرب جبريل الارض
فتنقلب وتنشف جميع الامياه من علي وجه الارض ومن تحتها

> The Lord Jesus the Messiah, glory to him, will appear upon his city with his angels and Gabriel will beat the earth, which will turn around and the waters of the surface of the earth and under it will disappear.

This Rabbinical tradition, also found in Eastern Christianity, must have been known to the Muslim *mufassirūn*, for al-Thaʿlabī, Ibn Muṭarrif and Ibn Kathīr also attribute the destruction of Sodom to the Archangel Gabriel, drawing on Q 1:83.[76] Finally, the last two groups of *suwar*, classified under this heading and the following one (§§VI–VII), are examples of narrative segments that do not correspond exactly to the other *suwar*, whose origin and function are different in each.

VI

The first group comprises three segments of the same kind. The three verses are independent in Qur'ānic intratextual terms, and reflect two different traditions: a) drawing on Gn 19:9, though explained in harmonization with Gn 19:12[77] (Q 7.82; 27:56); b) drawing on Josephus' *Antiquitates iudaeorum* I,11,4 (Q 15:76), which we shall be looking at later.

وَمَا كَانَ جَوَابَ قَوْمِهِۦٓ إِلَّآ أَن قَالُوٓا۟ أَخْرِجُوهُم مِّن قَرْيَتِكُمْ إِنَّهُمْ أُنَاسٌ يَتَطَهَّرُونَ	Q 7:82
فَمَا كَانَ جَوَابَ قَوْمِهِۦٓ إِلَّآ أَن قَالُوٓا۟ أَخْرِجُوٓا۟ ءَالَ لُوطٍ مِّن قَرْيَتِكُمْ إِنَّهُمْ أُنَاسٌ يَتَطَهَّرُونَ	Q 27:56
وَإِنَّهَا لَبِسَبِيلٍ مُّقِيمٍ	Q 15:76

76 Al-Bayḍāwī, *Anwār*, III, pp. 116–117. Cf. al-Thaʿlabī, *Qiṣaṣ*, p. 92; Al-Kisāʾī, *Qiṣaṣ al-anbiyāʾ*, ed. I. Eisenberg, p. 149, Ibn Muṭarrif al-Ṭarafī, *Qiṣaṣ al-anbiyāʾ*, ed. R. Tottoli, p. 54; Ibn Kathīr, *Tafsīr*, II, p. 436; Ibn Kathīr, *Qiṣaṣ al-anbiyāʾ*, p. 186.

77 Cf. L. Ginzberg, *The Legends of the Jews*, Philadelphia, 1901–1938, I, p. 254; F. Josephus AI I,12,3–4 (§§199–202).

VII

The second group consists of what we have labelled 'miscellaneous verses' with various narrative functions, depending on the context in which they appear. Several types of discourse are to be found: paraenetic segments[78] (15:72,75,77; 54:39), a rewriting[79] (26:167–169), homiletic discourse[80] (21:74–75; 29:30; 54:35–36), echoes of legend-narrative traditions[81] (37:137–138) and, again, the *reductio* of a Biblical referent (54:37), marking a *lectio unica* in the Qur'ān of Gn 19:5,11.

15:72,75,77	21:74–75	26:167–169	29:30	37:137–138	54:35–37; 39–40
لَعَمْرُكَ إِنَّهُمْ لَفِي سَكْرَتِهِمْ يَعْمَهُونَ ﴿72﴾ إِنَّ فِي ذَٰلِكَ لَآيَاتٍ لِّلْمُتَوَسِّمِينَ ﴿75﴾ إِنَّ فِي ذَٰلِكَ لَآيَةً لِّلْمُؤْمِنِينَ ﴿77﴾	وَلُوطًا آتَيْنَاهُ حُكْمًا وَعِلْمًا وَنَجَّيْنَاهُ مِنَ الْقَرْيَةِ الَّتِي كَانَت تَّعْمَلُ الْخَبَائِثَ إِنَّهُمْ كَانُوا قَوْمَ سَوْءٍ فَاسِقِينَ ﴿74﴾ وَأَدْخَلْنَاهُ فِي رَحْمَتِنَا إِنَّهُ مِنَ الصَّالِحِينَ ﴿75﴾	قَالُوا لَئِن لَّمْ تَنتَهِ يَا لُوطُ لَتَكُونَنَّ مِنَ الْمُخْرَجِينَ ﴿167﴾ قَالَ إِنِّي لِعَمَلِكُم مِّنَ الْقَالِينَ ﴿168﴾ رَبِّ نَجِّنِي وَأَهْلِي مِمَّا يَعْمَلُونَ ﴿169﴾	قَالَ رَبِّ انصُرْنِي عَلَى الْقَوْمِ الْمُفْسِدِينَ	وَإِنَّكُمْ لَتَمُرُّونَ عَلَيْهِم مُّصْبِحِينَ ﴿137﴾ وَبِاللَّيْلِ أَفَلَا تَعْقِلُونَ ﴿138﴾	نِعْمَةً مِّنْ عِندِنَا كَذَٰلِكَ نَجْزِي مَن شَكَرَ ﴿35﴾ وَلَقَدْ أَنذَرَهُم بَطْشَتَنَا فَتَمَارَوْا بِالنُّذُرِ ﴿36﴾ وَلَقَدْ رَاوَدُوهُ عَن ضَيْفِهِ فَطَمَسْنَا أَعْيُنَهُمْ فَذُوقُوا عَذَابِي وَنُذُرِ ﴿37﴾

78 For the vast literature on paraenesis, see for example John G. Gammie, 'Paraenetic literature: towards the morphology of a secondary genre', *Semeia* 50, 1990, pp. 41–77.

79 Cf. N. Sinai, 'Qur'ānic self-referentiality as a strategy of self-authorization', in Stefan Wild, ed., *Self-Referentiality in the Qur'ān*, Wiesbaden, 2006, pp. 125–126.

80 Cf. F.E. Peters, *The children of Abraham: Judaism, Christianity, Islam*, Princeton, 2004, p. 87. G.S. Reynolds, *The Qur'ān and Its Biblical Subtext*, pp. 230–253.

81 Cf. A. Neuwirth, 'Myths and Legends in the Qur'ān', in J.D. McAuliffe, ed., *Encyclopaedia of the Qur'ān*, III, pp. 477–497.

Rebulding the Story

Preliminary Step: An Eclectic Proposal

In view of the above, and through a comparison of the 69 *āyāt*, a tentative, eclectic and intertextual hypothesis can be advanced regarding a putative earlier version of the Story. The hypothesis takes as its basis the references in Q 11, which provide the text closest to Gn 19 in narrative terms. It additionally draws on three further references (Q 15:68, 54:37, 15:73) which serve to complete the Story.

The hypothesis includes a final reference (Q 15:76) not found in Gn 19, but which may have been part of the putative earlier text. The text and its English translation are as follows:

And when Our messengers came to Lot, he was grieved for them, and he lacked strength to protect them		11:77 وَلَمَّا جَاءَتْ رُسُلُنَا لُوطًا سِيءَ بِهِمْ وَضَاقَ بِهِمْ ذَرْعًا
And his people came to him, (as if) rushed on towards him, and already they did evil deeds He said: O my people! These are my daughters—they are purer—for you		11:78 وَجَاءَهُ قَوْمُهُ يُهْرَعُونَ إِلَيْهِ وَمِن قَبْلُ كَانُوا يَعْمَلُونَ السَّيِّئَاتِ قَالَ يَا قَوْمِ هَٰؤُلَاءِ بَنَاتِي هُنَّ أَطْهَرُ لَكُمْ
So guard against (the punishment of) God and do not disgrace me with regard to my guests	15:68 قَالَ إِنَّ هَٰؤُلَاءِ ضَيْفِي فَلَا تَفْضَحُونِ He said: These are my guests, so disgrace me not	فَاتَّقُوا اللَّهَ وَلَا تُخْزُونِ فِي ضَيْفِي

54:37 وَلَقَدْ رَاوَدُوهُ عَن ضَيْفِهِ
فَطَمَسْنَا أَعْيُنَهُمْ
And certainly they endeavoured to turn him from his guests, but We blinded their eyes

They said: O Lot, we are the messengers of thy Lord. They shall not reach thee	11:81 قَالُوا يَا لُوطُ إِنَّا رُسُلُ رَبِّكَ لَن يَصِلُوا إِلَيْكَ
So travel with thy people for a part of the night and let none of you turn back except thy wife. Surely whatsoever befalls them shall befall her. Surely their appointed time is the morning. Is not the morning nigh?	11:81 فَأَسْرِ بِأَهْلِكَ بِقِطْعٍ مِّنَ اللَّيْلِ وَلَا يَلْتَفِتْ مِنكُمْ أَحَدٌ إِلَّا امْرَأَتَكَ إِنَّهُ مُصِيبُهَا مَا أَصَابَهُمْ إِنَّ مَوْعِدَهُمُ الصُّبْحُ

15:73 فَأَخَذَتْهُمُ الصَّيْحَةُ
مُشْرِقِينَ
So the cry overtook them at sunrise

So when Our decree came to pass, We turned them upside down, and rained on them stones, as decreed, one after another	11:82 فَلَمَّا جَاءَ أَمْرُنَا جَعَلْنَا عَالِيَهَا سَافِلَهَا وَأَمْطَرْنَا عَلَيْهَا حِجَارَةً مِّن سِجِّيلٍ مَّنضُودٍ

Three of the segments are clearly no more than additions to the original text (11:77,81,82). But at the end of Q 11:78 (*a-laysa minkum rajulun rashīdun?*), which reflects the dialogue contained in Gn 18:23–32,[82] we catch echoes of a text which must have linked the visit of the three men to Abraham with the destruction of Sodom, as occurs in the Biblical account.[83] Interestingly, Josephus too makes use—albeit indirectly—of this allusion attributed to God, which serves to summarise the repetitive dialogue between God and Abraham in Gn 19:23–32: "To this God answered that not one of the Sodomites was good" (τοῦ δὲ θεοῦ φέσαντος μηδένα εἶναι τῶν Σοδομιτῶν ἀγαθόν).[84]

Q 54:37 (*wa-laqad rāwadūhu 'an ḍayfihi fa-ṭamasnā a'yunahum*, 'And they endeavoured to turn him from his guests, but we blinded their eyes') is a *reductio* of Gn 19:5–11. The latter phrase is an interesting exegesis of the HMT *sanĕwērîm* (סַנְוֵרִים 'sudden blindness'), an Akkadian loanword (*sinlurmā sinnūru*) meaning 'day- or night-blindness'.[85] Q 54:37 adheres to the traditional exegesis (*ṭamasnā a'yunahum*, 'we blinded their eyes')[86] also found among medieval Jewish commentators,[87] rather than the more novel exegesis offered by the Nestorian Ibn al-Ṭayyib,[88] who gives *āya* ('sign, portent'). The latter interpretation highlights the literal view of the Syriac tradition on which it draws, which in turn bases its exegesis on the term *shragrāgyātā* (ܫܪܓܪܓܝܬܐ),[89] a Persian loanword indicating a kind of visual delusion.[90] This interpretation of

---

82 See on this issue E. Ben Zvi, 'The Dialogue between Abraham and Yhwh in Gen. 18.23–32: a Historical-Critical Analysis', *Journal for the Study of the Old Testament* 17, 1992, pp. 27–46.

83 Cf. the commentary by Ibn Kathīr, *Tafsīr*, II, p. 434; cf. Ibn Kathīr, *Qiṣaṣ al-anbiyā'*, p. 182.

84 F. Josephus AI I,11,3 (§199).

85 M. Stol, 'Blindness and night-blindness in Akkadian', *Journal of Near Eastern Studies* 45, 1986, pp. 295–299.

86 Cf. Ibn Kathīr, *Tafsīr*, II, p. 435; al-Tha'labī, *Qiṣaṣ*, p. 92, Al-Kisā'ī, *Qiṣaṣ al-anbiyā'*, ed. I. Eisenberg, p. 148, and Ibn Muṭarrif al-Ṭarafī, *Qiṣaṣ al-anbiyā'*, ed. R. Tottoli, p. 54, who mention Gabriel intervention in this episode according to an old tradition (al-Ṭabarī, *Tafsīr*, XII, p. 518) in line with Origen, *Contra Celsum* I,66, II,67 (ed. M. Borret, *Origène. Contre Celse*, 4 vols, Paris, 1967–9).

87 Cf. Sĕ'adyah Ibn Danān, *Libro de las raíces*, ed. and trans. M. Jiménez Sánchez, p. 295 (nº 1326.1).

88 See on this issue J.P. Monferrer-Sala, 'The Lyre of Exegesis. Ibn al-Ṭayyib's analytical patterns of the account of the destruction of Sodom'.

89 Cf. Ephrem Syrus, *In Genesim*, ed. and trans. R.-M. Tonneau, I, p. 78 (Syriac), II, p. 63 (Latin), and Isho'dad of Merv, *Commentaire d'Iṣo'dad de Merv sur l'Ancient Testament. I. Genèse*, ed. J.-M. Vosté and C. van den Eynde, trans. C. van den Eynde, I, p. 163 (Syriac), II, pp. 176–177 (French).

90 *Shragragyathā* is glossed with Persian *abrōzišn* in *Le Commentaire sur Genèse-Exode 9,32 du manuscrit (olim) Diyarbakir 22*, ed. & trans. L. Van Rompay, I, p. 82 (Syriac), II, 104

sanĕwērîm is close to that provided by the Rabbis (GenR 50,8), who claim that the Sodomites 'were maddened' (אלאון היך) as a consequence of the blindness inflicted on them.

Another interesting segment is 15:76 with its parallel 37:137–138. The text of 15:76 *wa-innahā la-bi-sabīlin muqīmin* ("Surely it lies on road that exists") belongs to the old traditions alluded to by the compilers of *Qiṣaṣ al-anbiyāʾ*[91] and echoed in Josephus's assertion: "So far are the legends about the land of Sodom borne out by ocular evidence" (τὰ μὲν δὴ περὶ τὴν Σοδομῖτιν μυθευόμενα ἔχει πίστιν ἀπὸ τῆς ὄψεως)[92] or—with reference to the pillar of salt into which Lot's wife was changed—"I have seen this pillar which remains to this day" (ἱστόρεσα δ' αὐτήν ἔτι γὰρ καὶ νῦν διαμένει).[93] The text of 37:137–138 (*wa-innakum la-tamurrūna ʿalayhim muṣbiḥīna*, "Surely you pass by them in the morning and at nightfall"). This motif, though very popular among Christan writers,[94] probably entered Islam through the oral medium, possibly transmitted by merchants crossing the area where the city—according to Jewish and Christian tradition—had once stood.

Another interesting point is that of the four complete segments of Q 11 that together form the backbone of the textual reconstruction, two (11:77 *wa-qāla hadhā yawmun ʿaṣībun*; 11:81 *a-laysa al-ṣubḥu bi-qarībin?*) end with a sentence that concludes the earlier narration. These conclusions, which might be termed peripheral features of the text, are additions of a homiletic nature, and serve to mark the narrative tone of the text in question. If we are not mistaken, these additions provide discursive clues as to how the original text might have been split up for homiletic purposes.

Further Step: A Hypothetical Pre-Qurʾānic Version

In the light of the foregoing, we can now attempt to reconstruct the Story of the destruction of Sodom and Gomorrah by assembling the following seven segments: 11:77 + 11:78 + 15.68 + 54:37 + 11:81 + 15:73 + 11:82, to give the version and English translation shown below:

(French). Cf. R. Payne Smith, *Thesaurus syriacus*, III, col. 4326. On Persian *abrōzišn*, see Claudia A. Ciancaglini, *Iranian loanwords in Syriac*, Wiesbaden, 2008, p. 98.

91 Al-Kisāʾī, *Qiṣaṣ al-anbiyāʾ*, ed. I. Eisenberg, p. 149.

92 F. Josephus BI IV8,4 (§485), in Josephus, *The Jewish War*, books IV–VII. With an English translation by H. St. J. Thackeray, London – Cambridge, MA, 1928 (rep. 1961). Cf. Sozomen, *Historia ecclesiastica* II,24; Julius Africanus, *Chronographiae* (fragmenta), IX (ed. M.J. Routh, *Reliquiae sacrae*, Oxford, 1846 [rep. Hildesheim, 1974]).

93 F. Josephus AI I,11,4 (§§ 203–204).

94 *Ibn aṭ-Ṭaiyib. Commentaire sur la Genèse*, edité et traduit par J.C.J. Sanders, 2 vol., CSCO 274–275, Louvain, 1967, I, p. 72 (Arabic), II, p. 67 (French).

وَلَمَّا جَاءَتْ رُسُلُنَا لُوطًا سِيءَ بِهِمْ وَضَاقَ بِهِمْ ذَرْعًا وَجَاءَهُ قَوْمُهُ يُهْرَعُونَ إِلَيْهِ وَمِن قَبْلُ
كَانُوا يَعْمَلُونَ السَّيِّئَاتِ قَالَ يَا قَوْمِ هَٰؤُلَاءِ بَنَاتِي هُنَّ أَطْهَرُ لَكُمْ قَالَ إِنَّ هَٰؤُلَاءِ ضَيْفِي فَلَا
تَفْضَحُونِ وَلَقَدْ رَاوَدُوهُ عَن ضَيْفِهِ فَطَمَسْنَا أَعْيُنَهُمْ قَالُوا يَا لُوطُ إِنَّا رُسُلُ رَبِّكَ لَن يَصِلُوا
إِلَيْكَ فَأَسْرِ بِأَهْلِكَ بِقِطْعٍ مِّنَ اللَّيْلِ وَلَا يَلْتَفِتْ مِنكُمْ أَحَدٌ إِلَّا امْرَأَتَكَ إِنَّهُ مُصِيبُهَا مَا
أَصَابَهُمْ إِنَّ مَوْعِدَهُمُ الصُّبْحُ فَأَخَذَتْهُمُ الصَّيْحَةُ مُشْرِقِينَ فَلَمَّا جَاءَ أَمْرُنَا جَعَلْنَا عَالِيَهَا
سَافِلَهَا وَأَمْطَرْنَا عَلَيْهَا حِجَارَةً مِّن سِجِّيلٍ مَّنضُودٍ

And when our messengers came to Lot, he was grieved for them, and he lacked strength to protect them. And his people came to him, (as if) rushed on towards him, and already they did evil deeds. He said: O my people! these are my daughters—they are purer—for you. He said: These are my guests, therefore do not disgrace me. And they endeavoured to turn him from his guests, but we blinded their eyes. They said: O Lot! we are the messengers of thy Lord; they shall by no means reach thee; so remove thy family in a part of the night—and let none of you turn back, except thy wife, for whatsoever befalls them shall befall her; their appointed time is the morning; is not the morning night? So the rumbling overtook them (while) entering upon the time of sunrise. So when our decree came to pass, we turned them upside down and rained down upon them stones, of what have been decreed, one after another.

This hypothetical version, taking into account at all stages the *lectiones* transmitted by the *textus coranicus receptus*, might constitute, if not the exact text, at least an approximation to the pre-Qur'ānic version of the account of the destruction of Sodom and Gomorrah, i.e a version circulating before the Qur'anic text was assembled, closed, and authorized after the Prophet's death.[95]

Concluding Remarks

The irregular mosaic of *āyāt* containing information on the Story of the destruction of Sodom and Gomorra, referred to at the start of this paper, comprises a total of 69 segments of different narrative types. The final reconstruction

95 On this issue, see A.-L. de Prémare, *Aux origines du Coran*, Paris, 2004.

offered above is reduced to only 7 of those 69 segments. According to the present hypothesis, the brief initial account, a wholly-narrative text lacking in additional elements, clearly amassed various discursive accretions over time. These were of three kinds: narrative (26:167–169; 37:137–138), homiletic (21:74–75; 29:30; 54:35–36) and paraenetic (15:72,75,77; 54:39), their essential function being to enable people to learn lessons from the past.[96]

According to Nöldeke's classification, the 7 *āyāt* forming the reconstructed text belong to the Meccan period: the 3 segments comprising Q 54 and Q 15 belong to Mecca 2 and the four from Q 11 to Mecca 3. If Nöldeke's classification were wholly correct, the hypothesis advanced here would be untenable, since the reconstructed version would be the result of two different textual synchronies in compositional terms. However, as indicated at the outset with reference to the contributions of Sinai and Schmid, Nöldeke's classification does not successfully address all the problems of narrative diachrony posed by the Qur'ān. From the narrative standpoint, and thus for our present purposes, Hirschfeld's chronological arrangement is less hazardous, in that it groups the references used here into the same chronological sequence. In any event, while the chronological order of the Qur'ān is of primary methodological concern in textual analysis, not only for the Muslim tradition but also for much of Western textual criticism, its application gives rise to several textual drawbacks which are in some cases overcome by a diachronic textual approach.

Thus, while recognising the valuable contribution made by the chronological ordering of the Qur'ān, the present hypothesis is not bound by its constraints, but is governed instead by purely redactional criteria. The assumption is that those 7 *āyāt* represent the text closest to what might have been the original version of the Story in the Arab-Islamic milieu. That putative original pre-Qur'ānic Arabic version was subsequently adapted, disseminated and glossed to suit the requirements of the Qur'ānic text. Close examination of all the homiletic glosses and paraeneses will not only shed further light on this type of discourse in the Qur'ān, but may also—we believe—provide immensely-valuable supplementary information on the textual diachrony of glossed texts of the Story.

Finally, it should be stressed that this hypothetical pre-Qur'ānic version is not the only result of the Islamic reception of the account contained in Gn 19, even though the Biblical account is the direct referent on which the pre-Qur'ānic text is constructed. The Story of the destruction of Sodom and Gomorrah was known before the arrival of Islam, both in its Biblical form and in Jewish and Christian parabiblical literary developments. Moreover, the

96 T. Khalidi, *Arabic Historical Thought in the Classical Period*, Cambridge, 1994, pp. 8–10.

transmission of the Story coexisted alongside homiletic adaptations of the account produced—primarily for paraenetic and exegetic purposes—by Jewish and Christian writers. Thus, when the *textus coranicus receptus* assembled all the Story material, it included not only what we consider the pre-Qur'ānic text, but also additional elements of the story (narrative, homiletic, paraenetic), some of which must already have been in circulation prior to the arrival of Islam.

CHAPTER 3

Manipulation of the Qur'an in the Epistolary Exchange between al-Hāshimī and al-Kindī

Sandra T. Keating

The well-known text purporting to be an exchange of letters between the Muslim ʿAbd Allāh ibn Ismāʿīl al-Hāshimī and the Christian ʿAbd al-Masīḥ ibn Isḥāq al-Kindī written at the beginning of the ninth century has remained the subject of speculation among scholars. Little is known of its provenance, and important questions persist about the identity of its author(s), context and actual date. Because of these uncertainties, the text has been generally ignored by scholars until recently. A further difficulty is that the earliest Arabic manuscripts available, apparently copies of a 12th century text, are dated from the 17th century. To date, no critical edition has been made, and the only published versions of the Arabic text remain the 1977 dissertation thesis of George Tartar, which he also translated into French, and the edition of A. Tien.[1]

1 L. Bottini, '*The apology of al-Kindī*', in D. Thomas and B. Roggema, eds, *Christian-Muslim relations. A bibliographical history volume 1* (600–900), Leiden, 2009, pp. 590–1. French translation by G. Tartar, *Dialogue islamo-chrétien sous le calife al-Maʾmūn (813–834). Les épitres d'Al-Hashimî et d'Al-Kindî.* Paris, 1985. Tartar made use of four manuscripts in his edition: MS Paris, BNF–Syr. 204; MS Paris, BNF–Syr. 205; MS Paris, BNF–Ar. 5141; MS New Haven, Yale Landberg Collection–Ar. 56a, and the 1912 Cairo edition. The Arabic edition, likely based on MS Dublin, Chester Beatty–Ar. 4924 and MS Cairo, Dār al-kutub—ʿUlūm al-ijtimāʿiyya 1731 was made by A. Tien (*Risālat ʿAbdallāh ibn Ismāʿīl al-Hāshimī ilā ʿAbd al-Masīḥ ibn Isḥāq al-Kindī yadʿūhu bihā ilā l-Islām wa-risālat al-Kindī ilā l-Hāshimi yaruddu bihā ʿalayhi wa-yadʿūhu ilā l-Naṣrāniyya = The apology of al-Kindī*, London, 1880, repr. London 1885; Cairo, 1895; Cairo, 1912; Damascus, 2005). The most extensive studies of the text to date are F. González Muñoz, *Exposición y refutación del Islam : la versión latina de las epístolas de al-Hāšimi y al-Kindi.* A Coruña, 2005; P.S. van Koningsveld, 'The Apology of al-Kindī', in T.L. Hettema and A. Van der Kooij, eds, *Religious polemics in context*, Assen, 2004, pp. 69–02, and S.K. Samir, 'La version latine de l'Apologie d'al-Kindi (vers 830 ap. J.-C.) et son original arabe', in M. Penelas, P. Roisse and C. Aillet, eds, *¿Existe una identidad mozárabe? Historia, lengua y cultura de los cristianos de al-Andalus (siglos IX–XII)*, Madrid, 2008, pp. 33–82. I am currently in collaboration with Krisztina Szilagyi to prepare a critical edition and English translation of the complete text. For this chapter I will refer to Tartar's French edition and the Arabic edited by Tien recently reprinted.

 | DOI 10.1163/9789004360747_004

In spite of the paucity of information about the early history of exchange, it was apparently held to be of enough significance to be translated into Latin in the medieval period. As one of the few such texts known in the West, it played an unusually important role for Latin-speaking scholars by providing knowledge of earlier debates between Muslims and Christians in the Middle East. For example, we can be quite sure that the exchange was a source for Nicholas of Cusa (d. 1464) in writing his influential *Cribratio Alcorani* (1460/1). Jasper Hopkins in particular has argued that the Latin translation of the 'debate among those noble Arabs' mentioned by Nicholas is none other than the *Risāla al-Kindī*.[2] As far as is known, Nicholas had access to this text through the 'Toledan Collection', a group of Arabic texts commissioned for translation into Latin in the mid-12th century by Peter the Venerable, which also includes the earliest known Latin rendering of the Qur'an by Robert of Ketton.[3] In the past two decades, there has been renewed scholarly interest in the medieval Latin engagement with Islam, and as a consequence the Latin version of the letters of al-Hāshimī and al-Kindī has recently been edited and translated into Spanish.[4] This has prompted a fresh look at the Arabic original and search for answers concerning its origins.

The text as it has been preserved includes only the invitation of al-Hāshimī to Islam and the response of al-Kindī. The latter makes up nearly 85% of the translation, and makes no mention of a further response on the part of al-Hāshimī. As noted in the chapter in this volume by Fr. Emilio Platti, the text reveals a high level of knowledge about the origins and contents of the Qur'an on the part of the Christian author, whose identity has yet to be determined satisfactorily: is he a Christian who participated in actual exchanges with Muslims; to which denomination does he belong; how did he come to know so much about Islam? Even more intriguing is the question of whether the entire exchange was written by a single author as a hypothetical exercise, or represents an actual conversation between a Muslim and a Christian. The assumption among many scholars has been that the 'epistolary exchange'

2 Nicholas of Cusa, *Nicholas of Cusa's De Pace Fidei and Cribratio Alkorani: translation and analysis*, 2nd ed., and trans., Jasper Hopkins, Minneapolis, 1994, p. 75.

3 Thanks to Rita George-Turtković for pointing this out to me. Some of the earliest scholars to identify the source of the 'debate' were J. Kritzeck, *Peter the Venerable and Islam*, Princeton, 1964 and M.-T. d'Alverny, "Deux traductions latines du Coran au Moyen Âge", *Archives d'histoire doctrinale et littéraire du Moyen Âge*, n° 22–23, 1947–1948, pp. 69–131. More recently, Thomas Burman explored the question more extensively in 'The influence of the apology of Al-Kindi and *Contrarietas alfolica* on Ramon Llull's late religious polemics, 1305–1313', *Mediaeval Studies* 53, 1991, pp. 197–228.

4 Gónzález Muñoz, *Exposición*.

reflects a common literary device of the period and was constructed by one author who used the introductory letter as a foil for his arguments against Islam.[5] Nonetheless, there is some evidence that the texts do reflect a genuine exchange between a Christian and a Muslim that took place around the mid-820's. In fact, a specific link to the known debates of the period has been identified by Georg Graf, who noted the presence of large excerpts of Abū Rā'iṭa al-Takrītī's '*Risāla* on the Holy Trinity' in the letter from al-Kindī. Graf himself believed that it was Abū Rā'iṭa who had 'lifted' the material from al-Kindī.[6] This, however, seems rather unlikely.

At least three significant arguments undermine Graf's suggestion. First, one would need to presume that an author from whom nothing else has survived composed the brief but difficult theological defense of the Trinity found in al-Kindī's *Risāla*, and that it was then adopted by an established theologian. While this is not impossible, it seems more likely that passages of such complex thinking would have their origin with an author known for extensive theological treatises. Second, the much longer text of Abū Rā'iṭa does not show signs of being an elaboration of a shorter writing by another author; it is a complete exposition that systematically replies to Muslim challenges to the doctrine of the Trinity using primarily philosophical and theological reasoning. Al-Kindī's excerpt, on the other hand, has been tailored to fit the overall trajectory of his text and fit seamlessly into a presentation that speaks directly to Muslims. The primary purpose of al-Kindī's *Risāla* is to explain to Muslims why a Christian would not convert to Islam. When compared to Abū Rā'iṭa's extant *rasā'il* on the Trinity and Incarnation, which are intended to assist *Christians* in responding to Muslims and to give a clear account of Christian doctrine in the new

5 Among those who followed this view are A. Abel, 'L'apologie d'al-Kindī et sa place dans la polémique islamo-chrétienne', in *L'Oriente cristiano nella storia della civiltà. Atti de Convegno internazionale* (*Rome 31 marzo–3 aprile—Firenze, 4 aprile 1963*), coll. Problemi attuali de scienza e di cultura, Quaderno nº 62, Rome, Accademia Nazionale de Lincei, 1964, pp. 501–23; M. Ḥ. Al-Bakri, 'Risālat al-Hāšimī ilà l-Kindī, wa-radd al-Kindī ʿalay-hā', *Bulletin of the Faculty of Arts, Fouad I University of Cairo*, May 1947, pp. 29–49, and ʿA.M. Sharfī, 'Al-Fikr al-islāmī fī l-radd ʿalā l-naṣārā ilā nihāyat al-qarn al-rābīʿ al-ʿāshir', in *Kulliyyat al-ādāb wa-l-ʿulūm al-insāniyya, Tūnis, al-silsila al-sādisa* 29, Tūnis, 1986. G. Tartar refuted this position in 'L'authenticité des épîtres d'al-Hāsimī et d'al-Kindī sous le calife al-Ma'mūn (813–834)', in K. Samir, ed., *Actes du Ier Congrès international d'ètudes arabes chrétiennes* (*Goslar, septembre 1980*), coll. Orientalia Christiana Analecta, 118, Rome, 1982, pp. 207–21. See a summary of these arguments in Samir, 'La version latine', pp. 39–40.

6 Ḥabīb ibn Hidma Abū Rāiṭa, *Die Schriften des Jacobiten Ḥabīb ibn Hidma Abū Rāiṭa*, G. Graf, ed., and trans., Corpus Scriptorum Christianorum Orientalium 131, Louvain, 1951, pp. 32–6.

lingua franca of Arabic, it becomes apparent that the explication of the Trinity likely had its origin in the longer '*Risāla* on the Holy Trinity'.

Finally, Abū Rā'iṭa states that he wrote this treatise and the '*Risāla* on the Incarnation' in response to the request from an unknown Christian who is apparently engaged in discussion of these topics with Muslims.[7] Again, some have maintained the *rasā'il* follow a literary genre employing a hypothetical adversary and reader; yet the existence of another text that uses the material exactly in the way Abū Rā'iṭa recommends seems to support the thesis that this is more than a literary device. One might add that the beginning of the '*Risāla* on the Holy Trinity' gives advice to a person who has been invited by a Muslim to accept Islam on how to enter into the conversation. He states that Muslims will present a list of attributes that a Christian can certainly accept,[8] and that the response should be to first establish an understanding of what Christians mean by the doctrine of the Trinity, hence the first *Risāla*.[9] This is, in fact, what al-Kindī does in his *Risāla*, leading one to suspect he knew of Abū Rā'iṭa's advice.

A final observation may also help us establish the authenticity of al-Kindī's *Risāla* as a letter in an actual correspondence between two people. In keeping with the stated intention of the text, the format is an exposition, as one would expect in such an exchange and speaks to the reader more intimately. Indeed, al-Kindī's letter presumes that the reader knows him personally and his qualifications to address these questions. Abū Rā'iṭa, on the other hand, notes that the clearest way to present the information asked for by his reader is in the question and answer format typical of this period.[10] He expects his *risāla* to be used primarily for teaching purposes for Christians, even if it might be read by Muslims.

All of this, along with other corroborating points proposed by Samir Khalil,[11] remains circumstantial evidence. Yet, if these suggestions are correct, it may well be that al-Kindī was the intended recipient of Abū Rā'iṭa's *rasā'il* on the Trinity and Incarnation. One could then confidently identify the author of

7 S.T. Keating, *Defending the "People of Truth" in the early Islamic period: the Christian apologies of Abū Rā'iṭah*, History of Christian-Muslim relations 4, Leiden, 2006, pp. 164–5.

8 On the importance of this list for establishing common ground in debates between Muslims and Christians, see S.T. Keating, 'An Early List of the Ṣifāt Allāh in Abū Rā'iṭa al-Takrītī's "First Risāla On the Holy Trinity"', *Jerusalem Studies in Arabic and Islam* (Hebrew University) 36, 2009, pp. 339–355.

9 Keating, *Defending*, pp. 164–71.

10 Keating, *Defending*, pp. 164–5.

11 Samir, 'La version latine', pp. 34–41.

al-Kindī's *Risāla* as a Syrian Orthodox (Jacobite) Christian writing in the second half of the 820's, associated with the court of al-Ma'mūn, and in conversation with a Muslim who has invited him to Islam. But this thesis awaits further conclusive proof. Nonetheless, if this suggestion is in fact the case, the al-Hāshimī—al-Kindī exchange offers us a remarkable window into relations between Muslims and Christians in this period.

Whatever the historical relationship between the authors might be, a comparison between the writings of Abū Rā'iṭa and the *Risāla* of al-Kindī draws attention to some significant characteristics of al-Kindī's text that merit further investigation. For example, whereas Abū Rā'iṭa responds with treatises following traditional patterns to the Qur'anic command that Christians and Jews give a proof (*burhān*) of their beliefs and a rejection of Muḥammad's message (e.g. Q 2:111),[12] al-Kindī adds a lengthy and scathing historical account of Muḥammad's original message and its preservation by his followers. Al-Kindī moves beyond a simple defense and explanation of Christian faith and practice to a refutation of the very foundations of Islam. It is for this reason that this chapter will refer to his writing as a *risāla*, rather than an 'apology', as it is called in many translations. This is the term used most often in the extant manuscripts. The *risāla*, a letter-treatise form also found in Syriac writing, likely has its roots in the Greek *erotapokriseis* apologetical style. Christian writers in Arabic, including al-Kindī, exploit the form to its fullest, using an arsenal that includes theological, philosophical and historical arguments to make their case.

A second notable characteristic of the *Risāla* of al-Kindī is the approach that he takes to the charge that Jews and Christians have manipulated their scriptures. The accusation has its origin in the Qur'an and was later developed into the teaching of *taḥrīf*. Elsewhere I have argued that Abū Rā'iṭa's motivation for developing extensive non-scriptural evidence for Christian doctrine is to circumvent this accusation and to take advantage of the rising interest in the Greek philosophical tradition among Muslim intellectuals.[13] Al-Kindī combines this approach with a brilliant strategy—he turns the charge of *taḥrīf* against the Muslims, arguing that it is the Qur'an that was manipulated during its collection, and that the text the Muslims possess is not completely reliable.

The *Risāla* of al-Kindī became a significant resource for Christian apologetic writing against Islam in the medieval period. This is in large part because of his

12 See Keating, *Defending*, 'On the proof of the Christian religion and the proof of the Holy Trinity', pp. 82–145; 'The first *risāla* on the Holy Trinity', pp. 164–215; and 'The second *risāla* of Abū Rā'iṭah al-Takrītī on the Incarnation', pp. 222–97.

13 Keating, 'Refuting the charge of taḥrīf'.

detailed knowledge of the origins of the Qur'an and its contents. In an effort to better understand al-Kindī's method, this chapter will examine the numerous *āyāt* quoted in his *Risāla* and the arguments he makes about them.

The manuscripts edited by Tartar include the letter of ʿAbd Allāh ibn Ismāʿīl al-Hāshimī, which invites the reader to the true religion of Islam and presents its beliefs and practices. al-Hāshimī concludes with an invitation to respond to his request without pressure or fear of consequences. This letter is followed by ʿAbd al-Masīḥ ibn Isḥāq al-Kindī's lengthy *Risāla*, divided by Tartar into five parts: 'Theodicy, Unity and Trinity' (an extensive explanation of the Christian teaching of the One God revealed as Three in salvation history); 'Muhammad: Conqueror or Prophet—Messenger' (was Muhammad truly a prophet like other Old Testament prophets); 'Was the Qur'an revealed by God?' (what type of law does the Qur'an represent—divine, human or satanic law, and an account of its origin and collection); 'Islamic Practices and Traditions' (the effects of the coming of the Qur'an on its followers, and an examination of the traditions and practices of Muslims); and 'Exposition of the Christian Faith' (the revelation of God in Christ, with a special emphasis on authentic prophets and the truth of Christian teachings).[14]

Al-Kindī's general methodology becomes apparent in the development of his argument throughout the text. He hopes to demonstrate that while important common beliefs between Muslims and Christians exist, especially belief in the one God and recognition of the prophets of the Old Testament, Muslims have been misled by Muhammad and his followers into accepting a corrupted revelation. The result has been a deviation from the true revelation of the loving and merciful God Who has been manifested in Jesus Christ and witnessed by the ancient prophets and Christians. In the explanation of why he does not accept the call to submit to the one God, al-Kindī does not simply describe Christian faith; he seeks to undermine the very authenticity of Muhammad's prophethood and the authority of the Qur'an. To do so, he summarizes what he claims is widely known about the collection of the Qur'an, as well as the Qur'an itself as evidence. Although quotations from the Qur'an are found throughout the text to support his arguments, of particular interest to us here is the material contained in the third section of the *Risāla* on the divine revelation of the sacred text, which includes numerous references to and even direct quotations from the Qur'an.

14 Tartar, *Dialogue islamo-chrétien*, pp. 298–302.

Use of the Qur'an in al-Kindī's *Risāla*

What strikes one immediately is the sheer number of quotations found in this section—at least twelve extended quotations, with more partial quotations of five words or less. Further, the author makes explicit references to nineteen different *sūras*, some by name.[15] Even more remarkable is the fact that all are complete and accurate as to the received text of the Qur'an. Evidence of such extensive knowledge of the Qur'an is rarely found in Christian writings from this period, even when it may be hinted at. Al-Kindi does not tell us whether he is taking the excerpts from a written or oral source, but given the accuracy of the quotes, one suspects that he has at hand a written Qur'an. It might be suggested that the original text of the letter did not contain such complete references and that the material was added in a later redaction. If this were the case, though, one would expect more complete quotations in places they are missing. For example, when recounting the story of the relationship between the Christian monk Sergius/Nestorius to Muhammad, al-Kindī alludes to the Qur'anic verses that rebut this influence, yet he does not quote the *āyāt* specifically, even though they would help make his case.[16] In the available manuscripts, the author provides just enough of the verse to make his point, evidently with the expectation that his reader will understand his meaning and the fuller implications of his argument, and even to 'fill in the blanks'. This makes it likely that al-Kindī's *Risāla* is intended primarily for Muslim eyes, or perhaps other Christians who know the Muslim traditions well.

In the middle of this section, al-Kindī writes extensively about the collection of the Qur'an and the various Arabic readings that were present among the followers of Muḥammad before it was put into its final form. Here he presents what he believes is well-known about the early process of canonizing the scriptural text. His arguments are intended to remind the reader that for various reasons some *āyāt* were rejected or 'manipulated' by those responsible for their collection. Consequently, one cannot accept the version of the Qur'an as it has been received as the perfect word of God.

al-Kindī speaks to his reader as one whose account of the history carries some authority, and assumes his reader recognizes the significance of the arguments he is making. He draws attention to the verses in question and the names and events that played a key role in the early formation of the scripture, but does not write as if he is instructing someone who is not at least familiar with the outlines of the story and the importance of the references. Further,

15 *Sūras* noted specifically are: 2, 5, 8, 9, 12, 16, 17, 18, 24, 29, 33, 43, 44, 56, 59, 76, 88, 113, and 114.

16 Tartar, *Dialogue islamo-chrétien*, pp. 180–1; Tien, *Risāla*, pp. 82–3.

when he writes about the Arabic language and decisions made about different readings, he points out that he has some authority as an educated native Arabic speaker, one who understands the complexities of the early history and can see through, so to speak, the claim that the Qur'an in its received form has been miraculously sent from God.[17] Al-Kindī is confident he possesses the knowledge necessary to reject al-Hashīmī's invitation to Islam and perhaps even to convince his reader of its errors.

Divine Law, Human Law and Satanic Law

The first reference to the Qur'an in the third section of the *Risāla* comes in the question concerning the relationship of Muhammad's message to that of the law (*sharīʿa*) of Jesus and of Moses. Al-Kindī begins by making the case that divine law is greater and nobler than natural law, and that the Qur'an affirms divine law has come through Jesus, stating that his law contains guidance and light from God. Here we find one of the longest continual quotes from the Qur'an: 'And in [the prophets'] footsteps We sent Jesus the son of Mary, confirming what he [already] had of the Torah. And We sent him the Gospel, in it was guidance and light, and confirming what he [already] had of the Torah. A guidance and an admonition to the righteous' (Q 5:46).[18] The law of Jesus is one of generosity and, al-Kindī claims, above what reason demands of human beings, as one can see from Matthew 5:44–5, in which Jesus teaches the love of one's enemy and generosity to all people. The law of Moses, on the other hand, requires justice and equity, as is clear in the teaching of 'an eye for an eye' (Deut. 19:21; Exod. 21:23–4). This is the law of reason and what is recognized as natural law.

Already in this opening, al-Kindī draws his reader's attention to the Qur'anic claim at issue—God has sent prophets in succession, each with a revelation that confirmed what had come before. The implication is that, just as Jesus, who is accepted by the Christians, confirmed the Torah, Muhammad has received a revelation that confirms the Torah and Gospel. This most recent revelation is also a 'guidance and an admonition to the righteous'. It is al-Kindī's project to dismantle this claim by showing that, whatever truth might be found in the Qur'an, Muhammad was not a prophet like Moses and Jesus, and the Qur'an as Muslims currently possess it is not the pure revelation of God.

This aim becomes immediately clear with his explanation of the third type of law, Satanic law, which is that of injustice and inequity. Our author asks, to which of these three types of law of does Muhammad's message belong?

---

17 Tartar, *Dialogue islamo-chrétien*, pp. 196–8; Tien, *Risāla*, pp. 94–6.

18 Abbreviated quote found in Tartar, *Dialogue islamo-chrétien*, p. 175; the longer in Tien, *Risāla*, p. 78. All translations are my own, unless otherwise noted.

Here al-Kindī juxtaposes two apparently opposing verses in the Qur'an to represent the law of the Old and New Testaments, namely: 'Life for life, eye for eye, ... Tooth for tooth' (Q 5:45; abbreviated quote), and a reference to the recommendation on divorce from Q 2:237 that when one forgives he is 'closest to piety'. These two verses, al-Kindī argues, expose the inconsistency of the law of Muhammad, and, in short, reveal that he did not receive anything new from God, but rather stole the material from previous sources. al-Kindī strongly implies that Muhammad heard these verses from the Torah and Gospels, but did not understand that they represented the old law and the new. Thus, the Qur'an presents them as simultaneously valid, whereas Christians hold that the old law, i.e. natural law, has been superseded by the new law established by Jesus Christ. He concludes that the contents of the Qur'an are incoherent, leading one to presume that it has its source in Satanic law and that its own claims undermine its continuity with previous scriptures.[19]

Manipulation of the Revelation

The next section takes a rather different approach, asking whether the Qur'an is a revealed book from God. The main argument on the part of the Muslim, al-Kindī says, is that since Muhammad was illiterate, how could he have produced such a book whose beauty has no parallel? Here Q 17:88 is quoted in part, followed by two longer quotations. The first is Q 2:23,[20] which demands that the listener produce a text equal to it if he is in doubt as to its authenticity, while the second, Q 59:21, states that even a mountain would have recognized this as a true revelation and reacted accordingly.[21] al-Kindī is rather unimpressed by the challenge, sarcastically asking whether al-Hāshimī considers this feat on the same level as the miracles of Moses, Joshua and Jesus, who parted the sea, stopped the sun and raised the dead! Such a claim necessitates turning to the known history and origins of the Qur'an to ascertain whether it is truly a revelation from God. This prompts the next major section, which presents an extensive history of the relationship of Sergius the monk, who is later called Nestorius because of his adherence to Nestorian teachings, with Muhammad, and the collection and publication of the Qur'an

19 Tartar, *Dialogue islamo-chrétien*, pp. 176–9; Tien, *Risāla*, pp. 79–81.

20 'And if you are in doubt about what we have sent down to our servant, produce a sūra like it, and call your witnesses besides Allah, if you are truthful.'

21 'If we had sent this Qur'an down upon a mountain, you would have seen it humble itself and cleave apart from fear of Allah.'

in the first decades following Muhammad's death. Of interest to us here are the references first to Q 16:103 and then the quotation of Q 5:82 made at the beginning of this section.

Al-Kindī begins his account with an explanation of the relationship between Muhammad and the monk Sergius/Nestorius, reporting that it was the monk who turned him from the idolatry of his upbringing. Tartar rightly notes that this is surely an allusion to Q 16:102–3, which defends Muhammad against the charge that he was taught by a man, not the Holy Spirit, the proof being that the Qur'an is in a 'clear, Arabic tongue,' not the language of the foreigner.[22] Yet, al-Kindī does not quote the verse, even though it would help his argument. He then points out that Muhammad's relationship with Sergius/Nestorius is the reason why the Qur'an states that Christians are 'nearest to [the followers of Muhammad] in love, ... and that among them are priests and monks and that they are not arrogant.'[23] This positive view of Christians in the Qur'an is contrasted with the negative opinion it holds of the Jews, who he says have an 'ancient conflict' with the Christians.

The Jews are held responsible for a great deal of the confusion al-Kindī sees in the Qur'an, and he recounts a tradition that, after the death of Sergius/Nestorius, two of them pretended to be followers of Muhammad, but were only interested in undermining his message. Later, following Muhammad's death, the culprits slipped into the teaching of Muhammad parts of the Torah, some of its laws, etc., along with the verse alleging that 'The Christians say "the Jews are [standing] on nothing" and the Jews say "the Christians are [standing] on nothing", and they read the [same] Book'.[24] Although Abū Bakr was aware of Sergius/Nestorius' relationship with Muhammad, and even told 'Alī about it, the two Jews seized the book (*kitāb*) of Muhammad that 'Alī had in his possession which was based on the Gospel and mutilated it so as to obscure the correct teachings.

According to al-Kindī, the two secret Jews added other *sūras* and *āyāt*, such as al-Naḥl (16), al-'Anakbūt (29) and others he does not name specifically, to distort the pure text. He points out that the opportunity for this to happen came immediately after Abū Bakr was chosen as the successor, when 'Alī delayed in reporting to him with the excuse that he was 'occupied with collecting the Book of God, as the Prophet had commanded' him.[25] The result

---

22 Tartar, *Dialogue islamo-chrétien*, p. 181, n. 12.

23 Tartar, *Dialogue islamo-chrétien*, p. 181; Tien, *Risāla*, p. 83.

24 Q 2:113. The order of this verse is opposite in the Qur'an—the Jews are listed first. Tartar, *Dialogue islamo-chrétien*, p. 182; Tien, *Risāla*, p. 84.

25 Tartar, *Dialogue islamo-chrétien*, p. 182; Tien, *Risāla*, p. 84.

was that Abū Bakr and ʿAlī had two different collections of verses, which they subsequently decided to combine; thus, the distortions entered into the text without Muhammad's followers being aware of them. Here al-Kindī mentions *sūra* al-Barāʾa (9), also called al-Tawba, specifically as one that was known 'by heart'.[26]

Later, during an extended account of the collection of the Qurʾan, al-Kindī lists several other known discrepancies between the original text and the 'official' *muṣḥaf* (copy) promulgated by ʿUthmān. For example, at one time, *sūra* al-Nūr (24) was much longer than *sūra* al-Baqara (2) and some of *sūra* al-Aḥzāb (33) was cut, making it incomplete. al-Kindī states that originally *sūras* al-Anfāl (8) and al-Barāʾa (9), mentioned previously, were not separated. This is why al-Barāʾa does not begin with '*b-ismi-llāhi al-raḥmāni al-raḥīmi*', and is the only *sūra* that does not include this introduction. Further, it is known that Ibn Masʿūd, one of the first followers of Muhammad, said 'nothing should be added' with regard to the last two *sūras*, al-Falaq (113) and al-Nās (114).[27] Thus, it seems that Ibn Masʿūd, a reliable early witness, was protesting the addition of *āyāt* to the Qurʾan.

Al-Kindī goes on to remind the reader of several other disagreements among the followers of Muhammad, including the controversy over the 'stoning verse',[28] *mutʿa* (temporary marriage),[29] and further changes that came about because of variations in readings of the Qurʾan. Yet, the diverse texts and readings initially remained in existence, because they were preserved by many

26 Tartar, *Dialogue islamo-chrétien*, pp. 183–4; Tien, *Risāla*, p. 85.

27 Tartar, *Dialogue islamo-chrétien*, p. 188; Tien, *Risāla*, p. 87. These two sūras are also known as the 'two refuge prayers' (*al-muʿawwidhatayn*) because they both begin with 'I take refuge' (*aʿūdhu*). The *Tafsīr* of Ibn Kathīr states that according to Aḥmad Ibn Ḥanbal, Zirr Ibn Hubaysh reported that Ubai ibn Kaʿb told him that Ibn Masūd did not include these two sūras, along with the Fātiḥa, in his reading of the Qurʾan. (Ismāʿīl ibn ʿUmar ibn Kathīr, *Tafsīr al-Qurʾān al-ʿAẓīm*, Muṣṭafā al-Sayyid Muḥammad, ed., Jīza; Muʾassasat Qurṭuba, 2000, p. 516). Al-Qurtubī also states in his *tafsīr* that this position of Ibn Masʿūd was widely known (Muḥammad ibn Aḥmad al-Qurtubī, *al-Jāmiʿ li-aḥkām al-Qurʾān*, vol. 20, al-Qāhira, 1369/1950, p. 251). Thanks to Fr. Elie Estephan for pointing out the latter reference to me.

28 Although the verse commanding stoning as the punishment for adultery was apparently revealed to Muhammad, it was left out of the Qurʾan for an unknown reason. ʿUmar ibn al-Khaṭṭāb is recorded as confirming this as fact, but did not add the verse out of fear of being accused of adding to the Holy Book. The account is given in *Saḥīḥ* Bukhārī, vol. 8, bk. 82, no. 816 and *Saḥīḥ* Muslim, 1691 a.

29 The issue was whether *mutʿa* was allowed by the Qurʾan, since ʿAlī claimed that Muhammad had forbidden it at Khaybar. See Tartar, *Dialogue islamo-chrétien*, p. 189, n. 44; Tien, *Risāla*, p. 88.

of the followers, such as Ibn Masʿūd and ʿAlī, who kept them at their homes. But these readings were all suppressed, he says, and a final, official version was made, copied, and sent to various major cities to replace all others, along with the command to destroy all others. The result of this was that the manipulation of the text was not known to everyone after the *muṣḥaf* of ʿUthmān was promulgated.[30]

This section concludes with a list of some of those involved in the manipulation of the Qurʿan, especially the first four caliphs and their supporters, before it came to its final recension, and the known conflicts between them. Consequently, al-Kindī states, one cannot trace the manipulation to a single person, but rather it is the fault of many people, and quite complex. He rather sarcastically comments that this should not surprise anyone, since even the Qur'an itself notes that 'The Arabs of the desert are the worst in unbelief and the greatest hypocrites' (9:97).[31] Why, then, would one trust them concerning a revelation from God to a prophet?[32]

The Perfection of the Qur'an

This brings al-Kindī to a discussion of the assertion that the uniqueness of the Qur'an is proof of its veracity and of Muhammad's prophethood. Again, the verse from 17:88 is quoted, this time at length: 'Say: "If mankind and the jinns were to gather together in order to produce the like of this Qur'an, they could not produce its like, even if they helped each other."'[33] The claim, he argues, seems to rest on the perfection of the Arabic text, yet it is clear that there are more eloquent writings in other languages—Greek, Persian, Syriac and Hebrew. A part of the problem, al-Kindī states, is that his interlocutor is ignoring evidence from these other sources that he knows. In a very interesting passage, he states that this intentional ignorance is an inconsistency on the part of his addressee—al-Kindī himself has read and studied the sources and history, but simply ordered and well-presented narratives are not enough to convince him. He implies here that his Muslim reader has access to the same information as himself, but willfully overlooks evidence contrary to his beliefs and is thus taken in by falsehood.[34]

30 Tartar, *Dialogue islamo-chrétien*, pp. 188–90; Tien, *Risāla*, pp. 87–8.

31 Tartar, *Dialogue islamo-chrétien*, p. 191; Tien, *Risāla*, p. 89.

32 Tartar, *Dialogue islamo-chrétien*, pp. 190–2; Tien, *Risāla*, pp. 89–90.

33 Tartar, *Dialogue islamo-chrétien*, p. 193; Tien, *Risāla*, p. 91.

34 Tartar, *Dialogue islamo-chrétien*, p. 193; Tien, *Risāla*, p. 91.

Further evidence against the perfection of the Qur'an can be found in the language of the text itself. Although the Qur'an states that God 'sent down an *Arabic* Qur'an so that you might learn wisdom' (Q 12:2), it is clear that it contains many foreign words. Al-Kindī gives five terms as examples (*istabraq, sundus, abāraq, namāriq*, and *mishkāt*), which are found in at least six different *sūras*.[35] But these terms have their own equivalents in Arabic. Why, he asks, if the language is adequate, is it necessary to borrow terms from others to express the revelation? This question leads one to two possible answers—either God sent a revelation that was not expressed in Arabic as eloquently as it could have been, or Muhammad did not know Arabic well enough to express it perfectly. Al-Kindī suspects it is the latter, noting that the Qur'an alludes to Muhammad's recognition that the Arabs were well-known for engaging in discussion and making subtle arguments, as the Qur'an states, 'But they are a contentious people' (43:58).[36] Arabic is a very rich language, and poets ancient and contemporary exploited it beautifully. Thus, al-Kindī concludes, one must explain the presence of these foreign words in the Qur'an. He argues they are evidence of the complex formation of the text that included many hands, but not a divine origin.

The next longer sections of al-Kindī's text do not include references specifically to the Qur'an, but focus instead on the form of its *āyāt* compared to Arabic poetry, as well as the various material reasons why many have converted to Islam. This section of the text concludes by asking why Muslims give so much praise and honour to the family of Muhammad, which seems to be a contradiction to the statement by God found in several places in the Qur'an: 'O Children of Israel! Remember the favor which I bestowed upon you, and that I preferred you over the worlds.'[37] Should not, then, the Children of Israel, that is, all of the descendants of Abraham, be treated with favor? Even more so, al-Kindī asks, is it not the case that all human beings are equal before God, as descendants of Adam? The excessive praise and honor given to Muhammad and his family by Muslims, as well as particular obligations concerning them, are in direct opposition to the teachings that have been given about all human beings.[38]

This concludes the third section of the epistolary exchange, according to the translation of Tartar.

35 Tartar, *Dialogue islamo-chrétien*, p. 194; Tien, *Risāla*, pp. 91–92.

36 Tartar, *Dialogue islamo-chrétien*, p. 194; Tien, *Risāla*, p. 92.

37 Tartar, *Dialogue islamo-chrétien*, p. 205; Tien, *Risāla*, p. 102. Q 2:47; 2:122 ; 'He has preferred you over the worlds' in 7:140; 45:16; see also 6:86.

38 Tartar, *Dialogue islamo-chrétien*, pp. 204–6; Tien, *Risāla*, pp. 101 3.

Conclusion

The use and references to the Qur'an in al-Kindī's *Risāla* are unusual and unique in many respects. The section of the text under discussion in this presentation can offer us insights into at least two interrelated aspects of the period, the first historical and the second theological.

It has been noted by others already that the freedom al-Kindī apparently feels in making his arguments allows us to date the exchange fairly confidently during the reign of al-Ma'mūn (813–33 CE),[39] making it an important window into the period. Relations between Muslims and Christians must have been such that, at least within al-Kindī's context, the consequences of arguing against the authority and authenticity of the Qur'an and its Prophet were not dire. At the minimum, we can say that we have no reports that al-Kindī suffered for his position. That the text is written in Arabic by someone who professes to be an Arabic-speaking Christian further indicates the growing importance of Arabic as a theological language for Christians. Exchanges like that between al-Hāshimī and al-Kindī were probably the impetus for the great increase in theological writing in Arabic among Christians at the beginning of the ninth century as they felt an urgency to establish terminology and appropriate expression of doctrine and practice in the new language. Al-Kindī presents us with an example of a Christian writer who is familiar enough with the Qur'an and the history of its collection that he can make complex arguments about it, indicating that he recognized the importance both of the religion of his rulers and its foundational scripture. His arguments become a staple in later exchanges between Christians and Muslims about the truth of their respective religions. Such exchanges likely played an important role in the later ban on non-Muslims owning a Qur'an or teaching it to their children. Limited access to the text assured that non-believers could not use it to undermine settled teachings.

It is quite clear that al-Kindī himself had extremely detailed knowledge of the Qur'an and its early canonization. He states that his knowledge came through careful study, apparently not only from the examination of texts, but also in conversation with others. al-Kindī indicates that some of what was once common knowledge of the collection and canonization of the 'official' *muṣḥaf* of the Qur'an has now been lost because it was suppressed. The *Risāla* gives us a non-official witness to the redaction of the Qur'an, as well as its early collection, in a carefully ordered account. While the accuracy of this account might be questioned, there is no doubt that al-Kindī is not interested in supporting

39 See especially the articles by Samir, 'La version latine ', and Tartar, 'L'authenticité'.

the 'official version' of the origins of the Qur'an. This alone makes the *Risāla* a valuable text for understanding the early process of the reception of the Qur'an.

From a theological perspective, it is first notable that in this section al-Kindī does not choose to debate the presentation of Christianity (or Judaism) in the Qur'an, focusing instead on the integrity of the text itself and the claims Muslims make about it. The arguments he puts forward may now seem to be cliché, because they became so integral to Christian apologetical literature, especially in Europe, over the centuries. Yet within al-Kindī's *Risāla* they reveal a particularly interesting approach to apologetics. Nowhere in this section does the author argue that the content of the Qur'an is false; rather, the excerpts of Muhammad's text are treated as if they carry a degree of truth (unless we are to assume al-Kindī was being completely disingenuous in his writing!).

Al-Kindī's overarching argument in this section is that the Qur'an presents only 'part of the story' of God's revelation, the story that is known in its fullness to Christians. He argues that the deficiency of the Qur'an is likely the result of the limitations of Muhammad's own learning, as well as the garbled transmission and collection of the text after his death. Neither of these were Muhammad's fault. In the first case, Muhammad was limited by the shortcomings of his upbringing and historical context in pagan Arabia. Although he was taught by Sergius/Nestorius, after his death those who collected his teachings were unaware of this relationship, and so did not pass them on correctly. The problem was further exacerbated by the influence of the two Jews who intended to cause confusion and so deliberately violated its integrity. As a result, the current recension of the Qur'an must be regarded as 'imperfect' or somehow incomplete. It is not the scripture of the Christians that has been the victim of taḥrīf, it is the Qur'an.

As further evidence of this imperfection, al-Kindī calls into question the uniqueness and originality of the Qur'an. The tone in this section is not aggressive, but rather implies that those who, like al-Hāshimī, believe that the Qur'an is sent by God because of its perfection and uniqueness, are simply unaware of the writings of the great poets and rhetoricians of the Greeks, Persians, and others. He argues that much of its content can be traced back both to Jewish and Christian sources, yet it presents a truncated version of the stories and teachings they present. Without the 'whole story', one is in danger of misunderstanding God's revelation.

One sees this argument clearly in the opening of the section in which al-Kindī draws attention to the difference in teaching between the Old and New Testaments. Without making the problem explicit, he necessarily raises the question in the mind of the reader of the continuity between the two, a continuity that requires a fuller understanding of salvation history than is presented by the Qur'an's account of revelation to the prophets. A second example of this approach is found at the end of the section, where the reader is reminded of the Qur'an's affirmation that the Children of Israel have been favoured by God and honour has been bestowed upon them. Why, then, have they fallen from favour, as both Christians and Muslims claim? Additionally, what is the role of Muhammad and his extended family accounted in salvation history? It appears that al-Kindī wants to prompt the reader to reflect on sin, mercy and God's covenant with his people. In these instances, the full implications of the verses are not drawn out, but left for the reader's further consideration. Al-Kindī declares that he has carefully studied the texts and thought about the claims made by Muslims, and he is not convinced; thus, he is not obliged to submit to the religion of his rulers.

Much remains unknown about the *Risāla* of al-Kindī, its author, and its original purpose. But its significant impact on European thinking about Islam, as well the important role it has played for Christians in both East and West in responding to Muslim claims about its scripture and prophet makes it a continuing subject for serious study.

CHAPTER 4

ʿAbd al-Masīḥ al-Kindī on the Qurʾan

Emilio Platti

Introduction

The Letter written by ʿAbd al-Masīḥ ibn Isḥāq al-Kindī at the time of the Caliph al-Maʾmūn (d. 833), was the most influential Christian Arabic polemical text translated in Latin in the medieval West.[1] It seems obvious that even Thomas Aquinas' appreciation of Muhammad in his *Contra Gentiles* I, chapter 6, is directly or indirectly inspired by al-Kindī's *Apology*.[2] The main argument against Islam in al-Kindī's text is linked to the Prophet of Islam, and without any doubt, the Christian criteria for authentic prophecy presented by Aquinas, are the same criteria presented by al-Kindī: the signs and miracles, the authenticity of the Scriptures and the conformity of the prophetic law with God's will, in accordance with His nature.

As mentioned in our article, 'Criteria for Authenticity of Prophecy in ʿAbd al-Masīḥ al-Kindī's Risāla,'[3] we are convinced that there is no reason to question the information given in the al-Hāshimī-al-Kindī correspondence that ʿAbdallāh al-Hāshimī and al-Kindī were themselves high ranking dignitaries at al-Maʾmūn's court, as suggested by al-Kindī's report of a speech given by the caliph to those who attended his counsel.[4] Arguments presented by William

1 L. Bottini, 'The Apology of al-Kindī', in D. Thomas and B. Roggema, (eds), *Christian-Muslim Relations. A Bibliographical History I*, Leiden, 2009, pp. 587–94.

2 E. Platti, 'Il contesto teologico dell'apprezzamento dell'Islam di S. Tommaso', in D. Lorenz and S. Serafini, (eds), *Studi 1995*, Roma, 1995, pp. 294–307; and E. Platti, 'L'image de l'islam chez le Dominicain Vincent de Beauvais (m. 1264)', *Mélanges de l'Institut Dominicain d'Etudes Orientales* 25–26 (2004) pp. 65–140.

3 E. Platti, 'Criteria for Authenticity of Prophecy in ʿAbd al-Masīḥ al-Kindī's Risāla', in A. Rippin and R. Tottoli, (eds), *Books and Written Culture of the Islamic World. Studies Presented to Claude Gilliot on the Occasion of His 75th Birthday*, Leiden, 2015, pp. 3–25.

4 See G. Tartar, *Dialogue islamo-chrétien sous le calife al-Maʾmūn. Les épîtres d'al-Hāshimī et d'al-Kindī.* Thèse pour le Doctorat de 3e cycle, Strasbourg, 1977, for the Arabic text, pp. 94–5; and W. Muir, *The Apology of Al Kindy written at the court of al-Mâmûn (circa A.H. 215; A.D. 830) in Defence of Christianity against Islam*, London, Second Edition, 1887; for an English translation, pp. 29–31. See also Muir's summary, 'Our Apologist quotes a speech delivered at an assembly of his courtiers by the Caliph (Al-Mâmûn) in which he likens the hypocritical

 | DOI 10.1163/9789004360747_005

Muir are very convincing. al-Kindī's Apology is indeed 'a production written in so fearless and trenchant a spirit against Islam', … without being 'immediately suppressed', '… which a few years later would have been utterly impossible', but 'under the tolerant sway of the free-thinking al-Mâmûn, that was possible'. Muir refers here to the Muʿtazilite views of the caliph.[5]

According to Tartar's edition, al-Kindī's *Apology* has five chapters, but we can divide the work into three parts. The first chapter, which is also the first part, is a treatise on God's Unity and Trinity; the second, third and fourth chapters can be considered the second part, describing Islam in his fundamentals: Muhammad, the Qur'an, and Islamic Traditions and Practices; and the third part, the fifth chapter, is a description of the Christian Faith.

In our earlier article we studied the chapter on Muhammad, seen in the larger context of the *Risāla*.[6] Here we will analyse the third chapter in the second part of al-Kindī's work concerning the authenticity of Qur'an. It is clear that this subject is less important in the structure of the *Letter* as a whole. This can be seen in the first paragraphs of the chapter on the Qur'an, which are given the title by Tartar, *Le Coran est-il révélé de la part de Dieu?* (has the Qur'an been revealed by God?). Yet they actually concern three laws which form part of the *Sunna* of the Prophet of Islam. The third of these laws, brought by al-Hāshimī's 'master' (*ṣāḥib*) is, according to al-Kindī, nothing else than 'wrongdoing and violence', not the 'natural law' of Moses, or the 'divine law' of Jesus.

While the chapter on the Qur'an may not be the central theme of the *Letter*, Sidney Griffith's comment from 1983 is still valid:

> Unfortunately, thus far little scholarly attention has been paid to this valuable ninth century discussion of such an important issue. Perhaps the polemical character of the text makes it suspect as an historical document. But the fact remains that it is one of the earliest testimonies to the process of the Qur'an's canonization.[7]

---

conversion of the Magians, Jews and Christians of his own day, to that of the Jews and hypocrites in the time of Mahomet', p. 63.

5 Muir, *The Apology*, pp. 35–6.

6 Platti, 'Criteria'.

7 S.H. Griffith, 'The Prophet Muḥammad, his Scripture and his Message according to Christian Apologies in Arabic and Syriac from the first Abbasid Century', in *La vie du Prophète Mahomet. Colloque de Strasbourg (octobre 1980)*, (Bibliothèque des Centres d'Études Supérieures spécialisées), Paris, 1983, p. 105. See also P.S. van Koningsveld, 'The Apology of Al-Kindî', in T.L. Hettema & A. Van der Kooij, (eds), *Religious Polemics in Context*, Assen, 2004, pp. 69–92.

Griffith added that 'Unfortunately, there is not yet a satisfactory modern, critical edition of the Arabic text',[8] and Barbara Roggema repeated the same statement in 2009, 'It is to be regretted that no critical edition has yet appeared.'[9]

The current state of knowledge of the Arabic manuscripts is as follows. The oldest manuscript, Paris Arabic Karshūnī 205, which is said to be based on an older anonymous Cairo manuscript is from 1619. Gotha 2884 is from 1656, and Paris Arabic Karshūnī 204 is from 1657. Both are said to be based on a manuscript dated 1173. Tartar's Arabic edition was based on only four manuscripts; Paris Arabic Karshūnī 205 from 1619, Paris Arabic Karshūnī 204 from 1657, Yale Landberg 56a from 1874 and 1884, and Paris Arabic 5141 from 1887.

We have used the following versions for this article: the critical edition of the Arabic text by Georges Tartar, the critical edition of the 1142 Latin translation, published by Fernandez González Muñoz,[10] the French translation by Georges Tartar,[11] the Italian translation by Laura Bottini,[12] the (uncritical) Arabic edition by A. Tien,[13] and the partial English translation by Sir William Muir.

Al-Kindī on the Qur'an as Law

It is al-Kindī's final conclusion that none of the criteria concerning the authenticity of prophecy can be applied to the Prophet of Islam,[14] and this is particularly true because the Prophet's law, included in the Qur'an, mostly contradicts God's divine law of justice and generosity.[15] For al-Kindī, the Prophet's law is just the opposite; it is a law of injustice, and not divine law nor natural law (*ḥukm al-jawr, wa-huwa ḍidd al-ḥukm al-ilāhī wa-khilāf al-ḥukm al-ṭabīʿī*).

8 Griffith, 'The Prophet Muḥammad', p. 144.

9 B. Roggema, *The Legend of Sergius Baḥīrā: Eastern Christian Apologetics and Apocalyptic in response to Islam*, Leiden, 2009, p. 159, n. 24.

10 F.G. Muñoz (ed.) *Exposición y refutación del Islam: la versión de las epistolas de al-Hāšimī y al-Kindī*, La Coruña, 2005.

11 G. Tartar, *Dialogue islamo-chrétien sous le calife al-Ma'mūn. Les épîtres d'al-Hāshimī et d'al-Kindī*, Paris, 1985.

12 Al-Kindī, *Apologia del Cristianesimo*, Traduzione dall'Arabo, Introduzione a cura di Laura Bottini, Patrimonio Culturale Arabo Cristiano 4, Milano, 1998.

13 A. Tien, *The Apology of El-Kindi. A work of the ninth century, written in Defence of Christianity by an Arab*, London, 1880, 1885^2. See also the new non-critical edition with reference to two unidentified Egyptian manuscripts published in Damascus in 2005.

14 Tartar, Arabic text 99, 18–19: *Innanā innamā ṣaddaqnā al-anbiyā' wa-qabilnā qawlahum ʿindamā jā'ūnā bi-shurūṭ al-nubūwa wa-dalā'il al-risāla wa-aʿlām al-waḥy.*

15 Tartar, *Arabic text*, p. 102: 6 and 21.

But he adds some remarkable comments leaving the door open for a completely different interpretation of the Qur'anic texts concerning this subject. al-Kindī upholds the negative interpretation of the Islamic way of life on the path of God (*ilā sabīl Allāh*), but he is aware of the principle of abrogation in classical qur'anic exegesis, (*nāsikh wa-mansūkh*).[16] In this case, other verses of the Qur'an can *abrogate* the very negative verses mentioned and present a different, and more tolerant, interpretation of Islamic law. The 'tolerant' verse most quoted by al-Kindī is Q 2:256, '*lā ikrāh fī l-dīn*', 'no compulsion in religion'.[17]

Al-Kindī on the 'Sources' of the Qur'an

The second point analyzed by al-Kindī concerning 'the Book which is with you' (*al-kitāb alladhī bi-yadika*), is the main argument given by al-Hāshimī for the authenticity of the revelation of the Qur'an and the fact that it 'came down from God' (*munzal min ʿanda Allāh*).[18] The proof is, on the one hand, that Muḥammad was unable to read or write '*ummī ṣāḥibuka rajul ummiyyun*',[19] in the sense that he was not familiar with and had no knowledge of these stories (*lam yakun lahu maʿrifa wa-lā ʿilm bi-tilka l-akhbār*),[20] and on the other hand that nobody will be able to produce a similar Qur'an, according to the argument revealed in the three texts challenging anybody 'to produce the like thereof' in Q. 17:88, 2:23, and 59:21.

For al-Kindī, the content of the book itself is not original. In the first place, it cannot be denied that the text of the Qur'an borrowed stories and religious material from two sources, the Torah and the Gospel (*suriqa min mawḍiʿayn mukhtalifayn aʿnī al-Tawrāt wa l-Injīl*).[21] This can be explained by the twofold influence of Jews and Christians. Three Jews are named: ʿAbd Allāh ibn

16 Tartar, *Arabic text*, p. 148: 11. On this subject, see Platti, *Islam, Friend or Foe?* Louvain, 2008, pp. 79–80.

17 Platti, 'L'image de l'islam', pp. 125–8: the Latin translation of the more positive verses of the Qur'an 2:256; 10:99–100; 10:108–9: 11:118–9; 109; 29:46; 2:253; 3:20; 3:103.

18 Tartar, *Arabic text*, p. 106:12.

19 Tartar, *Arabic text*, p. 106:14.

20 These stories are 'the old stories coming from Moses and the Prophets and our Lord Christ' (*mā jāʾa fīhi min al-akhbār al-qadīma ʿan mūsā wa l-anbiyāʾ wa-ʿan sayyidinā al-masīḥ*) Tartar, Arabic text, 106: 13.

21 Tartar, *Arabic text*, p. 105:6.

Sallām (d. 663, sic for Salām),[22] Ka'b called al-Aḥbār (d. c. 652),[23] and Wahb Ibn al-Munabbih (d. 728),[24] who were already mentioned in the first part of the *Apology*.[25] For al-Kindī, they are the sources of Jewish practices introduced in Islam. Al-Kindī names one Christian, a monk called Sergius (*Baḥīrā*), who called himself Nestorius.[26]

In the Islamic tradition, there are two stories about Muhammad meeting a monk. The two occasions when Muhammad met a monk are mentioned in Ibn Isḥāq's *Sīra nabawiyya*. There is also a story about a monk called Baḥīrā[27] and another about an anonymous monk, who is called Nasṭūr in the *Kitāb al-ṭabaqāt al-kabīr* of Ibn Sa'd.[28] According to these episodes, the monks recognize the signs of prophethood in Muhammad. There is no mention of the

---

22 Tartar, *Arabic text*, p. 108:9. See also J. Horovitz, ''Abd Allāh Ibn Salām', *Encyclopaedia of Islam* 1:52, Leiden, 1979, and A. Guillaume, *The Life of Muḥammad: a Translation of (ibn) Isḥāq's "Sīrat Rasūl Allāh"*, London, 1955, pp. 240–1, *'Abd Allāh Ibn Salām accepts Islam.*

23 See also M. Schmitz, 'Ka'b al-Aḥbār', *Encyclopaedia of Islam* 4:316–7, Leiden, 1978. According to Muslim sources, Ka'b did not meet the prophet during his lifetime so there is an anachronism in al-Kindī's reference to Ka'b. This is true for Wahb as well. On the other hand, it is clear that Qur'an commentaries included well-known *Isrā'īliyyāt*. See Muqātil's commentary: *Tafsīr Muqātil Ibn Sulaymān. 80–150 Hijriyya I–V*, Cairo, 1979. It is likely that al-Kindī was mistaken about the chronology of the Jewish influence on the Qur'an and the *Isrā'īliyyāt.*

24 Tartar, *Arabic text*, p. 139:3.

25 Tartar, *Arabic text*, p. 46:15–6. See also Platti, '*Vincent de Beauvais*', p. 35.

26 Tartar, *Arabic text*, p. 107:18.

27 See Roggema, *The Legend of Sergius Baḥīrā*, and Guillaume, *The Life of Muhammad*, pp. 79–81, where Ibn Isḥāq mentions the monk Baḥīrā but does not call him Sergius.

28 Other (Muslim) traditions mention a monk called Nasṭūr. See Ibn Sa'd, *Kitāb al-ṭabaqāt al-kabīr* 1:1, (trans.) S.M. Haq, New Delhi, no date, pp. 145–7, and 177–9: (Muhammad) set out with (Khadīja's) slave, Maysara, 'till they reached Buṣrā, (a city) in Syria. They halted in the market of Buṣrā under the shade of a tree close to the monastery of a monk who was called Nasṭūr. The monk came to Maysara with whom he was acquainted and said: O Maysara, who is this man, that he halted under this tree? Maysara said: He is one of the Qurayshites, the people of the Sanctuary. The monk said to him: None but a prophet did ever halt under this tree. Then he said: Is redness in his eyes? Maysara said: Yes, it never leaves him. The monk said: He is the last of the Prophets. I wish I could be present when he would be forced to go in exile". (… On the market, a disputant said to Muhammad): "Swear by *al-Lāt* and *al-'Uzza*! The Apostle of Allāh—may Allāh bless him—said: I never swear by them, and whenever I happen to pass by them, I turn my face from them. The man said: Your word is true. Then (the monk) said to *Maysara* in confidence: O Maysara! By Allāh! He is a prophet. By Him in whose possession is my life! He is really the person who answers the description which our scholars find in their Scriptures.'

monks transmitting the contents of their Holy Book to Muhammad, but one of them says that Muhammad is the person who answers the description found in their Scriptures.

Al-Kindī on the 'Collection' of the Qur'an

Concerning the collection of the Qur'an itself, al-Kindī's information is in accord with some Islamic traditions,[29] as was the case for what he said about the episodes of the life of the Prophet. For this part of the third chapter, Tartar's edition refers to Ibn Abī Dāwūd's *Kitāb al-Maṣāḥif*, which contains several Traditions along with their *isnād* concerning this subject. Abū Bakr Ibn Abī Dāwūd al-Sijistānī was born in 844 and died in Baghdad in 929, so he was a contemporary of al-Ṭabarī (d. 923). Al-Kindī's *Epistle* appears to be older than Ibn Abī Dāwūd's collection of *Aḥādīth*, which is said to be the oldest in the genre.[30] A more detailed study of the Traditions referred to and connected with this subject is needed.

In any case, it will become clear from the following overview that it is al-Kindī's intention to demonstrate, from what Muslims themselves recognize to be authentic sources describing the 'collection' of the Qur'an after the Prophet's death, that Muhammad's 'original' Qur'an was not transmitted carefully. In this chapter, as in the last, al-Kindī uses Islamic sources to demonstrate that Muḥammad cannot be an authentic prophet.

Al-Kindī presents the following episodes concerning the collection of the Qur'an: the 'collection' of the Qur'an by 'Alī; the 'collection' of the Qur'an under Abū Bakr; the 'collection' of the Qur'an under 'Uthmān; the 'manipulation' of the original Qur'an resulting in the 'Uthmānic Qur'an; and the intervention of al-Ḥallāj ibn Yūsuf.

---

29 See V. Comerro, *Les traditions sur la constitution du muṣḥaf de 'Uthmān, Beiruter Texte und Studien*, 134, Beyrouth-Würzburg, 2012; and H. Motzki, 'The Collection of the Qur'ān', *Der Islam* 78 (2001) pp. 1–34, with reference to other collections of Traditions written in the ninth century, other than those in Bukhārī and Ṭabarī analysed by Comerro in chapters 1 and 2. It is obvious that we cannot compare the *isnād* introducing the *hadīth* in these collections, which are usually said to go back to al-Zuhrī, with the text of al-Kindī since he has no interest in the *isnād* of the Traditions.

30 According to A. Rippin, 'al-Sidjistānī', *Encyclopaedia of Islam* 9:546–7, Leiden, 1997.

The 'Collection' of the Qur'an by 'Alī

After mentioning that 'Alī Ibn Abī Ṭālib had been influenced by the two Jews 'Abd Allāh Ibn Salām and Ka'b called (*al-ma'rūf bi-*) al-Aḥbār, who added several texts to the Qur'an, such as *sūra* 16 (*al-Naḥl*-The Bee), *sūra* 29 (*al-'Anqabūt*-The Spider) 'and other texts', al-Kindī refers to different versions of a Tradition in which Abū Bakr asked 'Alī Abū l-Ḥasan why he didn't perform allegiance to him when others did, 'after forty days; and according to some others, after six months' (*qāla qawmun ba'da sittati shuhūr*). 'Alī answered: 'I was busy collecting God's Book, as the Prophet recommended me' (*Kuntu mashghūlan bi-jam' kitāb Allāh li-anna al-nabī kāna awṣānī bi-dhālika*).

According to the hadith transmitted by Ibn Abī Dāwūd, at that time 'Alī promised under oath not to wear any clothes, 'until he brought the Qur'an together in a volume' (*ḥattā yujmi 'al-Qur'ān fī muṣḥaf*). However, in Jeffery's edition of the *Kitāb al-Maṣāḥif*, there is a note saying that only one transmitter (Ash'ath) mentions *fī muṣḥaf*, and that *ajma'a al-Qur'ān* could simply mean *atamma ḥafẓahu*.[31] In the paragraph on 'Umar in Ibn Abī Dāwūd's book, it is said that he was the first to collect the Qur'an in a book *wa kāna awwal man jama'ahu fī l-muṣḥaf*.[32]

The 'Collection' of the Qur'an under Abū Bakr

According to al-Kindī, it was Abū Bakr who asked for the qur'anic material to be collected wherever it could be found. Sometimes people knew some verses by heart, as was the case with verses from *sūra* 9 (*al-Barā'a* or *al-Tawba*—Immunity or Repentance). al-Kindī says that it was a Bedouin from the desert who knew this text (*ka-sūrat al-Barā'a allatī katabūhā 'an al-a'rabī alladhī jā'ahum min al-bādiya*), while Ibn Abī Dāwūd mentions that it was Khuzayma Ibn Thābit who knew 'the end' (*ākhir*) of this *sūra*.[33] This conforms to the version in the *Ṣaḥīḥ* of Bukhārī (d. 870), (*ajma'uhu min al-'usub wa-l-likhāf wa ṣudūr al-rijāl ḥatta wajadtu ākhir sūrat al-tawba ma'a Abī khuzayma al-Anṣārī*),[34] which also mentions the fact that 'Umar 'started looking for the Qur'an and

31 A. Jeffery, *Materials for the History of the Text of the Qur'an: the old Codices* (*Kitāb al-Maṣāḥif* of Ibn Abī Dāwūd together with a collection of the variant readings), Leiden, 1937, p. 10, l. 8–10.

32 Jeffery, *Materials*, p. 10, l. 14–5.

33 Jeffery, *Materials*, p. 7, l. 19 with verses 128–9 from *sūra* 9.

34 Bukhārī, *Ṣaḥīḥ*, Cairo, 1959, Book 66, chap. 3.

collecting it from (what was written on) palm stalks and thin white stones, and from the men who knew it by heart'. But al-Kindī has a different reading, 'what was written on wood, palm branches and shoulder bones' (*wa-mā kāna maktūban ʿalā ṣaḥīfa wa-ʿalā khashab wa-jarīd al-nakhl wa-ʿaẓm al-katif*).

From these details it appears that al-Kindī has a different reading of the same story, and that it seems very likely that his information could be traced back to Islamic material. But it is remarkable that none of the terms used by al-Kindī in this particular case are actually found in one of the six authentic collections, nor even in Aḥmad Ibn Ḥanbal's *Musnad*. Ibn Abī Dāwūd's text mentions that they wrote it '*fī l-ṣuḥuf wa l-alwāḥ wa l-ʿusub*'. It is obvious that these differences are due to the oral transmission of these traditions.

al-Kindī mentions that people followed different readings of the Qur'an, readings according to 'Alī's text, or readings according to the Bedouin text (*al-aʿrābī*). Some people read according to Ibn Masʿūd's version of the text, according to the following Prophetic Tradition, 'Whoever wants to read the Qur'an in a tender and soft way, the way it came down, he has to read it according to the reading of Ibn Umm 'Abd' (*man arāda an yaqraʾ al-Qurʾan ghaddan layyinan kamā unzila, fa l-yaqraʾ bi-qirāʾat Ibn Umm ʿAbd*).[35] 'Abdallāh Ibn Masʿūd was called Ibn Umm 'Abd, 'the son of the mother of a slave'. This Tradition is also found in Aḥmad Ibn Ḥanbal's *Musnad*, (*man aḥabba an yaqraʾ al-Qurʾan ghaḍḍan kamā unzila, fa l-yaqraʾ alā qirāʾat Ibn Umm ʿAbd*).[36] There are only marginal differences between the versions of al-Kindī and Aḥmad Ibn Ḥanbal. Others followed the reading of Ubayy Ibn Kaʿb, according to the following tradition, also mentioned in Aḥmad's *Musnad*, 'He said that Ubayy Ibn Kaʿb Abū l-Mundhir is the lord of the readers' (*fa qāla Ubayy Ibn Kaʿb Abū l-Mundhir sayyid al-qurraʾ*).[37] The wording in the *Apology* is, 'the best of your readers is Ubayy' (*aqraʾukum Ubayy*).[38]

The 'Collection' of the Qur'an under 'Uthmān

According to al-Kindī, people were reading the Qur'an in so many different ways that the Caliph 'Uthmān decided to intervene and to ask some people to collect all available qur'anic material. al-Kindī's version is similar to those in Bukhārī's *Ṣaḥīḥ*, Book 66, chapter 3, and in Ibn Abī Dāwūd. The story of the

35 Tartar, *Arabic text*, p. 111:8.

36 Aḥmad ibn Ḥanbal, *Musnad*, Cairo, 1931, *hadith* 17729.

37 Aḥmad Ibn Ḥanbal, *Musnad, hadith* 3373.

38 Tartar, *Arabic text*, p. 112: 2.

collection in al-Kindī can be summarized as follows: 'Uthmān was informed that people read the text in different manners; so, he decided to bring together the qur'anic material, scrolls and parchment and what was already written (*al-adrāj wa l-riqāʿ wa-mā kutiba awwalan*). 'Alī was not consulted, and Ibn Masʿūd refused to collaborate, while Abū Mūsā al-Ashʿarī did. Zayd Ibn Thābit al-Anṣārī and 'Abdallāh Ibn al-'Abbās were asked to collect the material and to correct it. And they were told that if they both disagreed upon something, a term or a word, they had to write it 'according to the language of the Quraysh' *lisān Quraysh*. They disagreed about many things, such as *al-tābūt*, Zayd said, *huwa al-tābūh*, but Ibn al-'Abbās said, *bal huwa al-tābūt*, and they wrote it in the language of Quraysh. There were many things like that'.[39]

Ibn Abī Dāwūd's version is as follows;

> Khudayfa said that the people of Kūfa read according to the reading of 'Abdallāh (Ibn Masʿūd), and the people of Baṣra according to the reading of Abū Mūsā (al-Ashʿarī).'[40] "Uthmān sent (the following people) to transcribe (*an ansakhū*) the leaves into volumes (*al-ṣuḥuf fī l-maṣāḥif*): Zayd Ibn Thābit, Saʿīd Ibn al-'Āṣ, 'Abd al-Raḥmān Ibn al-Ḥārith Ibn Hishām and 'Abdallāh Ibn Zubayr. And he said to the group of three people from the Quraysh (*al-Qurashiyyīn*): When you disagree, you and Zayd Ibn Thābit, write it in the language of the Quraysh; it was indeed sent down in their language ... Al-Zuhrī said: one day they disagreed upon "al-tābūt" and "al-tābūh". And the group of the Quraysh said "al-tābūt", while Zayd said "al-tābūh"; and their disagreement went up to 'Uthmān, who said: write "al-tābūt", since this is the language of the Quraysh.[41]

Bukhārī's two accounts of 'Uthmān's collection are the best-known versions of this event, but he does not mention a disagreement about *al-tābūt* and *al-tābūh*. The first story is as follows:

> 'Uthmān ordered Zayd bin Thābit, Saʿīd Ibn al-'Āṣ, 'Abdallāh Ibn al-Zubayr and 'Abd al-Raḥmān Ibn al-Ḥārith Ibn Hishām to write it down in books (*maṣāḥif*) and he said to them: "In case you disagree with Zayd bin Thābit regarding any Arabic utterance of the Qur'an, then write it in the language of the Quraysh (*lisān Quraysh*), for the Qur'an came down in their language." And so they did.

39 Tartar, *Arabic text*, p. 112–3.
40 Ibn Abī Dāwūd, *Kitāb al-Maṣāḥif* (ed. Jeffery), p. 13.
41 Ibn Abī Dāwūd, *Kitāb al-Maṣāḥif* (ed. Jeffery), p. 19.

The second account is as follows:

> Hudhayfa Ibn al-Yamān came to ʿUthmān at the time when the people of Shām were waging war to conquer Armenia and Azerbaijan, together with the people of Iraq. Hudhayfa was troubled by their differences in the recitation (of the Qurʾan), so he said to ʿUthmān: "O Prince of the believers! Save this nation before they differ about the Book as the Jews and the Christians did before". So ʿUthmān sent a message to Ḥafṣa saying: "Send us the pages (*al-ṣuḥuf*) so that we may compile them into books (*maṣāḥif*); and we will return them to you". Ḥafṣa sent (this material) to ʿUthmān. And ʿUthmān then ordered Zayd bin Thābit, ʿAbdallāh Ibn al-Zubayr, Saʿīd Ibn al-ʿĀṣ and ʿAbd al-Raḥmān Ibn al-Ḥārith Ibn Hishām to write it in books. ʿUthmān said to the three Qurayshī men: "In case you disagree with Zayd bin Thābit on any point in the Qurʾan, then write it in the language of the Quraysh, since it came down in their language". And they did so. And when they had written the pages in books (*idhā nasakhū al-ṣuḥuf fī l-maṣāḥif*), ʿUthmān returned the pages to Ḥafṣa.[42]

The Copies of the Qurʾan Sent to the Cities

Bukhārī's version of the Tradition of the collection of the Qurʾan ends with a short sentence on the distribution of Qurʾanic copies; "Uthmān sent to every place (*ufuq*) one copy of what they had written down, and ordered that all the other Qurʾanic material, in pages or book form, be burnt.' Ibn Abī Dāwūd's *Kitāb* has conflicting details in this story.

Al-Kindī provides details about the *maṣāḥif* sent to four cities. Copies were sent to Mekka, Medina and Damascus (*Shām*), which was, according to al-Kindī, still in Malatiya (*Malaṭiyya*) at the time he wrote the *Apology*. A fourth copy was sent to Kūfa. The first copy, sent to Mekka, was destroyed by fire in the time of Abū l-Sarāyā. The one sent to Medina disappeared during the time of the troubles of al-Ḥīra, under Caliph Yazīd Ibn Muʿāwiya's reign. The fourth copy, sent to Kūfa, disappeared at the time of the revolt of al-Mukhtār. Abū l-Sarāyā, al-Sarī Ibn Manṣūr al-Shaybānī, died on 18th October, 815, after being captured. He headed the Shiʿa revolt in Kūfa, and had sent troops even to Mekka. Tartar's reading '*al-Ḥīra*' is a mistake,[43] because reference is made to the very famous battle of al-Ḥarra, when the people of Medina revolted against

42 Bukhārī, *Ṣaḥīḥ*, Book 66, chapters 2 and 3.

43 Tartar, *Arabic Text*, p. 114:11.

Yazīd Ibn Muʿāwiya, and the city was finally taken and ransacked by Muslim Ibn ʿUqba in August 683. The revolt of al-Mukhtār mentioned by al-Kindī[44] cannot be identified with that of Abū Ḥamza Ibn ʿAwf al-Azdī, called al-Mukhtār, who died in 748 under caliph Marwān II Ibn Muḥammad in a battle at Mekka. It must be the revolt of al-Mukhtār Ibn Abī ʿUbayd al-Thaqafī at Kūfa, where he was killed, probably in 687.[45]

Other sources mention four cities, Mekka, Damascus, Kūfa and Baṣra, so we can assume that a fifth copy 'remained' at Medina, with Caliph ʿUthmān himself. These five cities are the same five cities in which the seven readings originate. Some sources mention seven copies.[46]

The Members of the Group Asked to Copy the Qur'an

There is also some confusion in the sources about the names of the members of the group who were asked to transcribe what they found of the Qur'an. Zayd bin Thābit, ʿAbdallāh Ibn al-Zubayr, Saʿīd Ibn al-ʿĀṣ and ʿAbd al-Raḥmān Ibn al-Ḥārith Ibn Hishām are named by Bukhārī. Zayd Ibn Thābit al-Anṣārī and ʿAbdallāh Ibn al-ʿAbbās are named by al-Kindī. Régis Blachère points out that Ibn Abī Dāwūd recounts only two members of the group, Zayd Ibn Thābit and Saʿīd Ibn al-ʿĀṣ.[47] However, this might just be a shortened version of the group of four. Ibn Abī Dāwūd also has a story of twelve men brought together by ʿUthmān, but this could have been on another occasion.

Ibn Abī Dāwūd mentions two members of the group: 'They said: the most skillful in using the language are Saʿīd Ibn al-ʿĀṣ and Zayd bin Thābit' (*Qālū: afṣaḥ al-nās Saʿīd Ibn al-ʿĀṣ wa-aqra'ahum* (*aqra'uhum*) *Zayd Ibn Thābit*).[48] Ibn Abī Dāwūd mentions that the same two men were chosen by ʿUthmān to write the Qur'an because Zayd bin Thābit could write Arabic well and Saʿīd Ibn al-ʿĀṣ could recite it well: "Uthmān said: Which people can write? They said: the writer for the Messenger of God, Zayd Ibn Thābit. He said: Is anyone an Arab? They said: Saʿīd Ibn al-ʿĀṣ. ʿUthmān said: Let Saʿīd dictate and Zayd write' (*ʿUthmān*

44 Tartar, *Arabic Text*, p. 115:2.

45 See Platti, 'L'image de l'islam', pp. 107–8. correction for al-Ḥarra instead of al-Ḥīra, but not for al-Mukhtār, still identified with al-Mukhtār who died in 748.

46 See R. Blachère, *Introduction au Coran I*, Paris, 1947, p. 62, referring to al-Dānī, *al-Muqniʿ fī rasm maṣāḥif al-amṣār*, Istanbul, 1932, p. 10.

47 Blachère, *Introduction au Coran I*, p. 56. He is not sure about this since he argues that Saʿīd Ibn al-ʿĀṣ was at that time (around 650) governor of Kūfa and was too busy to do the job!

48 Ibn Abī Dāwūd, p. 22, l. 21 and p. 23, l. 1.

qāla: Man aktab al-nās? Qālū: Kātib rasūl Allāh Zayd Ibn Thābit, qāla fa-ayy al-nās aʿrab? Qālū: Saʿīd Ibn al-ʿĀṣ. Qāla ʿUthmān: Fal-yumli Saʿīd wal-yaktub Zayd).[49]

Ibn Abī Dāwūd records twelve people: ʿUthmān Ibn ʿAffān … gathered twelve men of the Quraysh, among whom were the companions Ubayy Ibn Kaʿb and Zayd Ibn Thābit. He sent them for the chest which was in the house of ʿUmar where the Qurʾan was (*ʿUthmān Ibn ʿAffān* (…) *fa-jamaʿa athnay ʿashar rajulan min Quraysh wa l-anṣār fī-him Ubayy Ibn Kaʿb wa-Zayd Ibn Thābit. Wa-arsala ilā al-rabʿa allatī kānat fī bayt ʿUmar fī-hi al-Qurʾan*).[50] Almost the same text is repeated with the word al-rabʿa added, 'who was in the house of ʿUmar'.[51] Bukhārī's version is well known: he mentions Ḥafṣa, daughter of ʿUmar, sister of ʿAbdallāh Ibn ʿUmar and widow of the Prophet.

The 'Manipulation' of the Original Qurʾan Resulting in the ʿUthmānic Qurʾan

Considering the material presented by al-Kindī in the preceding paragraphs, there was no doubt in al-Kindī's mind that a fundamental 'manipulation' occurred, resulting in a completely different text of the Qurʾan: 'your book that hands manipulated … indeed many hands manipulated it,' (*kitābuka alladhī qad tadāwalathu al-ayādī … wa-inna al-ayādī al-kathīra qad tadāwalathu*).[52] 'From (the original Qurʾan) nothing was left accounted for apart from some miscellaneous items' (*Fa-lam yabqa minhu shayʾ yuʿlam illā mutafarriqan*).[53]

To demonstrate further the reality of this manipulation, al-Kindī enumerates the following omissions and changes to the 'original text' of the Qurʾan.[54] With the exception of the first item, these items are all referred to from Islamic sources by Nöldeke and Blachère in their presentations of the History of the Qurʾan.[55]

49 Ibn Abī Dāwūd, p. 24, l. 5 and 15.

50 Ibn Abī Dāwūd, p. 25, l. 11.

51 Ibn Abī Dāwūd, p. 25, l. 20.

52 Tartar, *Arabic Text*, pp. 118:2 and 122:1.

53 Tartar, *Arabic Text*, p. 117:7.

54 Tartar, *Arabic Text*, pp. 115–117.

55 This seems to us enough to demonstrate that it was al-Kindī's purpose to show that his argumentation is based on Islamic traditions.

1. *Sūra* 24, *al-Nūr* (now 64 verses) was longer (*kānat aṭwal*) than *sūra* 2, *al-Baqara* (now 286 verses).
2. *Sūra* 33, *al-Aḥzāb* (now 73 verses) is mutilated and incomplete (*mubtawara laysat bi-tamāmihā*). According to Blachère, many Islamic Traditions confirm this fact.[56]
3. *Sūra* 9, *al-Barā'a* followed immediately after *sūra* 8, *al-Anfāl*, so that *sūra* 9 is not separated from *sūra* 8 by '*bi-sm Allāh al-Raḥmān al-Raḥīm*'. This is a well-known Tradition, commented on by Nöldeke and Blachère.[57]
4. Ibn Masʿūd refused to include in the Qur'an the two prayers called *al-Muʿawwidhatayn*, the two Incantation sūras, introduced by *aʿūdhu*—I seek refuge (with the Lord …), *sūra* 113, *al-Falaq* and *sūra* 114, *al-Nās*. Ibn Masʿūd said: 'Do not add to what is not there'.[58] There is a commentary by Blachère on this with references to Suyūṭī's *Itqān*.[59]
5. 'Umar said that a verse was missing, called '*āyat al-Rajm*', (*the Stoning*): 'If an adult man or woman commits adultery, stone them definitely, God is almighty and wise' (*al-shaykh wa l-shaykha idhā zanayā fa-rjamūhumā al-batta*).[60] In Ibn Isḥāq's *Life of the Prophet*, there is the following story: "Umar sat in the pulpit, and when the muezzins were silent he praised God … and said: God sent Muḥammad and sent down the scripture to him. Part of what he sent down was the passage on stoning; we read it, we were taught it, and we heeded it. The Apostle stoned (adulterers) and we stoned them after him. I fear that in time to come men will say that they find no mention of stoning in God's book and thereby go astray by neglecting an ordinance which God has sent down'.[61]
6. In another address, 'Umar declared that the verse concerning *mutʿa*, temporary marriage, was also part of what was read, and that he 'did not know anyone saying that *mutʿa* was not in God's Book' (*Innī lā aʿlam anna aḥadan qāla inna al-mutʿa laysat fī Kitāb Allāh*). But this verse also

56 Régis Blachère, *Le Coran I: Introduction au Coran*, Paris, 1947, p. 17 and *Le Coran III*, p. 982: 'Selon une tradition placée sous le nom de Ubayy (v. Nas. 223 fine), cette sourate, en sa forme primitive, aurait été au moins aussi longue que le n° 93 = II (i.e. sūrat al-Baqara); elle aurait notamment contenu le verset de la Lapidation aujourd'hui disparu du Coran'.

57 T. Nöldeke-F. Schwally, *Geschichte des Qorâns I*, Leipzig, 1909, p. 44, n. 1; Blachère, *Le Coran III*, p. 1075.

58 Tartar, *Arabic Text*, p. 115:13.

59 Blachère, *Le Coran I*, p. 44, referring to Jalāl al-Dīn al-Suyūṭī, *al-Itqān fī ʿulūm al-Qur'an*, Cairo, 1967.

60 Tartar, *Arabic Text*, p. 115:15–116:1.

61 Guillaume, *The Life of Muḥammad*, pp. 684–5, and note 2 with ref. Nöldeke-Schwally, *Geschichte I*, p. 248; Blachère, *Le Coran I*, pp. 190–1.

disappeared from the final text of the Qurʾan along with other texts: 'The one who falsified this (part), dropped many other things' (*faqad asqaṭa al-mumawwih ʿalayhi min al-Qurʾan ashyāʾ kathīra*).[62]

7. According to al-Kindī, it was ʿAlī who dropped temporary marriage (*al-mutʿa*), and prohibited the recitation of this verse: (*ka-dhālika āyat al-mutʿa, fa-inna ʿAliyyan kāna asqaṭahā battatan*).[63] This is in line with the fact that many *hadith*s state that *al-mutʿa* was allowed on certain occasions at first, but was then forbidden by the Prophet, according to ʿAlī, who narrates the following tradition: 'I said to Ibn Abbās: During the battle of Khaybar the Messenger of God forbade *al-mutʿa* and the eating of donkey's meat'.[64] Al-Kindī adds another story related to ʿAlī, translated by Muir in the following: 'They say that, while Caliph, (ʿAlī) overheard a man reciting the verse, and had him scourged for the same and forbade its further repetition. And this was one of the things for which ʿĀʾisha reproached ʿAlī after the battle of the Camel, when she had retired to the house of Khalaf ibn al-Khuzāʿī; for, among other things, she said that ʿAlī had beaten men in this matter of the Qurʾan, and forbade the repetition of certain passages, and tampered with the text'.[65] This translates (*innahu yajlid ʿalā l-Qurʾan wa-yaḍrib ʿalayhi wa-yunhī ʿanhu wa-qad baddala wa-ḥarrafa*).[66] Some details of this episode mentioned by al-Kindī are confirmed in Ṭabarī's *History*: 'Muḥammad (ibn Abī Bakr) took ʿĀʾisha out to Baṣra to stay in the house of ʿAbdallāh Ibn Khalaf al-Khuzāʿī.'[67]

8. Al-Kindī quotes ʿUmar again, referring to verses dropped by the same person, who most probably must be ʿAlī, according to the reference to the question of *al-mutʿa*: 'God had decided to make it easier for the people, as Muhammad was sent with an indulgent religion' (*wa-mā kāna ʿalayhi an*

62 Tartar, *Arabic Text*, p. 116:5–6.

63 Tartar, *Arabic Text*, p. 116:12.

64 See W. Heffening, 'Mutʿa', *Encyclopaedia of Islam* 7:757–9, Leiden, 1993, with reference to Bukhārī, 64 (*Maghāzī*), Bāb 38.21. See also G.H.A. Juynboll, *Encyclopaedia of Canonical Ḥadīth*, Leiden, 2007, pp. 242, 389, and 680. *Mutʿat al-nisāʾ* is the option that concerns the contracting of temporary relationships with local women and is not to be confused with the *tamattuʿ* or *mutʿa* option concerning the pilgrimage, referred to by Tartar, in *Dialogue*, p. 189, n. 44, according to Aḥmad Ibn Ḥanbal.

65 Muir, *The Apology*, p. 77, *Ibn Khalaf* (*at Bussora*); but according to Tartar, *Dialogue*, p. 190, n. 46, this man is ʿAbdallāh Ibn Khalaf al-Khuzāʿī who died at the battle of the Camel in 656.

66 Tartar, *Arabic Text*, p. 117:2–3.

67 *The History of Ṭabarī XVI. The Community divided* (trans. A. Brockett), Albany, 1985, p. 158.

yurakhkhiṣ Allāh li l-nās wa-innamā buʿitha Muḥammad bi l-dīn al-wāsiʿ).[68]

9. Ubayy ibn Kaʿb is quoted to have said that there were two other *sūras* in the Qurʾan which they used to recite (*Sūratān kānū yaqraʾūnahumā fīhi*): *sūra al-Qunūt* and *sūra al-Witr*, a prayer starting with the words 'O God, we seek Your help and Your forgiveness, we believe in You and we put our trust in You' (*Allāhumma, innanā nastaʿīnuka wa-nastaghfiruka wa-nuʾmin bi-ka wa-natawakkal ʿalayka*).[69] *Witr* is considered to be a prayer performed at night before dawn, and *Qunūt* is an invocation (*duʿāʾ*) in the *Witr* prayer.[70] The exact words quoted by al-Kindī are the first verses of one of the possible invocations used today as the *Qunūt* invocation. Ibn al-Nadīm in his *Fihrist* mentions the 116 *sūras* of Ubayy ibn Kaʿb's *muṣḥaf* in a different order than the *textus receptus* of ʿUthmān, with two *sūras* between *sūra al-Takāthur* (*Piling up*; in ʿUthmān's version 102) and *sūra al-Lumaz* (in ʿUthmān's version 104), *al-Humaza, the Scandal-monger*; according to Ubayy, before *Idhā zulzilat: When* (*the earth*) *is shaken* (in ʿUthmān's version 99). These two *sūras*, included in Ubayy's version, are called *al-Khalʿ* (*Taking off* (*or Denial*); *three verses*) and *al-Jayyid* (*The good; six verses* (*starting with*) *Allāhumma iyyāka naʿbudu* ... and finishing with *bi l-kuffār mulḥiq*).[71]

68 Muir, *The Apology*, p. 76: "*The Lord minded to deal gently with mankind, and verily he sent Mahomet with a wide and comprehensive faith*"; and see Tartar, Arabic Text, 116:6–7.

69 Tartar, *Arabic Text*, p. 116:10–11.

70 A.J. Wensinck, 'Witr', *Encyclopaedia of Islam* 11:213, Leiden, 2002, and 'Qunūt', *Encyclopaedia of Islam*, 5:395, Leiden, 1986.

71 Ibn al-Nadīm, *Al-Fihrist li-bn al-Nadīm* (ed.) G. Flügel, Beyrouth, 1964, p. 27, line 16; al-Nadīm, *The Fihrist of Al-Nadīm I* (ed.) A .F. Sayyid, London, 2009, p. 68: in this edition the two sūras are called *al-Khalʿ* and *al-Ḥafd* (*Running*); the text of these two sūras: note 1 and 2; See Blachère, *Le Coran I*, p. 38 and pp. 188–9: 'Le corpus d'Obayy et peut-être celui d'Ibn ʿAbbas contenaient en plus des cent-quatorze sourates du canon ʿothmanien, deux prières dont voici le texte: Le Reniement (…) La Course (…)'; See also Th. Nöldeke, *Geschichte des Qurâns*, Göttingen, 1860, pp. 228–9: Sūrat al-Qunūt: "Im Namen Gottes, des allbarmherzigen Erbarmers: (1) O Gott, Dich bitten wir um Hülfe und Vergebung; (2) Dich preisen wir, und gegen Dich sind wir nicht undankbar, (3) Und lassen fahren und verlassen Jeden, der wider Dich frevelt. Sūrat al-Witr, a prayer starting with the words "Allāhumma: "Im Namen Gottes, des allbarmherzigen Erbarmers: (1) O Gott (Allāhumma), Dir dienen wir; (2) Und zu Dir beten und Dir huldigen wir; (3) Und nach Dir eilen und streben wir, (4) Dein erbarmen hoffend, (5) Und Deine Strafe fürchend; (6) Wahrlich Deine Strafe erfafst die Ungläubigen"; referring to Jalāl al-Dīn al-Suyūṭī, al-Itqān fī ʿulūm al-Qurʾān 1, Cairo, 1967, p. 154.

It is obvious from all this material that al-Kindī has the intention to show that he is fully aware of what Muslims themselves recognize to be their authentic sources describing the 'collection' of the Qur'an. And in this context, it is important to consider the information given by al-Kindī concluding this paragraph, where he testifies that 'the Muṣḥaf of ʿAbdallāh ibn Masʿūd is still (this means: in the days of al-Kindī) transmitted by inheritance, in the same way the Muṣḥaf of ʿAlī ibn Abī Ṭālib is still in the hands of his family.'[72]

The Intervention of al-Ḥallāj ibn Yūsuf

The last intervention concerning the Qur'an mentioned by al-Kindī was by al-Ḥajjāj ibn Yūsuf al-Thaqafī (d. 714): 'Al-Ḥajjāj Ibn Yūsuf left no book without assembling it (anew), taking away something and adding some things' (*Innahu lam yatruk muṣḥafan illā jamaʿahu wa-asqaṭa minhu ashyāʾ kathīra wa-zāda fīhi ashyāʾ*). They say that some of these verses were revealed concerning the Banū Umayya, with the names of some of them, and others concerning the Banū l-ʿAbbās, with the names of some of them. Six copies were made in conformity with the wishes of al-Ḥajjāj, (*kutibat nusḥa bi-taʾlīf mā arāda al-Ḥajjāj fī sittati maṣāḥif*). One was sent to Miṣr, another to al-Shām, another to Medina, another to Mekka, another to al-Kūfa and another to al-Baṣra. The preceding copies were put in boiling oil; [al-Ḥajjāj did] what ʿUthmān had done before him.'[73] According to Ibn Abī Dāwūd: 'al-Ḥajjāj ibn Yūsuf changed (only) eleven *ḥarf* from ʿUthmān's *muṣḥaf*', all of them mentioned in detail.[74]

Conclusion

It has already been stated that it was al-Kindī's intention to demonstrate that the 'manipulation' of the original qur'anic text (*qad tadāwalathu al-ayādī*) was extremely important. From what we have seen, al-Kindī was using Islamic sources, just as he did in describing the life of prophet Muhammad. But it is also clear that al-Kindī's presentation is an interpretation, and that his conclusion that there is no ground to have faith in the text transmitted in his days, is

72 Tartar, *Arabic Text*, p. 117:4–5.

73 Tartar, *Arabic Text*, p. 117:6–7.

74 Ibn Abī Dāwūd, *Kitāb al-Maṣāḥif* (ed. Jeffery), pp. 49–50.

as such perhaps exaggerated.[75] Muslim authors themselves were aware of the facts described by the Christian author.

The polemical character of al-Kindī's presention is probably the reason why, according to Griffith, 'Thus far little scholarly attention has been paid to this valuable ninth century discussion of such an important issue.' As it seems to be clear that the material presented by al-Kindī is older than the Islamic material edited by Bukhārī (d. 870), Ṭabarī (d. 923) and Ibn Abī Dāwūd (d. 929), we are therefore convinced that this early material should be included in any research on the collection of the Qur'an.

---

75 According to early Shiʿa sources however, the term 'manipulation' is not at all exaggerated; see M.A. Amir-Moezzi, 'Le Coran silencieux et le Coran parlant: histoire et écritures à travers l'étude de quelques texts anciens', in M. Azaiez and S. Mervin, (eds), *Le Coran. Nouvelles approches*, Paris, 2013, p. 85: 'En récupérant son pouvoir, les adversaires de Muḥammad se sont vus contraints d'intervenir massivement dans le texte coranique afin d'en altérer les passages compromettants pour eux. Aidés par des hommes puissants de l'État et de lettrés professionnels (parfois les deux qualités étaient réunies chez un même individu, comme ce fut le cas de 'Ubaydallāh b. Ziyād ou d'al-Ḥaǧǧāǧ b. Yūsuf), ils mirent au point le Coran officiel connu.'

CHAPTER 5

ʿAmmār al-Baṣrī: Ninth Century Christian Theology and Qur'anic Presuppositions

Mark Beaumont

The early ninth century theologian and apologist ʿAmmār al-Baṣrī attempted the earliest known systematic theology in an Islamic context.[1] His method was to develop a thorough response to questions raised by Muslims concerning their perceptions of Christian beliefs that arose from the interpretation of the Qur'an. ʿAmmār al-Baṣrī tackles the Muslim rejection of the authenticity of the Christian Scriptures, the Incarnation, death and resurrection of Jesus the Messiah, and belief in God as one essence in three persons, Father, Son and Holy Spirit.

In two apologetic treatises, he offers justifications for these beliefs, not so much by referring directly to the teaching of the Qur'an, which he does rarely, but rather by appealing to Muslim assumptions based on their reading of Qur'anic texts. While his *Book of Questions and Answers* seems to have been written before his *Book of the Proof concerning the Course of the Divine Economy*, the latter is a fuller account of Christian theology. The former deals with God and the world, the authenticity of the Gospels, the Trinity and the Incarnation, and will be used here to provide additional evidence of ʿAmmār's handling of Qur'anic presuppositions.[2]

1 See M. Beaumont, "Ammār al-Baṣrī', in D. Thomas and B. Roggema, eds, *Christian-Muslim relations. A bibliographical history volume 1*, Leiden, 2009, pp. 604–10; and M. Hayek, "Ammār al-Baṣrī. La Première Somme de théologie chrétienne en langue arabe, ou deux apologies du christianisme', *Islamochristiana* 2, 1976, pp. 69–133.

2 ʿAmmār al-Baṣrī', 'The Book of Questions and Answers', (*Kitāb al-masā'il wa-l-ajwiba*) in M. Hayek, ed., *ʿAmmār al-Baṣrī. Apologie et controverses*, Beirut, 1977, pp. 93–265, and 'The Book of the Proof concerning the Course of the Divine Economy', (*Kitāb al-burhān*) in M. Hayek, ed., *ʿAmmār al-Baṣrī. Apologie et controverses*, Beirut, 1977, pp. 19–90. See Wageeh Mikhail's English translation of the Book of the Proof in the appendix to his PhD thesis; ʿAmmār al-Baṣrī's *Kitāb al-Burhān*: A Topical and Theological Analysis of Arabic Christian Theology in the Ninth Century, PhD dissertation, University of Birmingham, 2013. See also the German translation of the Book of the Proof by M. Maróth, in, *ʿAmmār al-Baṣrī: Das Buch des Beweises*, Piliscsaba, 2015.

 | DOI 10.1163/9789004360747_006

Christianity is a True Religion Based on Signs from God

In the opening section of his systematic defense of Christian beliefs and practices entitled *Book of the Proof concerning the Course of the Divine Economy*, ʿAmmār al-Baṣrī presents a proof of the truth of Christianity based on the Qurʾanic presupposition that a religion is truly from God if it is accompanied by signs from Him. He begins by noting that several communities claim to have the true religion revealed by God and that other religions are therefore not from God. 'We see people in our time disagreeing about their religions, divided in their communities, with each of them saying that their religion is the religion of God, and that what contradicts it is not from God. Yet we know that there is one religion of God among all of them.'[3]

Philosophers may have tried to use reason to determine the truth but this has not led to agreement among them. In such a situation how can the average person be any more certain than the intellectuals? Surely the answer lies in the conviction that 'God is above commanding human beings what they cannot bear.'[4] This is the first reference to a Qurʾanic text in the treatise, though ʿAmmār does not indicate chapter and verse to his reader. Q 22:78, 'He has chosen you and has not imposed difficulties on you in religious duties,' is the basis for ʿAmmār's argument, which he seeks to build on revelation rather than on reason.

He proceeds to back up this reliance on Qurʾanic teaching by announcing that the key to the solution of the search for the true religion is to be found in the principle that God has given signs to humanity of his reality and activity. ʿAmmār indicates that he has a Muslim audience in mind when he says, 'According to what you stubborn people have stated, God sent his messengers and revealed his signs through them, signs that could not be copied.'[5] He comes closer here to actual quotation from the Qurʾan, which in at least four places supports his interpretation. Q 2: 23–4, 10:38, 11:13, and 52:33–4, repeat the challenge to the hearers of the message of the Prophet to come up with their own message from God since they reject his, calling Muhammad a fraudulent forger of sayings. Yet they can only bring false messages from gods that do not exist. ʿAmmār concludes that, 'God wants to entrust to his people his signs that cannot be imitated.'[6]

3 Hayek, *ʿAmmār al-Baṣrī. Apologie et controverses*, pp. 26–7.
4 Hayek, *ʿAmmār al-Baṣrī. Apologie et controverses*, p. 28.
5 Hayek, *ʿAmmār al-Baṣrī. Apologie et controverses*, p. 28.
6 Hayek, *ʿAmmār al-Baṣrī. Apologie et controverses*, p. 28.

Furthermore, these signs have been revealed by several messengers. While the inimitability of the signs is taught in the context of challenges to Muhammad, Q 19:58, 22:52 and 57:25 emphasise that the signs being brought by the Prophet are in continuity with those revealed by previous messengers. ʿAmmār exploits this teaching to go on to compare and contrast the revelation of signs to the Jews and the Christians. God sent the Torah, the book of Moses, to the Children of Israel as his sign to them according to Q 3:3, 5:44, 6:91, 11:17, 46:12 and 62:5. While ʿAmmār does not identify these texts directly, he assumes their insistence on the granting of signs to the Jews. The advent of Christianity was also marked by the signs of God, but these were in fact 'greater' signs than those given to the Jews through Moses. These greater signs indicate that 'God did not intend the religion of the Torah for the whole of humanity.'[7] What God did intend was that the religion brought by the Messiah should be universal.

However, rather than rely on a Qur'anic text to back up his argument he appeals to Jesus' commissioning his disciples in Matt 10:9–10, and Luke 9:3, 'Do not take a rod, or a staff, or gold, or silver; do not wear sandals, or carry two tunics, or two sets of clothes.' ʿAmmār does not quote either of these texts exactly. His approach to the use of Christian Scripture is not unlike the way he refers to the Qur'anic text. He does not usually think it necessary to quote either Bible or Qur'an verbatim. The essence of the Scriptural teaching is his main concern. The point of Jesus' prohibitions is to insist that the proclamation of the message should not be contaminated by any worldly attachments of the preachers or by any incentives to accept the message given to their hearers. Thus, according to ʿAmmār, the first followers of Christ were attracted solely by the impact of the signs that they witnessed. 'There was no other cause for the acceptance of Christianity.'[8]

There are other causes for the acceptance of a religion, such as the use of force. ʿAmmār now introduces Islam into his discussion of the true religion based on the signs of God. Just as the Torah used the sword so did Islam, which 'spread in every direction by its use.'[9] But this was not the case with Christianity, which 'Did not conquer with the sword. Those who proclaimed it were weak fishermen who did not exercise rule or use the sword.'[10] ʿAmmār hardly needs to appeal to the Qur'an to verify the historical reality that the area from which he writes was taken by force early in the history of the Islamic movement, and that he is living in a situation where the exercise of Muslim

7 Hayek, *ʿAmmār al-Baṣrī. Apologie et controverses*, p. 30.

8 Hayek, *ʿAmmār al-Baṣrī. Apologie et controverses*, p. 30.

9 Hayek, *ʿAmmār al-Baṣrī. Apologie et controverses*, pp. 33–4.

10 Hayek, *ʿAmmār al-Baṣrī. Apologie et controverses*, p. 34.

rule has encouraged the migration of many Christians to the fold of Islam. Yet his implication is that God commanded the use of the sword to promote the spread of Islam according to the Qur'an. Q 2:190–3, 216–8, 244–6, 3:142, 4:74–7, 84, 95, 5:54, 8:72, 9:12–16, 29, 36, 38–9, 86–8, 111, 123, 16:110, 47:4, 48:15–7, 57:10, 59:6, and 61:4 all testify to this obvious difference from the command of Christ to leave the sword behind when preaching the gospel.

Another cause for the acceptance of a religion might be a permissive set of rules that make that religion appealing to people. In the case of the regulation of sexual desire of men for women, ʿAmmār accepts the premise that God made such desire 'natural' for men, such that David, the prophet (*al-nabī*) was so overcome with desire for a woman that he killed her husband, and that his son Solomon's desire for women undermined his wisdom.[11] While not openly discussing the permission in the Torah for a man to have more than one wife, ʿAmmār is attempting to engage a Muslim reader in the stories of two prominent men from the Bible whose names appear linked together in the Qur'an at Q 21:78–9, 27:15–6, 34:10–14, and 38:30. This is supported by the fact that he goes on to mention Samson's desire for a woman that led him into the hands of his enemies, but calls him merely 'A man who God set apart as a judge of the children of Israel.'[12] The name 'Samson' would be unfamiliar to a Muslim audience. ʿAmmār's use of the term 'prophet' for David is another indication of his awareness of Muslim sensibilities, since David is listed among the prophets (*al-nabiyyin*) in Q 4:163, and was chosen from among the prophets (*al-nabiyyin*) to be gifted with the psalms (*al-zabūr*) in Q 17: 55. His readiness to cite three stories of sexual permissiveness from the Bible that are not found in the Qur'an shows that ʿAmmār is trying to build a Biblical case on a Qur'anic foundation.

Immediately after referring to the power of desire in David, Solomon and Samson, ʿAmmār gives another illustration from his own period of 'a man from among the kings in our time who set out from his kingdom with his whole army for Rome in search of a woman in a fortress.'[13] Michel Hayek, the editor of *The Book of the Proof*, believes this man is the Caliph al-Muʿtaṣīm who was reputed to have captured Amorium for the sake of a woman in 838, and that this provides the only solid clue to the date of the writing of this work.[14] The function of these stories is to highlight the way that rulers, whether from among the Jews or the Muslims, can be led astray by sexual desire. There is also the implication that Judaism and Islam, in allowing a man to marry more

11 Hayek, *ʿAmmār al-Baṣrī. Apologie et controverses*, p. 38.

12 Hayek, *ʿAmmār al-Baṣrī. Apologie et controverses*, p. 38.

13 Hayek, *ʿAmmār al-Baṣrī. Apologie et controverses*, p. 38.

14 See Hayek's footnote on page 38 and his introduction on pages 19–20.

than one woman, not only make religion easier to accept, but also take human beings away from focusing on the signs of God. ʿAmmār concludes emphatically, 'Those who proclaimed the Christian religion, whether to rulers or those who were ruled, commanded that a man should control his desire for women by marrying only one woman.'[15] Thus both Judaism and Islam are less than adequate expressions of the signs of God.

The upshot of these discussions of the use of the sword to promote a religion and the permission of more than one wife by a religion is that only Christianity as promoted by the disciples of Christ in the story found in the gospels fully displays the signs of God. 'We have made clear that the Christian religion was established by signs and that the gospel (*al-injīl*) is God's book (*kitāb allāh*) that is well known among the nations to have promoted these signs.'[16] ʿAmmār uses the Qur'anic term *injīl* in the singular rather than the plural form *anājīl* normally used within the Christian community, showing his apologetic purposes in writing this work. The Qur'an teaches that the *injīl* was sent down by God in Q 3: 3–4, 65, 5:46–7, 66, and 57:27, as a book. This appeal to the unitary character of the four gospels via Qur'anic terminology will be tested by the charge that the gospels in the possession of Christians are not fully authentic versions of that divinely sent book.

The Christian Gospels are the Authentic Revelation of God

At the fifth Mingana Symposium in September 2005 I presented a paper entitled "Ammār al-Baṣrī on the alleged corruption of the Gospels', which was subsequently published in volume 6 of the series *The History of Christian-Muslim Relations*.[17] There I examined in some detail ʿAmmār's approach to defending the authenticity of the Gospels as God's book. In the context of the present study of ʿAmmār's construction of Christian theology on the basis of Qur'anic presuppositions, I analyse his interpretation of the charge of corruption of the Scriptures of the People of the Book made in the Qur'an. Firstly, he never quotes the Qur'an directly, but merely notices that Muslims ascribe corruption to God's book the *injīl*. He is not interested in defending the Hebrew Scriptures and does not intimate that the Qur'an appears only to allege that the Jews had been involved in corrupting their scriptures, in Q 3:78, and 7:162. Thus for

15 Hayek, *ʿAmmār al-Baṣrī. Apologie et controverses*, pp. 38–9.

16 Hayek, *ʿAmmār al-Baṣrī. Apologie et controverses*, p. 41.

17 See M. Beaumont, "Ammār al-Baṣrī on the alleged corruption of the Gospels', in D. Thomas, ed., *The Bible in Arab Christianity*, Leiden, 2007, pp. 241–256.

him the Book of God is not so much the Bible as a whole but the four gospels in particular.

He begins his defense of the gospels by a *reductio ad absurdum* argument. Given that the gospels demonstrate the signs of God as already argued, it is inconceivable that those who brought the message of the *injīl* should wish to corrupt it. But if it is argued that the gospels were altered in some way after the nations had accepted them as true then this is simply absurd because we have in our hands the same documents that the nations had when they received them at first. He develops the absurdity of this accusation in the following scenario.

> Why did people not invent for themselves a book that they wanted, establishing in it that when the Jews wanted to kill the Messiah, they told lies about him, and conceit swelled up and consumed them, and that he was raised up to heaven alive without death having touched or affected him.[18]

This forthright polemical stance is somewhat unusual for ʿAmmār, whose typical handling of Islamic conceptions is more cautious and not overtly critical. Why does he do this here? Perhaps he felt that the way the story of the ending of Jesus' life is told in the Qur'an in Q 4:157–8 was so objectionable that he needed to use irony to discredit it. In the context of his argument that the gospels are authentically revealed scripture, he probably adopted this ironical tone to disturb the confidence of Muslims that their version of Jesus' life was more accurate than the Christian one.

Indeed, he continues to underpin his confidence in the reliability of the gospel accounts by pointing out that the disciples of Jesus 'Did not remove difficulties such as their being called to worship a crucified man' from the gospel accounts. ʿAmmār then asks the question, 'Is there anything more difficult for kings, and those who have authority, power and glory, than belief in the worship of a crucified man?'[19] The question is rhetorical since the presupposition of Muslims is that no wise ruler would be led astray by such falsehood.

ʿAmmār raises another difference between the teaching of the Qur'an and the gospels concerning marriage. Jesus prohibits his disciples from marrying more than one woman. While not quoting from the Qur'an directly, he obviously has in mind the permission granted to a Muslim to marry up to four wives in Q 4:3. In his *Book of Questions and Answers* ʿAmmār takes this difference one

18 Hayek, *ʿAmmār al-Baṣrī. Apologie et controverses*, p. 44.

19 Hayek, *ʿAmmār al-Baṣrī. Apologie et controverses*, p. 44.

step further by proposing that the gospel makes the rules for marriage much stricter than men would naturally prefer by denying remarriage after divorce. He quotes the saying of Jesus found in Matthew 19:9, 'Whoever divorces his wife and takes another commits adultery, and whoever leaves his wife except for her adultery commits adultery.' Then he comments, 'It is clear that a man is forbidden from marrying a woman other than the one he has married.'[20] This is stricter than the freedom for men to divorce given in the Qur'an at Q 2:227–42, 33:4, 49, 58:2–4, and 65:1–7. Once again, ʿAmmār does not refer directly to the Qur'an.

ʿAmmār is aware that some Muslims merely argue that Christians have misinterpreted their gospels rather than including data contradictory to the teaching of the Qur'an. He dismisses this apparent concession by drawing attention to further teaching in the gospels that is opposed in the Qur'an. He actually quotes verbatim, Q 19:90–91 and 2:18 to challenge this friendlier attitude. These texts demonstrate God's anger at Christians and his threat to punish them for calling Jesus God's Son. He poses a series of stark challenges to Muslim readers concerning the language found in the Qur'an about the Word and Spirit of God.

> You do not know the Father because you deny the Son. You say the Spirit comes by command from the Lord whereas God's book says that the Spirit is the Lord. You say that the Word is created whereas the gospel says the Word is eternal and is God.[21]

Apart from the texts already quoted concerning the Son, Q 17:85 is referred to concerning the Spirit being commanded by God. Q 4:171 is alluded to with respect to Jesus being called God's word at his conception. How then can Muslims attempt to soften the reality of these flagrant contradictions between the gospels and the Qur'an by telling Christians that if only they read their gospels in the light of the Qur'an they would arrive at the truth? No, the gospel was not corrupted either in its original state or in its meaning. His final word on the accusation of corruption is that the gospel is 'God's book and the whole world should believe and obey it.'[22]

In his *Book of questions and answers* ʿAmmār develops another argument for the authenticity of the gospels based on the fact that there is no difference between the teaching in the Qur'an and the preaching of Muḥammad about

---

20 Hayek, *ʿAmmār al-Baṣrī. Apologie et controverses*, p. 139.

21 Hayek, *ʿAmmār al-Baṣrī. Apologie et controverses*, p. 45.

22 Hayek, *ʿAmmār al-Baṣrī. Apologie et controverses*, p. 45.

idolatry (*shirk*), the unity of God (*tawhīd*), and the rules for living (*sharāʾiʿ*). Any difference would have meant that people would not have accepted his religion or his book. He applies this reality to the one who preached the gospel and the gospels that were written by his disciples. 'Since you confirm that the sending down (*tanzīl*) of what is in our hands is expanded by everything that is in your hands, then what we have testifies to what you deny and denies what you proclaim.' Here ʿAmmār appeals to Q 5:48, 'We sent down to you the book confirming the book in your hands.' In other words far from the Qurʾan demonstrating that the previous book is corrupted, it affirms the truth of the gospel. As Hayek points out, ʿAmmār is arguing that the charge of corruption rebounds on Muslims who must concede that it is they who have corrupted the true teaching of the gospel.[23]

The Trinitarian God

The above quotation introduces the next section of ʿAmmār's systematic theology in dialogue with Islamic presuppositions on the Christian belief in God as three in one.[24] He begins by going on the offensive with the Islamic insistence on oneness. If a Muslim insists that the attributes of God do not adhere in his essential nature, then he denies that God has life and speech in his essence. 'He does not call God "living" since he does not affirm that God has life and speech … He deprives God of life and makes him inanimate. May God be greatly exalted above that!'[25] ʿAmmār here summarises his longer argument in his *Book of questions and answers*, written earlier in his career. Since Abū al-Hudhayl al-ʿAllāf (d.c. 845) wrote a 'refutation of ʿAmmār the Christian in his reply to the Christians' it is probable, as Sidney Griffith argues, that ʿAmmār was attempting to answer this leading Muʿtazilī thinker.[26]

---

23 Hayek, *ʿAmmār al-Baṣrī. Apologie et controverses*, p. 146.

24 See my analysis of ʿAmmār's defence of the Trinity from his *Book of Questions and Answers*, in 'Speaking of the Triune God: Christian defence of the Trinity in the early Islamic period', *Transformation* 29, 2012, pp. 111–127. See also Sara Husseini's analysis of ʿAmmār's handling of the Trinity in S.L. Husseini, *Early Christian-Muslim Debate on the Unity of God*, Leiden, 2014, pp. 105–40.

25 Hayek, *ʿAmmār al-Baṣrī. Apologie et controverses*, p. 47.

26 See S.H. Griffith, 'The concept of *al-uqnūm* in ʿAmmār al-Baṣrī's apology for the doctrine of the Trinity', in S.K. Samir, ed., *Actes du premier congrès international d'Études arabes Chrétiennes*, Rome, 1982, pp. 169–191, pp. 180–1, and "Ammār al-Baṣrī's *Kitāb al-Burhān*: Christian kalām in the first Abbasid century' *Le Museon* 96, 1983, pp. 145–181, pp. 169–72.

'Ammār builds his argument on current Muslim discourse about whether the names of God refer to actions of God. Abū al-Hudhayl al-'Allāf is reported to have denied that the names did refer to actions of God. The statement 'God is knowing' means 'There is an act of knowing that is God' and 'There is an object that he knows.'[27] Abū al-Hudhayl defended God's unity (*tawḥīd*) by denying that there could be an entity called 'knowledge' which is identified in God. 'Ammār attacks this conception by arguing that there are inherent qualities in God, life and speech, which are quite different from actions that God performs but that are not inherent in him.

In *The Book of the Proof*, 'Ammār appeals to the books of God to back up his case, which he did not do in the earlier apologetic work, *The Book of Questions and Answers*. 'God, in his books, condemns those who worship idols because they worship gods that do not have life or speech. He describes himself in all of his books as having Spirit and Word.'[28] While he goes on to quote directly from the Bible but not directly from the Qur'an, 'Ammār presupposes Q 21:65–6, where Abraham challenged his family to turn from the worship of idols to submission to the Lord of heaven and earth. Eventually they admitted to Abraham, 'These idols do not speak.' Abraham replied, 'Why do you worship what does you neither good or harm?' The reference to God's Spirit is Q 21:91, 'We breathed our Spirit into her (Mary)', and Q 4:171, 'The Messiah, 'Isa, son of Mary, messenger of God, and His word given to Mary, and his spirit.' Here too God's word is particularly connected with God's spirit.

'Ammār's reference to God having Spirit and Word in the Qur'an was an already established theme in Christian defence of the Trinity. John of Damascus (d.c. 750) is the earliest known Christian theologian to have made reference to this. In his *Heresy of the Ishmaelites*, John rebuts the accusation of Muslims that Christians are guilty of associating Christ with God when they call him Son of God by drawing attention to the fact that Muslims call Christ Word and Spirit of God. He argues, 'If the Word of God is in God, then it is evident that he is God as well. If, however, the word is outside of God, then, according to you, God is without Word and Spirit. Consequently, by avoiding the association of a partner with God, you have mutilated him.'[29] John's argument can be seen

27 See R.M. Frank, *Beings and their attributes; the teaching of the Basrian school of the Mu'tazila in the classical period*, Albany, 1978, p 12.

28 Hayek, *'Ammār al-Baṣrī. Apologie et controverses*, p. 48.

29 The Greek text of *The heresy of the Ishmaelites* is edited by B. Kotter in *Die Schriften Des Johannes Von Damaskos, IV*, New York, 1981, pp. 60–7. This text is reproduced and translated by D.J. Janosik in his unpublished 2011, London School of Theology PhD, *John of Damascus: first apologist to the Muslims*, appendix 1, pp. 281–6. Here p. 283.

in the way ʿAmmār challenges the Muslim belief that the attributes of God do not adhere in his essential nature, as noted already. The result of this denial is that the Muslim removes speech and life from God and renders him lifeless. John's accusation that Muslims mutilate God has become an accusation that Muslims empty him of life.

Another appeal to the Spirit and Word in the Qur'an is found in an anonymous Apology for Christianity, not in Greek but in Arabic, which comes from the same Chalcedonian community to which John belonged.[30] The writer says at the end of the treatise that 'If this religion was not truly from God, it would not have stood firm nor stood erect for seven hundred and forty-six years', so it may have been composed in the middle of the eighth century around the same time as John's work.[31] There is a detailed presentation of the Trinity using language taken from the Qur'an which suggests that the unknown writer is attempting to set out Christian belief for a Muslim reader, with the parallel purpose of showing fellow Christians a way to communicate their faith with Muslims. The fact that it is composed in Arabic demonstrates that the language of the Muslim rulers was becoming used in some Christian communities, for example in Palestinian monasteries.[32]

After a lengthy prayer, the writer addresses a Muslim reader by declaring, 'We do not distinguish God from His Word and His Spirit. We do not worship another god alongside God in His Word and His Spirit.'[33] The first sentence echoes John's argument that Christians do not mutilate the Triune God by separating His Word and Spirit from Him. The second sentence alludes to

30 The Arabic text (Sinai 154) is edited and translated into English by M.D. Gibson as *A treatise on the Triune nature of God*, London, 1899.

31 S.K. Samir discovered this statement on one of the pages of the manuscript not included in the printed version by Gibson who said that she was unable to photograph 'a few pages from the end.' Samir believes that this dates the writing to just before 750. See S.K. Samir, 'The earliest Arab apology for Christianity (c. 750)' in S.K. Samir and J.S. Nielsen, eds, *Christian Arabic apologetics during the Abbasid period (750–1258)*, Leiden, 1994, pp. 57–116, p. 61. M. Swanson calculates the date not from the birth of Christ but from the beginning of the church and suggests 788. See M. Swanson, 'Some considerations for the dating of *Fī tathlīth Allāh wāḥid* (Sinai Ar. 154) and *al-gāmiʿ wugūh al-īmān* (London, British Library op. 4950)', *Parole de L'Orient* 18, 1993, pp. 118–141. However, S.H. Griffith argues that Palestinian scribes were more likely to compute the date from the beginning of the year of the Incarnation, thus placing the composition around 755. See S.H. Griffith, *The church in the shadow of the mosque*, Princeton, 2008, p. 54.

32 See S.H. Griffith, 'The monks of Palestine and the growth of Christian literature in Arabic' *The Muslim World* 78, 1988, pp. 1–28.

33 *A treatise on the triune nature of God*, ed., M.D. Gibson, p. 75.

Q 5:72–3 which alleges that Christians worship gods alongside the One True God and reshapes the terminology to include Christ the Word and the Holy Spirit in the definition of God. 'We do not say three gods ... But we do say that God and His Word and His Spirit is One God and One Creator.'[34] Obviously here is a rebuttal of Q 5:73, 'They are unbelievers who say that God is one third of a Trinity', and Q 4:171, 'Believe in God and His messengers and do not say "Trinity."' He quotes from Q 4:171 and 16:102 to challenge his Muslim reader to accept this truth.

> Believe in God and His Word; and also in His Holy Spirit; surely the Holy Spirit has brought down from your Lord mercy and guidance ... You find in the Qur'an that God and His Word and His Spirit is One God and One Lord. You have said that you believe in God and His Word and His Spirit, so do not reproach us, you people, for believing in God and His Word and His Spirit.[35]

ʿAmmār's appeal to the Qur'anic references to God's word and spirit is part of an established Christian discourse. But his use of these texts is particular to him. Having connected the Word and Spirit with the essence of God, ʿAmmār proceeds to quote verbatim from Ps 33:6, 'The heavens were created by God's word,' Job 33:4, 'God's spirit created me,' Isa 40:8, 'God's word lasts forever,' Ps 119:89, 'The word of our God stands firm in heaven,' and Ps 56:4 'I praise God for his word' to show that the Bible, or more especially the Old Testament, is full of references to God's Word and Spirit.[36] It is noteworthy that ʿAmmār does not think he should refer to New Testament texts at this point. He does, however, turn to the Christian conception of God as Father, Son and Holy Spirit. This might well be explained by the fact that the Old Testament texts do not call God Father and do not connect God's Word with his Son as New Testament texts would do.

When he does refer to Father, Son and Holy Spirit he instantly deals with the Muslim concerns with numerical threeness in God and the attribution of a female partner to him.

> We are not guilty before God of speaking of three gods, but in our speaking of the Father, the Son and the Holy Spirit, we only want to confirm the truth that God is living and speaking. The Father, we mean to say, is

34 Gibson, p. 76.

35 Pp. 77–8.

36 Hayek, *ʿAmmār al-Baṣrī. Apologie et controverses*, p. 48.

> he who has life and word. The life is the Holy Spirit and the word is the Son. This is not the same as the allegation of our opponents that we make a female partner for God and a son from her. May God be greatly exalted above that![37]

Two Qur'anic texts are referred to by ʿAmmār here. Q 4:171, 'Do not say 'three'. Stop it! It will be better for you. God is one God,' contains the accusation which ʿAmmār seeks to deny by arguing that the Trinity affirms the oneness of God. Q 72:3, 'God has taken neither a female partner nor a son,' was used by Muslims to discredit the Christian belief in the divine sonship of Jesus, and ʿAmmār joins in an already established tradition of denial of the accusation by forming his own version of Q 4:171, 'Far exalted is God above having a son' in 'May God be greatly exalted above that.'

ʿAmmār was probably familiar with the text of the Dialogue in Baghdad between Patriarch Timothy I of his own denomination, the East Syrian Diophysites (Nestorians), and The Caliph al-Mahdī, who had summoned Timothy to answer questions about Christian beliefs around 781–2. The Caliph opened his questioning about Christ with the following; 'How can someone like you, knowledgeable and wise, say that the Most High God took a wife and had a son?'[38] The Caliph accused Christians of believing in a biological connection between God and Jesus through physical union with Mary. The fact that Christians would never have said such a thing demonstrates that this idea arose from the interpretation of the texts such as Q 4:171 and 72:3. Timothy reacted by exclaiming, 'Who has uttered such blasphemy?' and avoiding sonship terminology altogether, spoke of his belief in 'The Word of God appearing in the flesh for the salvation of the world.'[39] ʿAmmār's language of incredulity at Muslim accusations has a distinguished history.

This refutation frames ʿAmmār's discussion of the Trinity in *The Book of the Proof*. He returns to it before beginning his treatment of the Incarnation, advising his Christian readers to refute this allegation of Muslims who 'Stirred up people against us by their accusation that we say that God took a female companion and a son from her. May God be greatly exalted above that!'[40]

37 Hayek, *ʿAmmār al-Baṣrī. Apologie et controverses*, pp. 48–9.

38 The Arabic text (c. 795) edited by L. Cheikho in *Al-Machriq* 19, 1921, pp. 359–374 and pp. 408–418 is reproduced as *A dialogue between the Caliph al-Mahdī and the Nestorian Patriarch Timothy I* in the appendix of H. Putman, *L'Église et l'Islam sous Timothée I (780–823)*, Beirut, 1975. Here, appendix, p. 7.

39 Putman, *L'Église et l'Islam sous Timothée I (780–823)*, appendix, p. 7.

40 Hayek, *ʿAmmār al-Baṣrī. Apologie et controverses*, p. 56.

The Incarnation

ʿAmmār opens his defence of the Incarnation by answering the charge that belief in a divine Son brings the pure nature of God into disrepute by associating created flesh and blood with the very essence of the creator.

> We are blameless before God concerning all of this, because the Son, according to us, has no body, no members, no flesh and no blood. His eternal birth was not from a woman's body … The Son is timeless and he had no beginning in time.[41]

According to ʿAmmār, the accusation found in the Qur'an that Christians believe God took a wife and had a son with her misses the mark precisely because Christians hold a completely different view of the sonship. The Son always existed and never began in time. It is the failure of Islam to recognize this fundamental belief that causes so much misunderstanding between Muslims and Christians. This was also the burden of Patriarch Timothy before the Caliph al-Mahdī, who asked why Christians called the Messiah 'Son of God.' Timothy answered by separating Christ's eternal sonship from his temporal one; 'The Messiah was born of the Father as His Word and he was born of the Virgin Mary as a man. His birth from the Father is eternal before time and his birth from Mary took place in time without a human father.'[42]

The same problem arises with the concept of fatherhood. Does not the use of such terminology drag God, the timeless, and unlimited one into the same created and circumscribed world that humans inhabit? The usual sense of fatherhood and sonship is that one precedes the other in time, and that the physical body of the father is seen anew in the bodily characteristics of the son. However, the Christian understanding of fatherhood and sonship is altogether different, argues ʿAmmār. There is no physical relationship between the Father and the Son and there is no priority in time for the Father over the Son.

God does not have a body from which another body was created. Fatherhood and sonship are two properties created together in us humans. Neither of them can exist without the other, since human fathers and sons are created in time. We must understand that the fatherhood and sonship in the essence of the Creator are eternal, neither preceded the other. There is nothing in the essence of the Creator that is created or which precedes or follows.[43]

---

41 Hayek, *ʿAmmār al-Baṣrī. Apologie et controverses*, p. 57.

42 Putman, *L'Église et l'Islam sous Timothée I (780–823)*, appendix, p. 7.

43 Hayek, *ʿAmmār al-Baṣrī. Apologie et controverses*, p. 58.

Nevertheless, this Christian conceptualization of eternal, non-physical fatherhood and sonship is contradicted by the Qur'an, which alleges that Christians confuse created and uncreated categories. ʿAmmār quotes Q 112:3, 'He does not beget and is not begotten' and asks whether the Muslim interpretation of this text is that God is exalted beyond the creaturely activity of begetting. If the answer is affirmative then there are consequences for our understanding of procreation in the world.

> If the honour and the exaltation are in the saying that "He does not beget and is not begotten" ... then he must have granted exaltation to the trees and plants, and to what does not have life; grains, seeds, rocks and stones, since each of these does not beget and is not begotten.[44]

In this *reductio ad absurdum* argument, ʿAmmār attempts to challenge the reading of this Qur'anic text by insisting that begetting is characteristic of only some aspects of the created world that reproduce by begetting in the way that humans do. By making non-generation an honourable and exalted characteristic, Muslims have put themselves in an indefensible position.

> If that which was not generated is the most exalted thing, then Eve, who was not generated, would have been the most exalted over all things; and Satan, who does not generate nor is generated, would have been more exalted than Abraham, the friend of the Most Merciful.[45]

The references to Eve, Satan and Abraham are chosen because they are intelligible to a Muslim interlocutor. Abraham is named friend (*khalīl*) of God in Q 4:125, an epithet unique to him among the named believers in the Qur'an. Selecting the human being who is given the high privilege of being regarded by God as very near to him, enables ʿAmmār to contrast such an exalted status granted to a human being who had been subject to the usual means of begetting with the utterly dishonourable state of the angel Satan, who was not begotten. In Q 19: 44–5, Abraham pleads with his father not to worship Satan, God's enemy, lest he be punished by God for making Satan his ally (*walīy*). ʿAmmār is clearly playing on the opposite descriptors of Abraham and Satan found in the Qur'an, by his use of irony in interpreting the significance of this pair.

---

44 Hayek, *ʿAmmār al-Baṣrī. Apologie et controverses*, p. 60.

45 Hayek, *ʿAmmār al-Baṣrī. Apologie et controverses*, p. 61.

While the wife of Adam is not actually named as Eve in the Qur'an, the choice of the first woman as an example of a non-begotten human alongside Adam is prescient. In Q 36: 60–3, God says to rebellious humans on the Day of Judgement, 'Did I not command you, O children of Adam, not to worship Satan, because he was your clear adversary?' But their failure to listen and obey results in their being cast into hell (*jahannam*). The fact that Adam and his wife, Eve, exemplify this rejection of God's way by listening to Satan and following him, as reported in Q 2:35–6, 7:19–25, and 20:117–23, allows ʿAmmār to paint a powerful picture of dishonour and shame. Seven times in the Qur'an, at Q 2:34, 7:11, 15:30–2, 17:61, 18:50, 20:116, and 38:72–6, it is reported that Satan is the only angel that does not bow before Adam at God's command. If the disreputable human being, Eve, and the antagonistic angel, Satan, are models of beings that are not generated or begotten then how can Muslims hold that the absence of generation and begetting is the epitome of honour?

ʿAmmār drives home his argument that begetting is not only suitable to humans but also to God himself.

> Since we have found that man is the most dignified of all things, and that he is more honoured by God than them or even the angels, we know that dignity and glory are in what is generated and generates … We are certain that our dignity and our high rank occur by the application of the names of fatherhood and sonship to us. They are properties (*khawāṣ*) of the Creator, may His praise be exalted, as He said in his pure and holy book, which was confirmed in the world by the resurrection of the dead and miracles beyond description.[46]

If a Muslim protests that fatherhood and sonship are not attributed to God in the Qur'an, then he should be reminded that the names of God found there are given to humans as well. God has called us by his names, such as living, knowing, wise, speaking, king, powerful, mighty, strong, able, generous, kind, and merciful. Only humans in God's created world are called by these names. It is not logical for Muslims to argue that what belongs to humans cannot be attributed to God.

> We say that if a human being is called living, knowing, beneficent, generous, gracious, kind, or the like, then they cannot call the Creator by them as well. If they say: "All of this belongs to the Creator, yet he has been kind

46 Hayek, *ʿAmmār al-Baṣrī. Apologie et controverses*, p. 61.

> and generous to us by calling us by these names." We say: "Why then do you not include fatherhood and sonship as well?"[47]

Here is an argument for fatherhood and sonship as properties of God based on the divine revelation found in the New Testament, revealed by God, and proved to be authentically divine by the most astonishing sign, the resurrection of Christ from death. But this historical truth depends on the life and death of Christ as told in the gospels.

ʿAmmār does not attempt to develop an argument for the appropriateness of the Incarnation based on the Qur'anic conception of God sitting on a throne, which is used by two other ninth century theologians, Theodore Abū Qurra and Ḥabīb ibn Khidma Abū Rā'iṭa. Abū Qurra (d.c. 830), at one time Chalcedonian Bishop of Harran in northern Mesopotamia, had a reputation for debating with Muslims. In a treatise entitled 'A reply to the one who refuses to attribute the Incarnation to God,' he attempts to answer the following question posed by an anonymous Muslim, 'How can the divine Son take a body and experience suffering?'[48] Abū Qurra replies that 'God is not effaced or cancelled out by appearing to His creation.'[49] He appeals to texts from the Bible that speak of God sitting on His throne and argues that God is both seated on His throne and in control of the whole universe. While he does not refer to any of the eighteen passages in the Qur'an that refer to God sitting on His throne, it is probable that Abū Qurra is aware of discussions among Muslims about the interpretation of these texts.[50] He seems to be asking Muslims to agree that God can sit in one location yet control everything since the Qur'an affirms this. On this basis he argues that God can both be in Jesus and in control of everything. 'The eternal Son is in every place ... He is not at all limited or restricted, apart from being in the body in which he experienced pain and suffering.'[51]

47 Hayek, *ʿAmmār al-Baṣrī. Apologie et controverses*, p. 61.

48 Abū Qurra, 'A reply to the one who refuses to attribute the Incarnation to God' (*Maymar fī-i-radd ʿalā man yankaru li-llāh al-tajassud*), in C. Bacha, *Les oeuvres Arabes de Théodore Aboucarra Évêque d'Harran*, Beyrouth, 1904, pp. 180–186.

49 Bacha, p. 180.

50 *Sūras* 7:52, 9:130, 10:3, 13:2, 17:44, 20:4, 21:22, 23:88 and 117, 25:60, 27:26, 32:3, 39:75, 40:15, 43:82, 57:4, 81:20, 85:15. See further, S. Rissanen, *Theological encounters of oriental Christians with Islam during early Abbasid rule*, Åbo, 1993, pp. 120–123, and M. Beaumont, *Christology in dialogue with Muslims*, Carlisle, 2005, pp. 33–36.

51 Bacha, p. 182.

The Jacobite (Syrian Miaphysite) theologian, Abū Rāʾiṭa (d. c. 835) associated with Takrit, was active in the early decades of the ninth century.[52] His *Letter on the Incarnation* contains forty four answers to questions about the Incarnation which might typically be asked by Muslims. Question twenty nine is posed to the Muslim: 'Do you not describe God as being in heaven and on the Throne?' Abū Rāʾiṭa makes direct reference to the Qurʾan here, and proceeds to argue that a Muslim must accept that God 'Is in heaven and on the Throne and in everything', and therefore there is no contradiction in the Christian belief that 'The Word was incarnated in its entirety yet is still in everything.'[53]

If ʿAmmār was familiar with their use of the throne texts as an analogy for the Incarnation he did not follow their lead. Perhaps he was already aware that Muslim reaction to this appeal to God sitting on a throne yet still being present everywhere would not be favourable to the Christian cause. He may have encountered Muslims like Al-Qāsim ibn Ibrāhīm (d. 860), who argued in his *Refutation of the Christians*, written as a result of debating with Christians in Egypt between 814 and 826,[54] that associating the created with the Creator weakens His power, and believing that God should take a body is to limit Him. 'He is God the Creator … who has no partner in his power or timelessness … who is not, composed of various parts, weak, embodied, or limited.'[55] For Muslims, allowing for limitations to God by analogy with his session on a throne is simply unacceptable. ʿAmmār may have decided that using this Qurʾanic detail was counter productive.

The Death of Christ by Crucifixion

Whatever might be said about God becoming human, the biggest difficulty about the Christian view of Christ for Muslims, according to ʿAmmār, is the denial of his death by crucifixion. 'They condemn us for saying that the Messiah

52 He was named as a participant in a synod held in 828 in The Chronicle of Michael the Syrian. See J.-B. Chabot, *Chronique de Michel le Syrien: Patriarche Jacobite d'Antioche*, vol. 3, Paris, 1899–1910, p. 50.

53 Abū Rāʾiṭa, 'The second letter of Abū Rāʾiṭa on the Incarnation' (*'al-Risāla al-thānīa li-Abī Rāʾiṭa fī-l-tajassud'*) in S.T. Keating, ed., *Defending the 'People of Truth' in the early Islamic period: The Christian apologies of Abū Rāʾiṭah*, Leiden, 2006, pp. 217–97, p. 259.

54 See W. Madelung, 'Al-Qāsim ibn Ibrāhīm', in D. Thomas and B. Roggema, eds, *Christian-Muslim relations. A bibliographical history volume 1*, Leiden, 2009, pp. 540–543.

55 Al-Qāsim ibn Ibrāhīm, 'Refutation of the Christians', (*'Al-radd ʿalā al-Naṣārā'*), in I. Di Matteo, ed., 'Confutazione contro i Christiani dello Zaydati al-Qāsim b. Ibrāhīm, *Revista degli Studi Orientali* 9, 1921–2, pp. 301–31, p. 309.

was crucified, and they accuse us of introducing weakness to God or humiliation to the Messiah.'[56] 'Ammār joins together the factual denial of the historicity of the death of Christ by crucifixion in Q 4:157, with a Muslim rationale for rejecting the possibility of it having ever happened. This combination of denying the facticity of the cross and challenging the dishonour of God and Christ if the death took place that way was by now traditional in Muslim thinking, as is shown by the Calph al-Mahdī in his interrogation of Patriarch Timothy. The Caliph quoted Q 4:157 as proof that Jesus Christ did not die by crucifixion, and then said to Timothy that being executed on the cross would dishonour Jesus and that it is inconceivable that God should have handed him over to the Jews to kill him.[57]

'Ammār repeats the verbatim quotation from Q 19:90–91 already cited in his defence of the authenticity of the gospels.

> They hold it against us that we slander God and attribute to him "what makes the heavens almost split apart because of it, the earth crack open, and the mountains become completely flattened" ... How do we introduce weakness to God when we say that Christ was crucified, yet he, according to them, is a prophet lower than their prophet in rank, and is not so exalted by them that the heavens are almost split apart by this happening to him? As he is exalted above what they accuse us of saying about God, then neither weakness nor imperfection has been introduced to God.[58]

Q 19:90–1, comes in the context of the claim in Q 19:88 that the most Merciful has taken to himself a son. The response is deafening because it is an outrageous belief. 'The heavens are on the point of splitting apart, the earth cracking open and the mountains becoming completely flattened because they claim that the Most Merciful has a son.' Here 'Ammār applies the text to the crucifixion of the Son, because presumably he understood that for Muslims the humiliating nature of the cross is the worst form of slander of the divine character. It is bad enough for Muslims that Christians claim that Jesus was more

56 Hayek, *'Ammār al-Baṣrī. Apologie et controverses*, p. 79.

57 H. Putman, *L'Église et l'Islam sous Timothée I (780–823)*, appendix, pp. 45, 48. For a detailed examination of Muslim and Christian responses to these concerns in the eighth and ninth centuries see M. Beaumont, 'Debating the cross in early Christian dialogues with Muslims', in D.E. Singh, ed., *Jesus and the cross: reflections of Christians from Islamic contexts*, Oxford, 2008, pp. 55–64.

58 Hayek, *'Ammār al-Baṣrī. Apologie et controverses*, p. 79.

than a prophet, it is far worse if Christians exalt God for asking his divine son to die for the sake of humans who have rebelled against God.

The comparison of Jesus with Muhammad is used by ʿAmmār to show that he is aware of Muslim sensibilities concerning the status of Jesus. Q 33:40 calls Muhammad 'The seal of the prophets.' He is the one who had been sent to the Christians to challenge their deification of Jesus, according to Q 4:171, 5:72–3, 116–7 and 9:31–3. ʿAmmār then compares Jesus and John the Baptist. Muslims accept that John the Baptist was beheaded. They recognize that John was favoured by God, but they do not claim that John's execution makes God weak. Yet they say that the execution of Jesus makes God weak. 'They introduce weakness to God, through prejudice, bias and lack of justice.'[59]

Three prophets in the Qur'an, Jesus, John and Muhammad are set up for comparison. Why should Muslims be offended that Jesus has a humiliating end to his life when they are able to accept an equally humiliating end to John's life? The story of the beheading of John is not related in the Qur'an, but ʿAmmār appears to be confident that Muslims do not challenge the version of John's life taken from the gospels. Yet they do exactly that with the gospel account of the death of Jesus on the cross.

ʿAmmār devotes a section of *The Book of the Proof* to defending Christian veneration of the cross from Muslim critique. The public display of the cross in processions and on the outside of churches had been a point of contention after the Islamic conquest of the Middle East. Muslims had tended to want to privatize these public displays to remove them from view. From a Muslim perspective, the taint of idolatry was attached to the Christian fondness for embracing the cross. He begins his defence by asking why Muslims kiss a stone in Mecca. 'As for their mocking us for venerating the cross, we will return the argument back to them. It is much more surprising to see them venerating a stone, which the polytheists had honoured and venerated.'[60]

The same comparison between Christians venerating the cross and Muslims venerating a stone is found in John of Damascus' *Heresy of the Ishmaelites*, where John says, 'They accuse us of idolatry because they say we worship the cross which they despise. So we say to them, "Why do express your adoration for the stone by kissing it?"'[61]

If Muslims say that the stone is venerated because it came down from heaven, ʿAmmār recommends that Christians should ask them,

59 Hayek, *ʿAmmār al-Baṣrī. Apologie et controverses*, p. 80.

60 Hayek, *ʿAmmār al-Baṣrī. Apologie et controverses*, p. 87.

61 Janosik, *John of Damascus: first apologist to the Muslims*, appendix 1, pp. 283–4.

> We heard that God has forbidden the honouring of stones he had created in this world, and has forbidden humans from taking them as idols to worship. So, what makes honouring and venerating that which came down from heaven more worthy than that which is from the things of this world; for God is the Creator of it all?[62]

ʿAmmār has in mind the description in Q 5:90, of sacred stones as an abomination of Satan. The worship of objects as deities is attacked forthrightly in the Qur'an, particularly in the recounting of Abraham's challenge to his family to give up worshipping their idols in Q 6:74, 14:35, 19:41–50, 21:51–71, 26:69–86, 29:16–26, and 37:83–99. So when ʿAmmār goes on to quote the Muslim interlocutor defending the kissing of the black stone 'Because of Abraham', he implies without spelling it out that Muslims are capable of outright contradiction in their beliefs, and replies, 'So, you venerate a stone because of Abraham, and reject the veneration of wood because of the veil of the Creator, I mean the human nature of Christ!'[63] In other words, Muslims who accuse Christians of idolatry because they adore a wooden model of the cross ought to look to their own blindness in their adoration of a stone in the Meccan mosque. It is a blindness that prevents them from seeing the glory of the divine nature under the veil of the human nature of Jesus Christ.

If ʿAmmār was aware of John of Damascus' argument he decided not to include John's references to Abraham's connection to the stone. John reports that some Muslims say that Abraham had sexual relations with Hagar on the stone and that others say that he tied his camel to it when he was going to sacrifice Isaac on the stone. John asks Muslims, 'Are you not ashamed for kissing this thing just because Abraham had sexual relations with a woman upon it, or that he tied a camel to it? Yet you convict us of venerating the cross of Christ, through which the power of demons and deception of the devil have been destroyed?'[64] ʿAmmār's approach is much more respectful to Muslim sensibilities, and he seeks to engage in serious dialogue rather than in diatribe.

The last recourse of the Muslim is to say that God required them to venerate the stone. ʿAmmār goes on the attack. 'You should not say God has commanded us to do this, since you confess that he prohibited you from doing such a thing, and he ordered you to fight the polytheists because of it.'[65] He refers to Q 9:3, 5, 7–9, 12–14, 17, 28–29, 33, and 36, where Muḥammad is commanded to fight

62 Hayek, *ʿAmmār al-Baṣrī. Apologie et controverses*, p. 88.
63 Hayek, *ʿAmmār al-Baṣrī. Apologie et controverses*, p. 88.
64 Janosik, *John of Damascus: first apologist to the Muslims*, appendix I, p. 284.
65 Hayek, *ʿAmmār al-Baṣrī. Apologie et controverses*, p. 88.

polytheists until they submit to Islam. ʿAmmār believes he has the upper hand and finishes by saying to his Christian reader he does not think that Muslims can give a reasonable answer.

Eating and Drinking in the Afterlife

The final section of ʿAmmār's systematic theology deals appropriately with the afterlife. He already drew attention to the distinctive teaching of the gospels concerning the manner of life for believers in the hereafter. In his defence of the authenticity of the gospels as revealed scripture, he mentioned that if Christians had wanted to corrupt their scriptures, 'they would have put into them what they thought would be pleasant in the hereafter; marriage, eating, drinking and such things.'[66] Christ taught that there would be no marriage in heaven in Matt 22:30 and Luke 20:35–6. However, in Matt 26:29 he promised that his disciples would drink wine with him in his Father's kingdom and in Luke 22:30 he looked forward to eating and drinking with his disciples at his table in his kingdom. The testimony of the fourth gospel is rather different. In John 3:14, Jesus told the woman at the well that if she drank the water he could give her then she would never thirst again. In John 6:27, Jesus challenged those who had eaten the food he had multiplied to believe that he was the bread of life, and that those who came to him would never go hungry. Paul's argument in Rom 14:17, that the kingdom of God is not about eating and drinking could be taken in a Johannine sense to depict eternal life as the absence of physical food and drink. ʿAmmār shares a developed tradition of reading the New Testament with Johannine and Pauline eyes.

ʿAmmār repeats the point twice more in the conclusion to his section on the authenticity of the gospels. 'See if your book agrees with the gospel … that there will be no marriage, food or drink in the hereafter,' and 'You hold to marriage, eating and drinking in the hereafter whereas the gospel annuls them.'[67] The Qur'an does depict believers eating, drinking and enjoying sexual pleasure in Q 37:45–8, 38:51–2, 44:54–5 and 52:19–20.

When he returns to this issue at the end of his work he lays out the Christian conception of heaven.

> God has shown in his book that he will make human bodies in that world perfectly strong and not weak. They will not need food or drink … They

66 Hayek, *ʿAmmār al-Baṣrī. Apologie et controverses*, p. 44.

67 Hayek, *ʿAmmār al-Baṣrī. Apologie et controverses*, p. 45.

> will be sustained by the power of the Creator ... in a state that is not sustained by the taste of one kind of food or drink after another, or of sexual intercourse time and again.[68]

He then invites Muslims to compare the experience of believers with that of angels in the afterlife. Both Christians and Muslims believe that humans will join with angels in the experience of heaven, 'Sharing in rank, power, dignity, endurance, and eternal joy with God's holy angels forever and ever.'[69] Yet Muslims hold that humans will continue to have physical needs and desires while angels will not. ʿAmmār cannot imagine that Muslims truly believe that the reward of Gabriel, Michael and all the other angels is inferior to the reward of humans.

Conclusion

ʿAmmār developed a systematic theology for his Christian community based on an apologetic interaction with the dominant Islamic culture of the early ninth century. The truth of Christianity was defended by arguing that the first Christian disciples spread the faith not by human means but by reliance on divine signs that, according to the Qur'an, could not be copied. When Muhammad brought signs from God they were in continuity with earlier signs, such as the gospel that Jesus brought. Therefore, Muslims must accept that Christianity was accompanied by these signs to which the Qur'an testifies.

However, the message of the Qur'an is not actually in continuity with the message that Jesus brought in the Christian Gospels. Since Muslims allege that Christians must have corrupted the pure teaching of Jesus, ʿAmmār mounted a defence of the authenticity of the Gospels by expressing astonishment that the disciples would have invented such a distasteful religion that centred on the worship of a crucified man, or such a narrow- minded religion that prohibited re-marriage after divorce. The accusation of corruption is rather turned against Muslims who have to account for how the Qur'an has altered the teaching of the Gospels.

The Muslim denial of threeness in God is dealt with by appealing to the Qur'anic references to God's word and spirit in a now established Christian apologetic tradition. But ʿAmmār has his own distinctive use of these references

68 Hayek, *ʿAmmār al-Baṣrī. Apologie et controverses*, p. 89.

69 Hayek, *ʿAmmār al-Baṣrī. Apologie et controverses*, p. 89.

to construct an argument for God's spirit and word to be essential attributes rather than merely actions of God. Refashioning the logic of John of Damascus, he accuses Muslims of rendering God lifeless and speechless if the word and spirit are not essential properties of God.

His treatment of the Incarnation is built on the foundations of the Qur'anic statements that God did not take a wife and have a son and that God does not beget nor is begotten. Like his illustrious East Syrian theological predecessor, Patriarch Timothy I, ʿAmmār makes a case that Muslims have not appreciated the difference between time and eternity in the relationship between God the Father and God the Son. But ʿAmmār takes the defense a step further by arguing that the concept of begetting is actually more dignified than Muslims seem to believe. If humanity is the crown of creation, according to the Qur'an, much superior to the angels, then God himself has elevated begotten humans above non-generated angels.

At the heart of the Incarnation is the death of the Incarnate one by crucifixion, and ʿAmmār's forthright rebuttal of the denial of the facticity of the death of Jesus on the cross is based on the parallel of the execution of John the Baptist. If the beheading of John is accepted as historically true by Muslims, then why should they baulk at the execution of Jesus? Then if God is thought be weakened by allowing the monstrous crucifixion of Jesus then why did he allow John's head to be removed? The flaw in the argument is the absence of the beheading from the Qur'anic account of John.

Muslim distaste for Christian veneration of the cross is dealt with by turning attention to the kissing of the black stone by Muslims on pilgrimage to Mecca. In a comparison first mentioned by John of Damascus, ʿAmmār's handling of the argument is much more respectful of Muslim sensibilities but like John of Damascus he does not think that the kissing of the stone can be defended by Muslims from the taint of idolatry.

The contrast between physical and spiritual bodies in the afterlife closes ʿAmmār's theological dialogue with Muslim believers. The signs of God revealed in the New Testament show that humans who are granted life in the heareafter do not have the same bodily needs there. The Qur'an's vivid description of eating, drinking and sexual relations runs counter to the earlier testimony of the signs of God.

This a theology of engagement that demonstrates attention to Muslim concerns relating to Christian beliefs that seem to be challenged by the Qur'an. There is a reliance on carefully reasoned argument rather than on diatribe. Such an approach models a respectful apologetic stance that does not refrain from asking Muslims the most difficult questions about the Qur'an.

CHAPTER 6

'They Find Him Written with Them.' The Impact of Q 7:157 on Muslim Interaction with Arab Christianity

Gordon Nickel

Many passages in the Qur'an relate explicitly to Christians and their scriptures, both Old and New Testaments.[1] Stories of biblical figures such as Moses, Abraham and Noah appear frequently in the Qur'an in multiple and diverse versions. Important Christian doctrinal beliefs known from the Bible are variously affirmed or denied in the Muslim scripture. The Torah, Psalms and Gospel are named a number of times, and then in only the most positive and respectful terms. At the same time, a series of verses makes dark and obscure accusations against the 'people of the book' for somehow tampering with the scriptures in their possession.

The Qur'an passages that arguably set up the greatest opportunities for interaction between Muslims and Arab Christianity, however, are those passages that seem to claim that references to the messenger of Islam would be found in the previous scriptures. There is a persistent tradition in Muslim thought and practice to search for verses in the Bible that can be claimed as prophecies of Islam's messenger. The practice stretches in time from writings in Islam's second century all the way to the latest YouTube videos on the Internet. On the other hand, often at the same time and sometimes from the same writers, a Muslim accusation of biblical falsification has been based on the perception that no prophecies of Islam's messenger are to be found in the Bible.

Muslims, as well as many non-Muslim scholars, often indicate three main passages in the Qur'an that seem to claim that references to the messenger of Islam would be found in the Bible.[2] The first passage has Ibrāhīm praying, 'Our Lord, and raise up in their midst a messenger from among them who will recite to them your signs' (Q 2:129). A second passage describes 'Īsā, the Qur'anic

1 S.H. Griffith, 'Christians and Christianity', *Encyclopaedia of the Qur'ān*, (ed.) J.D. McAuliffe, Leiden, 2001, vol. 1, pp. 307–16. G. Nickel, *Narratives of tampering in the earliest commentaries on the Qur'ān*, Leiden, 2011, pp. 39–50.

2 J.D. McAuliffe, 'The prediction and prefiguration of Muḥammad', in *Bible and Qur'ān: Essays in scriptural intertextuality*, (ed.) J.C. Reeves, Atlanta, 2003, pp. 107–31.

 | DOI 9789004360747_007

Jesus, as saying that he brings 'Good tidings of a messenger who comes after me, whose name is *aḥmad*' (Q 61:6). The third passage, however, is the only one that actually names the books in which the alleged references to the messenger would be found: 'The messenger, the *ummī* prophet, whom they find written with them in the *tawrāt* and the *injīl*' (Q 7:157).

This chapter is an exploration of how this expression from Q 7:157 was understood in the Islamic interpretive tradition, and an enquiry into the Muslim need to claim biblical attestation to the messenger of Islam. In addition to major commentaries of the classical period, works of other early Muslim genres are consulted for their contributions to this theme. Beginning in the formative period of Islam, Muslim claims for prophecies of their messenger in the Bible became 'a constant theme through the ages and across the immense geography of the Islamic world'.[3] Academic scholars of Muslim polemic have commented on the relationship between the Muslim claim of attestation and the accusation of falsification, and their observations will be brought into the analysis.

Three particular questions are focused in the following discussion. What is the relationship of the claim for attestation in Q 7:157 to the Muslim accusation of biblical falsification? Is it true, as Arthur Jeffery suggested, that 'The commonest charge of alterations in the Gospel is that the name of Muḥammad was there, but the Christians removed it'?[4] Secondly, did the continuing search for biblical passages that might be claimed as references to the messenger of Islam represent a need in Muslim thought for attestation to the messenger to be found in the earlier scriptures? Was there a deliberate effort in the first centuries of Islam 'to legitimize the authority of the new religion's founder by placing him in *continuity* and *fulfillment* of previous respected traditions'?[5] Finally, are there any indications that the understanding of Q 7:157 influenced the ways in which Muslims interacted with Arab Christians in daily life? Did

---

3 J.P. Monferrer-Sala, 'Maimonides under the messianic turmoil: Standardized apocalyptic *topoi* on Muḥammad's prophecy in *al-Risālah al-yamaniyyah*', in *Judæo-Arabic Culture in al-Andalus: Proceedings of the 13th Conference of the Society for Judæo-Arabic Studies, Cordoba 2007*, (ed.) A. Ashur, Cordoba, 2013, pp. 173–196, p. 174.

4 A. Jeffery, 'Ghevond's text of the correspondence between 'Umar II and Leo III', *Harvard Theological Review* 37 (1944), pp. 269–321, p. 293, note. 41.

5 M. Accad, 'Muḥammad's advent as the final criterion for the authenticity of the Judeo-Christian tradition: Ibn Qayyim al-Jawziyya's *Hidāyat al-ḥayārā fī ajwibat al-yahūd wa-'l-naṣārā*', in *The Three Rings: Textual studies in the historical trialogue of Judaism, Christianity and Islam*, (eds) B. Roggema, M. Poorthuis, and P. Valkenberg, Leuven, 2005, pp. 217–236, p. 235 (italics Accad's).

the perception that the Bible did not match Q 7:157 lead to a Muslim tendency to shut down conversation with Christians when it was based on the Bible?[6]

Qur'anic Text and Context

The verse containing the claim of reference to 'the *ummī* prophet' in the Torah and Gospel, Q 7:157, comes near the end of a long Qur'anic narrative about Moses. The narrative begins at Q 7:103 with 'Then after them we sent Moses with our signs to Pharaoh'. The passage continues until Q 7:171, after which there is a change of subject to the 'Children of Adam'.

This passage about Moses is one of the most extensive of the Qur'an's various Moses narratives. The version in Sura 7 contains many elements that are familiar from the Torah. For example, the Sura 7 version begins with God sending Moses to Pharaoh. There is a scene in Pharaoh's court (vv. 104–126). God delivers the Children of Israel from Pharaoh (vv. 136–138), then provides manna and quails in the wilderness (v. 160). There are familiar elements in this version that do not appear in any other 'variant tradition' of the Moses story in the Qur'an: God sends the plagues (vv. 130–135); Moses appoints 70 leaders (v. 155); God gives Moses the tablets (v. 145); and Moses asks to see God (v. 143). There are also narrative elements in this version that are not found in the Torah: God commands the Children of Israel to enter a town prostrate (v. 161); a 'mount' is raised over the people (v. 171); and the Children of Israel transgress the Sabbath (v. 163).

In the immediate context of Q 7:157, Moses prays to 'the Lord' (*al-rabb*) on behalf of the 70 men he chose (Q 7:155). His prayer continues into verse 156. God answers in the first person singular, though God's name is not given here. God's answer continues into verse 157:

> Those who follow the messenger, the *ummī* prophet, whom they find written down with them in the Torah and the Gospel, bidding them to honour, and forbidding them dishonour, making lawful for them the good things and making unlawful for them the corrupt things, and relieving them of their loads, and the fetters that were upon them. Those who believe in him and succour him and help him, and follow the light that has been sent down with him—they are the prosperers.[7]

6 W.M. Watt, *Muslim-Christian encounters: Perceptions and misperceptions*, London, 1991, p. 30.

7 Translation of A. Arberry, *The Koran interpreted*, Oxford, 1955, except for the phrase 'the ummī prophet'.

The meaning of the phrase *al-nabī al-ummī* in both 7:157 and 7:158 is surrounded by uncertainty and became a flashpoint of polemic in itself.[8] The term *ummī* seems to indicate a nation or a people who do not yet have a divinely inspired book, but for many Muslims it came to mean that the messenger of Islam could neither read nor write. This meaning, according to Isaiah Goldfeld, was 'probably put forward to uphold the idea of complete originality and inspiration of Muḥammad in the face of eventual hostile reference to eclecticism on his part.'[9] Norman Calder characterized the polemical dimension of the interpretation of *ummī* as 'a development almost certainly the product of sectarian dispute about the probative value of miracle in the Muhammadan biography.'[10]

The phrase 'believe in Allāh and his messenger' in Q 7:158 is one that readers might expect to find in so-called 'Medinan' suras. It seems out of place in the midst of a Moses narrative in a sura understood by Muslims to be 'Meccan'. In her examination of the golden calf story in Q 7:148–154, Angelika Neuwirth indeed describes Q 7:156–7 as a 'Medinan insertion'.[11]

In the Islamic Interpretive Tradition

The interpretation of Q 7:157 during the earliest period of Qur'anic exegesis was brief and straightforward, in the nature of a gloss. It is only with the first of the great classical commentators, al-Ṭabarī (d. 923), that the interpretation of this verse became more substantial. Muqātil ibn Sulaymān (d. 767), writing during the second Islamic century, interpreted the *ummī* prophet as meaning 'Muhammad', but offered no suggestion for how or where he would be found 'written with them' in the Torah and Gospel.[12] Muqātil's wider interpretation of Qur'anic passages that he connected to the Torah and/or Gospel, however, is remarkable for the frequency of the claim that the content in view is 'the

8 Y. Goldfeld, 'The illiterate prophet (*nabī ummī*): An inquiry into the development of a dogma in Islamic tradition', *Der Islam* 57 (1980), pp. 58–67. N. Calder, 'The *ummī* in early Islamic juridic literature', *Der Islam* 67 (1990), pp. 111–123.

9 Goldfeld, 'The illiterate prophet', p. 58.

10 Calder, 'The *ummī* in early Islamic juridic literature', p. 111.

11 A. Neuwirth, 'Meccan text—Medinan additions? Politics and the re-reading of liturgical communications', in *Words, texts and concepts cruising the Mediterranean Sea*, (eds) R. Arnzen and J. Thielmann, Leuven, 2004, pp. 71–93, pp. 84–5.

12 Muqātil ibn Sulaymān, *Tafsīr Muqātil ibn Sulaymān*, (ed.) 'A.M. Shihāta, Beirut, 2002, 5 vols, vol. 2, p. 67.

matter of Muhammad'. For example, almost all his explanations of a series of 11 verses containing verbs of concealment focus on Muhammad as the object.[13]

In this sense the commentary of al-Ṭabarī echoes an early exegetical pattern. Al-Ṭabarī understands the concealment verses very much like Muqātil. According to him, the object of concealment in 10 out of the 11 verses is the description of Muhammad. Indeed, this is virtually the only object of concealment in eight of his passages.[14] Also remarkable in al-Ṭabarī is the frequency of occurrence of the exact phrase from Q 7:157, 'they find him written with them in the Torah and the Gospel'. In his exegesis of the concealment verses, the phrase appears 12 times in this wording, and another 16 times in similar expressions.[15]

The Messenger Who is Not Crude

For Q 7:157 itself, al-Ṭabarī offered an extensive interpretation around the end of Islam's third century.[16] On the first part of the verse, al-Ṭabarī provided 15 exegetical traditions in addition to his opening statement that God's 'mercy' that 'embraces all things' (Q 7:156) means the community of Muḥammad.[17]

One of the traditions is a story about a conversation between God and Moses after Moses has appointed 70 men for a meeting with God (Q 7:155).[18] God offers to Moses to make a place of worship and a means of purification for the people. God will place the *sakīna* in the houses of the people and enable all of the people to recite the Torah by heart. When Moses tells the people about purification and the place of worship, they say they only want to pray in churches (*kanāʾis*). When he tells them that God will place the *sakīna* in their houses, the people say they want it to stay in the ark (*al-tābūt*). When Moses says God will enable them all to recite the Torah from memory, they say, 'We only want to recite it looking at it'. So God says, 'I will ordain it for those who are godfearing' (Q 7:156).

Al-Ṭabarī also transmitted a tradition about Torah attestation to Muhammad that he attributed to 'Aṭā' ibn Yasār. According to al-Ṭabarī, 'Aṭā' ibn Yasār asks

13 Nickel, *Narratives of Tampering*, pp. 88–96, p. 112.

14 Nickel, *Narratives of Tampering*, p. 146.

15 Nickel, *Narratives of Tampering*, p. 147.

16 al-Ṭabarī, *Jāmiʿ al-bayān fī taʾwīl al-qurʾān*, 12 vols, vol. 6, Beirut, 2005, pp. 82–7.

17 al-Ṭabarī, *Jāmiʿ al-bayān*, vol. 6, pp. 82–5.

18 al-Ṭabarī, *Jāmiʿ al-bayān*, vol. 6, p. 83.

ʿAbd Allāh ibn ʿAmr ibn al-ʿĀṣ to tell him the reference to the messenger of Islam in the Torah. ʿAmr ibn al-ʿĀṣ replies that it says in the Torah,

> O Prophet, We have sent you as a witness, an announcer of good tidings and a warner and as a refuge for the *ummiyyīn*. You are my servant and my messenger. I have called you *al-mutawakkil*. He is not crude (*faẓẓ*), nor uncouth (*ghalīẓ*), nor clamorous (*ṣakhkhāb*) in the markets; does not repay evil with evil but pardons and forgives. We will not grasp him in death until through him we make the crooked religion straight, so that they say, 'there is no god except Allah'. By him we will open hardened hearts, deaf ears and blind eyes.[19]

According to al-Ṭabarī, 'Atā' then meets Kaʿb and asks him whether these were the right words. Kaʿb does not disagree with a single letter, except that he pronounces the endings of three of the words differently.

Several versions of this tradition appear in works that are dated before al-Ṭabarī.[20] Scholars have commented that parts of this tradition resemble phrases from the Hebrew Bible. In particular, the phrase 'he is not crude, nor uncouth, nor clamorous in the markets (*laysa bi-faẓẓin wa lā ghalīẓ wa lā ṣakhkhāb fī 'l-aswāq*)' has made a good number of scholars think of Isaiah 42:2.[21]

Proof of his Prophethood

The commentary of Fakhr al-Dīn al-Rāzī (d. 1209) on Q 7:157 is also fairly extensive, and here the master of Herat did not disappoint.[22] He began his

---

19 al-Ṭabarī, *Jāmiʿ al-bayān*, vol. 6, p. 84. Translation by McAuliffe, 'Prediction and Prefiguration', p. 118.

20 Ibn Saʿd, *Kitāb al-ṭabaqāt al-kubrā*, Beirut, 1937, 8 vols, vol. 1, pp. 360–62. A. Guillaume, 'New Light on the Life of Muhammad', *Journal of Semitic Studies*, Monograph No. 1 (Manchester University Press, n.d.), p. 32 (Ibn Isḥāq). Al-Bukhārī. *Ṣaḥīḥ al-Bukhārī*, Cairo, 1955, 8 vols, vol. 6, pp. 44–5 (*kitāb al-tafsīr*, bāb 273, on Q 48:8).

21 J. Horowitz, 'Tawrāt', *The Encyclopaedia of Islam*, (eds) M.Th. Houtsma et al., Leiden, 1934, vol. 4, pp. 706–707, p. 706. Guillaume, 'New Light on the Life of Muhammad', p. 32. W.M. Watt, 'The early development of the Muslim attitude to the Bible', *Transactions of the Glasgow University Oriental Society* 16 (1955–56), pp. 50–62, p. 57. H. Lazarus-Yafeh, *Intertwined worlds. Medieval Islam and Bible criticism*, Princeton, 1992, p. 78. U. Rubin, *The Eye of the beholder: The life of Muḥammad as viewed by the early Muslims: a textual analysis*, Princeton, 1995, p. 30. McAuliffe, 'Prediction and Prefiguration', pp. 118–19.

22 *Al-Tafsīr al-kabīr li-imām al-Fakhr al-Rāzī*, Beirut, 1973, 32 vols, vol. 15, pp. 22–25.

comments on the verse with a query as to the nature of the 'following' of the messenger by the Children of Israel. Does it mean merely that they believed in the prophethood of the messenger after finding his mention in the Torah, or does it mean that they followed his laws (*sharāʾiʿ*) as well? Al-Rāzī believed it more likely that they followed his law as well, including the command to give *zakāt* (cf. Q 7:156).

In any case, for al-Rāzī, the *ummī* prophet indicated in Q 7:157 was emphatically the messenger of Islam. The major part of his exegesis is a presentation of nine characteristics (*ṣifāt*) by which Allah describes Muhammad in this verse, according to al-Rāzī. He begins with the characteristics of being a messenger, a prophet, and an *ummī*.[23] The significance of *ummī* for al-Rāzī is the miraculous way in which the messenger of Islam can neither write nor read, and yet can recite precisely, without changing the words. Al-Rāzī cross-references Q 29:48, 'And you were not a reader of any *kitāb* before it, nor did you write it with your right hand, for then might those have doubted who follow falsehood'.

It is al-Rāzī's fourth *ṣifa*, however, that most directly addresses the meaning of the phrase, 'whom they will find written with them in the Torah and Gospel'. Al-Rāzī offers an interesting piece of reasoning about the certainty of the Qur'an's claim of references to Islam's messenger in the Bible:

> This means that his description (*naʿt*) and the veracity (*ṣiḥḥa*) of his prophethood is written in the Torah and the Gospel, because if that were not written, that would greatly disincline the Jews and the Christians from accepting his message. This is because insisting (*iṣrār*) on lying and falsehood (*buhtān*) is greatly disinclining. Indeed, a wise man does not seek degrading matters (*nuqṣān*) and matters that disincline people from accepting his message. Since [the verse] said so, it means that that description was mentioned in the Torah and the Gospel. That is one of the greatest proofs (*dalāʾil*) of the veracity of his prophethood.[24]

Al-Rāzī indeed pictured an interaction between the Qur'an and Christians and Jews, but it is with the messenger of Islam. Tracing the line of al-Rāzī's reasoning is relevant to the theme of this article. Al-Rāzī assumed the messenger of Islam to be a wise prophet who wanted the Jews and Christians to accept his message. To lie to the Jews and Christians would turn them away from the messenger. Therefore, the Qur'an's claim that the messenger would be found

23 al-Rāzī, *Al-Tafsīr al-kabīr*, vol. 15, p. 23.
24 al-Rāzī, *Al-Tafsīr al-kabīr*, vol. 15, p. 23.

in the Torah and Gospel must be true. In turn, the asserted description of the messenger in the Torah and Gospel provides a major proof of the messenger's prophethood!

From a different angle, the passage indicates both the importance al-Rāzī attached to the alleged mention of the messenger in the earlier scriptures and the confidence he places in those scriptures as a source of authority and attestation. There is no mention here of an 'original' Torah and Gospel corrupted already by the time of the messenger or later. Rather, as is the case many times in *tafsīr* and other early Muslim genres,[25] al-Rāzī's 'proof' of the prophethood of the messenger relies for its narrative dynamic on the assumption of intact texts of the Torah and Gospel in the hands of the Jews and Christians who encountered the messenger. The 'veracity' of his prophethood in this case depends on the integrity of the Torah and Gospel.

His People Pray in Ranks

Al-Qurṭubī (d. 1272) opened his comments on Q 7:157[26] with two versions of the tradition already encountered above in the commentary of al-Ṭabarī: the conversation between God and Moses about a place of worship and a means of purification.[27] He interprets the meanings of the words 'apostle', 'prophet' and *ummī*, explaining the distinction between 'apostle' and 'prophet'. Like al-Rāzī, he explains the term *ummī* through Q 29:48.

On 'whom they find written with them in the Torah and Gospel', al-Qurṭubī reports the tradition about a messenger 'neither crude nor uncouth' in substantially the same form as found above in al-Ṭabarī.[28] Al-Qurṭubī credits al-Bukharī as his source, again from 'Aṭā' ibn Yasār questioning 'Abd Allāh ibn 'Amr ibn al-'Āṣ. The confirmation of Ka'b is also given here, along with a reference to al-Ṭabarī saying that Ka'b's dialect was Himarite.

According to Qurṭūbī, however, Ka'b added to the description of the prophet, supposedly also from the Torah, saying:

25 G. Nickel, 'Erzälungen über zuverlässige Texte—vergnügliches Lesen, bei dem der islamische Fälschungsvorwurf geprüft wird', In *Der Islam als historische, politische und theologische Herausforderung*, (eds) C. Schirrmacher and T. Schirrmacher, Bonn, 2013, pp. 23–34.

26 al-Qurṭubī, *Al-Jāmiʿ al-aḥkām al-qurʾān*, 26 vols, vol. 9, Beirut, 2006, pp. 351–57.

27 al-Qurṭubī, *Al-Jāmiʿ al-aḥkām*, vol. 9, pp. 351–52.

28 al-Qurṭubī, *Al-Jāmiʿ al-aḥkām*, vol. 9, p. 354.

> His place of birth is in Makka, his place of migration in Ṭāba, his rule in Syria, and his *umma* those who praise. They praise Allah in all circumstances and in every dwelling; they clean their limbs and clothe themselves to the middle of their legs. They abide by the sun, performing the ritual prayer wherever they are, even on top of the garbage. Their rank in battle is like their rank in ritual prayer.[29]

Then, wrote Qurṭūbī, Ka'b recited, 'Allah loves those who fight in his way as if they were a solid structure' (Q 61:4).

'We Find Your Description in Our Book'

One other major Muslim commentator who offered substantial interpretation of Q 7:157 was Ibn Kathīr (d. 1373).[30] On the opening phrase of Q 7:157, Ibn Kathīr immediately writes that this is about the description of Muhammad in 'the books of the prophets'. 'They gave good tidings of his coming to their communities and commanded them to follow him. His characteristics had not lapsed (*zalla*) [but were] present in their books. Their scholars and rabbis know them'.[31]

Ibn Kathīr then offers a tradition that he traced back to the visit of a Bedouin man to Medina during the time of Islam's messenger there. While trying to meet the messenger, the Bedouin witnesses a scene in which the messenger and his companions pass by a Jewish man. The Jewish man is 'reading from an open copy of the Torah' while mourning a son who is dying. The messenger of Islam asks the father, 'I ask you by the one who sent down the Torah, do you find my description and my advent in your book?' The Jewish man shakes his head in the negative. His son, however, says, 'Rather, yes, by him who sent down the Torah, we find your description and your advent in our book. I bear witness that there is no god except Allah and that you are the messenger of Allah'.[32] The messenger of Islam then removes this boy from his father and personally takes care of the boy's funeral.

It is striking that at this late stage of classical commentary on the Qur'an, in the 14th Century, Ibn Kathīr was still reporting this kind of narrative, first seen in the *tafsīr* of Muqātil and in the *Sīra* of Ibn Isḥāq. The story puts 'an open

29 al-Qurṭubī, *Al-Jāmiʿ al-aḥkām*, vol. 9, pp. 354–55.
30 Ibn Kathīr, *Tafsīr al-qur'ān al-ʿaẓīm*, Beirut, 1996, vol. 3, p. 229.
31 Ibn Kathīr, *Tafsīr al-qur'ān al-ʿaẓīm*, vol. 3, p. 229.
32 Ibn Kathīr, *Tafsīr al-qur'ān al-ʿaẓīm*, vol. 3, p. 230.

copy' of the Torah and the messenger of Islam together in the same scene. There is some uncertainty suggested in the messenger's question. Neither the messenger, nor his companions Abū Bakr and 'Umar, can read the Hebrew Torah. The Jewish father denies the truth, an illustration of Jewish perfidy. However, the confident exclamation of the dying Jewish boy, one who knows the contents of the Torah, turns the messenger's question into a verification of prophethood. There is no mention here of an 'original' Torah already corrupted at the time of the messenger or later. Rather, the story depends for its narrative dynamic on an intact Torah in the hands of the Jewish father.

Ibn Kathīr also tells a long story about a meeting of Muslim messengers with Heraclius in Damascus, in which a succession of biblical figures are discussed.[33] Then Ibn Kathīr presents the tradition of a Torah attestation to the messenger of Islam from 'Aṭā' ibn Yasār, citing both al-Ṭabarī and al-Bukhārī as sources. Here he also adds an expression to the tradition, which he attributes to al-Bukhārī: 'It was common in the speech of many of our *salaf* that they described the books of the People of the Book as the Torah'.[34]

Though this exploration has revealed a number of interesting interpretations of Q 7:157, it has not produced an abundant harvest of suggested passages from the Torah and Gospel that could be alleged to be prophecies of Muhammad. Meanwhile during this entire period, from before al-Ṭabarī up to the contemporaries of Ibn Kathīr, writers of other Muslim genres were providing many actual passages. However, in the commentary of the lesser-known al-Biqāʿī (d. 1480), we have an example of an exegete who knew the Bible well and what might be claimed as attestations to the messenger of Islam.[35] Al-Biqāʿī very quickly quotes Deuteronomy 18:15–18 from the Torah, as well as the *paraclete* passage from the Gospel according to John, chapters 14–16.

In Works of Dialogue and Polemic

Though the interpretations of Q 7:157 in the classical commentaries show signs of the polemical dimensions of the claim of attestation, works of dialogue and polemic give a stronger indication of what these claims may have meant for Muslim interaction with Arab Christianity. Muslim polemicists, and

33 Ibn Kathīr, *Tafsīr al-qur'ān al-ʿaẓīm*, vol. 3, pp. 230–32.

34 Ibn Kathīr, *Tafsīr al-qur'ān al-ʿaẓīm*, vol. 3, p. 232.

35 Al-Biqāʿī, *Naẓm al-durar fī tanāsub al-āyāt wa 'l-suwar*, Beirut, 1995, vol. 3, pp. 124–133 (on 7:157).

participants in dialogues, sometimes also made an explicit connection between their arguments and their understanding of Q 7:157.

The dialogue of Timothy the Patriarch with the caliph al-Mahdi illustrates well how Muslim-Christian interaction may have gone, based on the phrase in Q 7:157. The caliph asks Timothy, 'How is it that ... you do not accept Muḥammad from the testimony of the Messiah and the Gospel'.[36] Timothy explains how Christians find Jesus to be the fulfillment of many Old Testament prophecies, and then concludes, 'So far as Muḥammad is concerned I have not received a single testimony either from Jesus the Messiah or from the Gospel which would refer to his name or to his works'.[37] The caliph then asks about 'the paraclete', and Timothy explains why in his view this could not refer to the messenger of Islam. Finally the caliph says, 'There were many testimonies but the books have been corrupted, and you have removed them'.[38] Even after this, the caliph claims references to the messenger of Islam in the Hebrew Bible, such as Isaiah 21:7 and Deuteronomy 18:18, and considerably later again declares, 'If you had not corrupted the Torah and the Gospel, you would have found in them Muḥammad also with the other prophets'.[39]

Though the caliph does not quote Q 7:157 as the reason for his questions,[40] his persistence in proposing biblical passages as references to the messenger of Islam makes a connection to Q 7:157 reasonable. It is also interesting to note how easily, purely on the basis of Timothy's denials, the caliph moves to accusations of falsification and removal of references. Other early Christian-Muslim dialogues portray Christians as needing to respond to Muslim claims of biblical attestation to Muḥammad, for example the correspondence between Leo III and 'Umar II (Isaiah 21:7);[41] and the answers of Theodore Abū Qurra (d.c. 825) to the allegations of his fictitious Muslim interlocutor (based on Q 61:6).[42]

36 A. Mingana, 'The Apology of Timothy the Patriarch before the Caliph Mahdi', *Bulletin of the John Rylands Library* 12, 1928, pp. 137–226, p. 168.

37 Mingana, 'Apology of Timothy', p. 169.

38 Mingana, 'Apology of Timothy', p. 171. Translator A. Mingana comments at this point, 'The bulk of Muslim testimony, based on the Ḳur'ān, vii. 156, is to the effect that the name of Muḥammad is found in the Gospel.' 'Apology of Timothy,' p. 171, note. 2.

39 Mingana, 'Apology of Timothy', p. 191.

40 Mingana immediately connects the caliph's initial question with Q7:157. 'Apology of Timothy', p. 168, note. 1.

41 A. Jeffery, 'Ghevond's text of the correspondence between 'Umar II and Leo III', *Harvard Theological Review* 37 (1944), pp. 269–321, pp. 327–8.

42 A.-T. Khoury, *Polémique byzantine contre l'Islam* (*VIIIe–XIIIe S.*), Leiden, 1972, pp. 213–14. D.J. Sahas, 'The Formation of Later Islamic Doctrines as a Response to Byzantine Polemics:

One of the earliest Muslim writers to make use of actual passages from the Bible was Ibn Qutayba (d. 889) in his *Dalāʾil al-nubuwwa*. He presented verses from Isaiah and other Old Testament prophets, from the Torah and Psalms, as well as from the Gospel accounts of Matthew and John, in order to make the case that the coming of Muhammad is foretold in the Bible.[43] Ibn Qutayba did not accuse the Bible of corruption; after citing many verses from the Bible, he writes, 'This is what is in the earlier books of Allah that remain in possession of the people of the book'.[44] He seems to have followed the lead of ʿAlī ibn Rabban al-Ṭabarī in both content and approach. However, he invokes the Qur'an as the ultimate authority, and simply reasons that if the Qur'an said that descriptions of Muhammad would be found in the earlier scriptures, it must be true. 'If these accounts were not in their books, then there would not be any evidence of what the Koran says is contained in them, as in these words of His: "Whom they find written down with them in the Torah and the Gospel"' [Q 7:157].[45]

During the century before Ibn Ḥazm, one writer who made a case for the corruption of the text of the Bible was al-Maqdisī (d. after 966). Al-Maqdisī took an ambivalent attitude toward the Torah, because while accusing it of corruption he also searched in its pages for annunciations of Muhammad.[46] In contrast to Ibn Ḥazm, al-Maqdisī wrote in a courteous tone and was generally fair and accurate in his descriptions of the beliefs and practices of the Jews. Al-Maqdisī was also candid about his motivation for making a case to Muslims for the alteration of the text of the Torah: 'He tells his readers not to get discouraged when the Jews say that the Prophet is not mentioned in the Torah, for after all, it is explicitly stated in the Koran and is therefore beyond any doubt'.[47] Al-Maqdisī's statement seems to indicate an actual Muslim interaction with

---

The miracles of Muhammad', *Greek Orthodox Theological Review* 27 (1982), pp. 307–324, p. 313.

43 D. Thomas, 'Dalāʾil al-nubuwwa', *Christian-Muslim relations. A bibliographical history*, (ed.) D. Thomas, Brill Online, 2013. G. Lecomte, 'Les citations de l'Ancien et du Nouveau Testament dans l'œuvre d'Ibn Qutayba', *Arabica* 5 (1958), pp. 34–46. Further on Ibn Qutayba's claim of biblical prophecies, see S. Schmidtke, 'The Muslim Reception of Biblical Materials: Ibn Qutayba and his *Āʿlam al-nubuwwa*', *Islam and Christian-Muslim Relations* 22 (2011), pp. 249–274.

44 C. Adang, *Muslim writers on Judaism and the Hebrew Bible from Ibn Rabban to Ibn Hazm*, Leiden, 1996, p. 275.

45 Adang, *Muslim writers on Judaism and the Hebrew Bible*, pp. 276, and 150.

46 C. Adang, 'Medieval Muslim Polemics against the Jewish Scriptures', in *Muslim perceptions of other religions. A historical survey*, (ed.) J. Waardenburg, Oxford, 1999, pp. 143–159, p. 149.

47 Adang, *Muslim writers*, p. 155, from al-Maqdisī's *Kitāb al-badʾ wa l-taʾrīkh*.

non-Muslims concerning claims of the mention of the messenger, as well as his source for such claims in Q 7:157.

A similar motivation is found in the *Shifāʾ al-ghalīl* of al-Juwaynī (d. 1085). The Qurʾan states that there are references to the messenger of Islam in the Torah and Gospel, explains al-Juwaynī at the beginning of his short but significant work. Since the existing texts of the Torah and Gospel do not mention Muhammad, al-Juwaynī decides to make the case that alteration to the originals was both possible and actual.[48] Al-Juwaynī thinks it enough to suggest that alterations could have taken place, and to support his suggestions by indicating differences between biblical accounts. If alterations took place in this way, he argues, then it is possible that references to Muhammad present in the original may have been removed.[49] During the same century, however, al-Māwardī (d. 1058) had no difficulty finding texts in the Hebrew Bible that he then claimed to be prophecies of the messenger. In chapter 15 of his *Kitāb aʿlām an-nubbuwwa*, al-Māwardī cites 25 passages allegedly predicting the coming of the messenger, from Genesis to Zephaniah.[50]

Again from the non-Muslim side, a work of Maimonides (d. 1204) offers a glimpse of the arguments that some Muslims may have been making, as well as connecting the accusation of falsification explicitly to the assertion of references to the messenger of Islam. Writing in his *Epistle to Yemen*, Maimonides attempted to deal with the claims of Jewish apostates to Islam who 'believe the statement of the Koran that Mohammed was mentioned in the Torah'.

> Inasmuch as the Muslims could not find a single proof in the entire Bible nor a reference or possible allusion to their prophet which they could utilize, they were compelled to accuse us saying, 'You have altered the text of the Torah, and expunged every trace of the name of Mohammed therefrom'. They could find nothing stronger than this ignominious argument

48 D. Thomas, 'Shifāʾ al-ghalīl fī bayān mā waqaʿa fī l-Tawrāt wa-l-Injīl min al-tabdīl', *Christian-Muslim relations. A bibliographical history*, (ed.) D. Thomas, Brill Online, 2013.

49 D. Thomas, 'The Bible and the *kalām*', in *The Bible in Arab Christianity*, (ed.) D. Thomas, Leiden, 2007, pp. 176–91, p. 189.

50 S. Schmidtke, 'The Muslim reception of the Bible: al-Māwardī and his *Kitāb aʿlām an-nubbuwwa*', in *Le Sacre Scritture e le loro interpretazioni*, (eds) C. Baffioni, R.B. Finazzi, A.P. Dell'Acqua and E. Vergani, Milan/Rome, 2015, pp. 71–97, pp. 77–93. Al-Māwardī also quoted Bible passages in his Qurʾan commentary, *al-Nukat wa ʾl-ʿuyūn*, at Q 7:157. Schmidtke, 'The Muslim reception of the Bible', p. 74.

the falsity of which is easily demonstrated to one and all by the following facts.[51]

After proposing a couple of responses to the Muslim argument, Maimonides concluded, 'The motive for their accusation lies therefore, in the absence of any allusion to Mohammed in the Torah'.[52]

Two other Jewish authors wrote about experiencing the Muslim claims in similar ways. Al-Qirqisānī, who lived in the first half of the tenth century, wrote in his *Kitāb al-anwār*, 'The Muslims say: the prophets have announced Muḥammad, and the Torah mentioned him. This is what the Qur'ān says explicitly'.[53] Ibn Kammūna (d. 1284) characterized his Muslim antagonist as saying, 'There were annunciations about the advent of Muhammad in the books of the prophets before his time. For Muhammad claimed that he had been mentioned in the Torah and in the Gospel, as witness the verse: "who follow the messenger, the gentile prophet whom they find mentioned in their Torah and Gospel"'.[54] These are Jewish voices rather than the voices of Arab Christians. However, as fellow *dhimmis* within the Muslim Empire, Jews and Christians sometimes made common cause in defending the Torah,[55] and Christians sometimes even acknowledged when Jews did a better job of answering Muslim accusations that both communities faced.[56] These examples also suggest that in the course of interaction with Jews and Christians, Muslims held Q 7:157 very close to both the claim of biblical attestation and the accusation of biblical falsification.

The same pattern of Muslim claim and accusation continues up to the present day. In a recent scholarly work that compares the Qur'an to the Bible,

51 *Moses Maimonides' epistle to Yemen: The Arabic original and the three Hebrew versions*, (ed.) A.S. Halkin, English trans. B. Cohen, New York, 1952, pp. 40 (Arabic), 40–41 (Hebrew), viii (English).

52 *Moses Maimonides' epistle to Yemen*, p. viii. See also Monferrer-Sala, 'Maimonides under the messianic turmoil', pp. 184–5.

53 H. Ben-Shammai, 'The Attitude of Some Early Karaites Towards Islam', in *Studies in Medieval Jewish History and Literature, Volume II*, (ed.) I. Twersky, Cambridge, Mass., 1984, pp. 3–40, p. 31.

54 Ibn Kammūna, *Examination of the Three Faiths*, trans. M. Perlmann, Berkeley, 1971, p. 137.

55 Monferrer-Sala, 'Maimonides under the messianic turmoil', p. 178. Ben-Shammai, 'The Attitude of Some Early Karaites', p. 32. From the Christian side, A. Tien, trans., 'The Apology of Al-Kindi', in *The Early Christian-Muslim Dialogue: A Collection of Documents from the First Three Islamic Centuries (632–900)*, (ed.) N.A. Newman, Hatfield, 1993, p. 498.

56 M. Perlmann, 'The medieval polemics between Islam and Judaism', in *Religion in a Religious Age*, (ed.) S.D. Goitein, Cambridge, Mass., 1974, pp. 103–138, p. 122.

M.M. al-Azami quotes Q 7:157 and writes that this verse 'explicitly states that even the corrupted texts of the Old and New Testaments contained clear references to the forthcoming prophet'.[57] Al-Azami claims such references were seen by many of the earliest Muslims, 'but have since then been largely cleansed'.[58] For support, he refers to Ibn Kathīr's commentary on Q 7:157. Al-Azami, remarkably, is willing to accuse Christians and Jews of falsifying the Bible in the seventh century or later. For this he takes as his basis the Qur'anic statement about biblical references to the '*ummī* prophet', and he is content to rely for examples on a 14th-century commentary.

Modern Scholarly Highlighting of Q 7:157

Academic scholars of Muslim *tafsīr*, polemic and other genres have often noted the claims in Muslim literature for references to the messenger of Islam in the Bible. Some scholars have made connections from the claim for references to the need for biblical attestation on the one hand, and to the accusation of falsification on the other.

Ignaz Goldziher was the first scholar of Muslim polemic to observe the connection between the accusation of biblical falsification and the Muslim claim that the 'announcement of the sending of Muhammad' would be found in the earlier scriptures.[59] Goldziher called the accusation of Christian and Jewish falsification of the Bible the 'central point' and 'principle polemic moment'.[60] The first systematic treatment of the accusation of falsification Goldziher attributed to Ibn Ḥazm (d. 1064).[61] Until the 10th century, however, there was only the assumption that attestation to the mission of Islam's messenger would be found in 'the unfalsified writings of revelation'.[62]

Hava Lazarus-Yafeh further pinpointed the accusation to the Qur'anic claim that the *ummī* prophet would be 'written down with them' in the Torah and Gospel: 'The contradictions between the Ḳur'ānic and Biblical stories, and the denial of both Jews and Christians that Muḥammad was predicted in their

57 M.M. al-Azami, *The history of the Qur'ānic text from revelation to compilation*, Leicester, 2003, p. 262.

58 al-Azami, *The history of the Qur'ānic text*, p. 262.

59 I. Goldziher, 'Über muhammedanische Polemik gegen Ahl al-Kitab', *Zeitschrift der Deutschen Morgenländischen Gesellschaft* 32 (1878), pp. 341–87, p. 348.

60 Goldziher, 'Über muhammedanische Polemik', pp. 364, and 344.

61 Goldziher, 'Über muhammedanische Polemik', p. 363.

62 Goldziher, 'Über muhammedanische Polemik', p. 348.

Holy Scriptures, gave rise to the Ḳur'ānic accusation of the falsification of these last by Jews and Christians respectively'.[63] Though Lazarus-Yafeh considered the accusation Qur'anic, she also suggested a causative relationship between Jewish and Christian denial and Muslim accusation, in the context of polemical interaction.

W. Montgomery Watt also pictured a situation in which early Muslims discovered the differences between the Qur'an and the Bible related to the place of Muhammad.[64] Watt highlighted Q 7:157 as the source of Muslim expectations that Muhammad was foretold in the Bible. This perception of the Bible was shown to be inadequate, Watt wrote, but Muslims could not abandon it without rejecting the Qur'an. In response, Muslim scholars began to develop the doctrine of the corruption of the earlier scriptures. 'This made it easy to rebuff any arguments based by Christians on the Bible'.[65]

In quite recent publications, Camilla Adang arrives at a similar conclusion: 'What may be at the root of these allegations is that the Jews denied that Muḥammad was mentioned in their scripture'.[66] Adang explicitly mentions Q 7:157 as a crux of contention, and writes that Muslims who accused the Bible of deliberate tampering believed the Jews were motivated by a desire to delete or obscure the scriptural references to Muhammad.[67] Shari Lowin expresses the same thought from a different angle: 'This claim [of textual alteration] explains why Muḥammad does not appear in either the Hebrew Bible or New Testament, despite the Muslim claim that his arrival and mission had originally been predicted there'.[68]

In early Muslim works of *tafsīr* and *sīra*, notes John Wansbrough, 'Haggadic embellishment of the charge [of conscious and malicious distortion of the word of God] turned mostly upon the absence from Hebrew scripture of

63 H. Lazarus-Yafeh, 'Tawrāt', *The Encyclopaedia of Islam*, New Edition, P.J. Bearman et al., eds. (Leiden: Brill, 2000), Vol. x, p. 394. Whether the accusation is Qur'anic, as Lazarus-Yafeh wrote, may be disputed; but the dating of the accusation to the beginning of Jewish and Christian denial of references to the messenger of Islam in their scriptures seems to be supported by the available evidence.

64 W.M. Watt, 'The early development', p. 51.

65 W.M. Watt, *Muslim-Christian encounters: Perceptions and misperceptions*, London, 1991, p. 30.

66 C. Adang, 'Torah', *Encyclopaedia of the Qur'ān*, (ed.) J.D. McAuliffe, Leiden, 2006, Vol. 5, p. 304.

67 C. Adang, 'Polemics (Muslim-Jewish)', *Encyclopedia of Jews in the Islamic World*, (ed.) N.A. Stillman, Brill Online, 2010.

68 S. Lowin, 'Revision and Alteration', *Encyclopaedia of the Qur'ān*, (ed.) J.D. McAuliffe, Leiden, 2004, vol. 4, p. 450.

proof-texts announcing the mission of Muhammad'.[69] Wansbrough specifies Q 7:157 as the 'point of departure' for the allegation that Islam's messenger had been referred to in the Bible,[70] and documents the development of the theme of 'alleged prognosis of Muhammad in Jewish scripture' in the *Sīrat al-nabawiyya* of Ibn Isḥāq.[71] 'The use and abuse of "scripture" was thus a polemical concept', Wansbrough concludes, 'adduced in support of the Muslim claim that God's salvific design had been achieved only with the revelation granted Muhammad'.[72]

Uri Rubin conducts an extensive investigation into biblical annunciation in his book *The Eye of the Beholder*. Rubin notes the verses in the Qur'an that seem to claim attestation for Islam's messenger in the Bible, especially 7:157 and 61:6,[73] and also indicates some of the biblical passages that Muslims have claimed for their messenger, such as Isaiah 42 and John 15–16. He suggests that a need for attestation to the messenger of Islam arose out of apologetic in relation to Jews and Christians. He writes, 'The Muslims had to sustain the dogma that Muḥammad did indeed belong to the same exclusive predestined chain of prophets in whom the Jews and the Christians believed'.[74] The aim was to convince the People of the Book to recognize Muḥammad as a prophet like their own. Therefore, according to Rubin, Muslims searched for attestation in previous sacred scriptures and identified their own messenger with those references.

Accusation of Falsification

Muslim interaction with Arab Christianity, if influenced by Q 7:157, would tend to move in two main directions. In the case of Christian denial that references to Islam's messenger can be found in the Bible, one response would be to accuse Christians that the reason they don't find the references is that Christians and/or Jews have changed or removed the references. Another response would be to persist in a search for biblical references that could then be claimed for

69 J. Wansbrough, *Quranic studies: Sources and methods of scriptural interpretation*, Oxford, 1977, p. 189.

70 Wansbrough, *Quranic studies*, p. 63.

71 J. Wansbrough, *The Sectarian milieu: Content and composition of Islamic salvation history*, Oxford, 1978, pp. 14–16, and 40.

72 Wansbrough, *Sectarian milieu*, p. 109.

73 U. Rubin, *Eye of the beholder*, pp. 22–3.

74 Rubin, *Eye of the beholder*, p. 21.

the messenger of Islam. This is indeed how the interaction seems to have proceeded. In fact, in many cases the accusation of falsification and the claim of attestation came at the same time.

When accusations of Jewish and Christian falsification of the Bible first appear in early Muslim writings, the main object of falsification is alleged references to the messenger of Islam. For example, in the commentary of Muqātil, the earliest complete extant commentary, accusations of falsification come at Q 2:79 and Q 3:78.[75] On the expression, 'those who write the *kitāb* with their hands' in Q 2:79, Muqātil wrote, 'This is about how the chiefs of the Jews of Medina erased the description of Muhammad … from the Torah'.[76] The messenger of Islam is also the object of alteration in the occasion of recitation for Q 2:79 offered by al-Wāḥidī (d. 1075).[77]

The Muslim accusation of falsification seems to have taken on a life of its own in the writings of Ibn Ḥazm (d. 1064). However, this is not where Ibn Ḥazm's polemic began. Ibn Ḥazm is best known for the case he made against the Bible in his *Kitāb al-fiṣal*. Interestingly, some years earlier he had argued for the fulfillment of biblical prophecy in the messenger of Islam in his work *al-Uṣūl wa 'l-furūʿ*.[78] There Ibn Ḥazm had devoted an entire section to biblical quotations—as well as expressions falsely attributed to the Bible—that he claimed were 'signs of the prophet in the Torah'. The *Kitāb al-fiṣal* has been thoroughly examined and described by scholars,[79] so its extensive attack on the Bible need not detain the present study. However, the paradox within Ibn Ḥazm's polemic may be noted. "Ibn Ḥazm argues that, despite other biblical passages being corrupt, [the alleged references to Muhammad] have been preserved by God to provide a testimony for Muslims against the other religions. As Adang observes, it is maybe not surprising that these are missing from the

75 Nickel, *Narratives of tampering*, pp. 100–101, and 97–8.

76 *Tafsīr Muqātil*, vol. 1, p. 118. The same tendency to specify Muhammad as the object of falsification at these two verses is shown in the commentaries of Ibn ʿAbbās, al-Ṭabarī, al-Zamakhsharī, al-Qurṭubī, Ibn Kathīr, the Jalālayn, and even the 19th-century exegete al-Shawkānī. G. Nickel, *The gentle answer to the Muslim accusation of scriptural falsification*, Calgary, 2015, pp. 77–80.

77 al-Wāḥidī, *Asbāb al-nuzūl*, Beirut, 2006, p. 15.

78 C. Adang, 'Some Hitherto Neglected Material in the Work of Ibn Ḥazm', *Al-Masāq: Studia Arabo-Islamica Mediterranea* 5 (1992), pp. 17–28.

79 Among many other treatments, Lazarus-Yafeh, *Intertwined Worlds*, pp. 26–35. T. Pulcini, *Exegesis as polemical discourse: Ibn Ḥazm on Jewish and Christian scriptures*, Atlanta, 1998.

Kitāb al-fiṣal, given Ibn Ḥazm's intention there to destroy any credibility of the scriptures of Judaism and Christianity".[80]

It also seems unlikely that in the *Kitab al-fisal* Ibn Ḥazm based his accusations against the Bible on Q 7:157 or on Christian and Jewish denials that biblical references to the messenger of Islam could be found (though this seems to have been the approach of his contemporary al-Juwaynī). Ibn Ḥazm had other ways of alleging the Bible's corruption. However, it is interesting to note that later Muslim writers who made use of Ibn Ḥazm's arguments from *Kitāb al-fiṣal* did not for that reason neglect the claim that attestation to Muhammad would be found in the Bible.[81] It is also interesting that the 'common' Muslim inquirer in the *Hidāyat al-ḥayāra fī ajwibat al-Yahūd wa 'l-Naṣāra* of Ibn al-Qayyim al-Jawziyya (d. 1350), still contends that the Jews and Christians had erased Muhammad's name from the Bible.[82]

The References Remain

In addition to the accusation that the Bible is corrupt and falsified, Muslim controversial writings have also made the claim that references to the messenger of Islam can be found in the Bible as it is. The accusation and the claim often exist side by side, sometimes in the works of the same author. Jane McAuliffe writes that 'two parallel trajectories can be traced through the centuries-long interplay of polemic and apologetic which launched these works. One line of exegetical analysis has occupied itself principally with scorning the Jewish and Christian scriptures, while the other set about searching them.'[83] McAuliffe finds that this 'inherent tension' has never been directly addressed in the corpus of classical Islamic thought, nor has that tradition found a way to resolve 'this lingering contradiction.'[84]

Ordinarily, an accusation of corruption against the Bible would seem to forfeit the right to claim attestation to Islam's messenger in the same scripture. Such is the nature of polemic, however, that even contradiction can be brought into use. Andrew Rippin notes that:

80 J.P. Monferrer Sala, 'Ibn Ḥazm', *Christian-Muslim relations. A bibliographical history*, (ed.) D. Thomas, Brill Online, 2013. Adang, 'Some hitherto neglected material', p. 18.

81 Accad, 'Muḥammad's advent', p. 219.

82 J. Hoover, 'The Apologetic and Pastoral Intentions of Ibn Qayyim al-Jawziyya's Polemic against Jews and Christians', *Muslim World* 100 (2010), pp. 476–89, p. 486.

83 J.D. McAuliffe, 'The Qur'ānic Context of Muslim Biblical Scholarship', *Islam and Christian-Muslim Relations* 7 (1996), pp. 141–158, p. 144.

84 McAuliffe, 'The Qur'ānic Context', p. 153.

> Despite what would seem to be the consequence of [the] stance that there would ... be no references to Muḥammad found in the Bible, Muslims were quick to try to isolate any evidence of 'fulfillment' of earlier scripture that could be proclaimed by the coming of Muḥammad. The stimulus for this was undoubtedly Christian polemical pressure to provide proof of the validity of Islam.[85]

Rippin writes that the earliest Muslim apologetic treatises claimed references to Muhammad in the Bible. He cites as an example *The Book of Religion and Empire* by 'Alī ibn Rabban al-Ṭabarī (d. c. 860), a work that presents separate chapters of alleged prophecies of Islam's messenger from a range of Old Testament figures as well as from Jesus. Most extensive is the chapter on 'The prophecies of Isaiah about the prophet'.[86]

Other early Muslim authors brought forward biblical references that they claimed were fulfilled in Muhammad. The earliest Arabic collection of biblical references claimed for the messenger of Islam appears to be the *Risāla* of Ibn al-Layth, written between 790 and 797.[87] Ibn al-Layth included the references as part of a larger argument for the prophethood of Muhammad made to the Byzantine emperor Constantine VI. Barbara Roggema writes that 'The text bears witness to the intense debates regarding the prophethood of Muḥammad in the early decades of the 'Abbasid caliphate and to the need to respond to an ever more sophisticated anti-Muslim polemic coming from Christians living in Dār al-Islām'.[88] For Ibn al-Layth, the response included the claim that Muhammad was prophesied in the Bible.

However neither of these early works, nor the writing of Ibn Qutayba, accused the Bible of textual corruption, only that Jews and Christians did not understand it properly.[89] 'Ibn Rabban could ill afford to reject the Torah as a forgery, for this would deprive him of the main proof he adduces for

---

85 A. Rippin, 'Interpreting the Bible through the Qur'ān', in *Approaches to the Qur'an*, (eds) G.R. Hawting and A.A. Shareef, London, 1993, pp. 249–259, p. 254.

86 'Alī al-Ṭabarī, *The Book of Religion and Empire*, trans. A. Mingana, Manchester, 1922, pp. 93–116.

87 B. Roggema, 'Risālat Abī l-Rabī' Muḥammad ibn al-Layth allatī katabahā li-l-Rashīd ilā Qusṭanṭīn malik al-Rūm', *Christian-Muslim relations. A bibliographical history*, (ed.) David Thomas, Brill Online, 2013.

88 Roggema, 'Risālat Abī l-Rabī' Muḥammad ibn al-Layth'.

89 Adang, *Muslim writers*, p. 21 (Ibn al-Layth). Lecomte, 'Les citations de l'Ancien et du Nouveau Testament dans l'œuvre d'Ibn Qutayba', pp. 44–5. D.S. Margoliouth, 'On "The book of religion and empire" by 'Ali b. Rabban al-Tabari', *Proceedings of the British Academy* 16 (1930), p. 170.

Muhammad's veracity: the frequent occurrence of his name and description in the Jewish—and Christian—scriptures'.[90]

It seems that individual Muslim authors began to combine accusation of biblical corruption and the claim of biblical attestation to Muhammad only after the ninth century. In his *Kitāb al-bad' wa l-ta'rīkh*, al-Maqdisī accused Christian and Jewish scholars of removing 'the characteristic signs and proofs' of Muhammad's prophethood from the Bible while simultaneously adducing Gen 17:20 and Deut 33:2 as proofs that Muhammad was prophesied in the Bible.[91] Two centuries later, the Egyptian jurist Aḥmad ibn Idrīs al-Qarāfī (d. 1285) combined a sharp attack on the Bible with claims of biblical attestation to Muhammad in his *al-Ajwiba l-fākhira 'an al-as'ila l-fājira fī l-radd 'alā l-milla l-kāfira*.[92]

The most extensive example of combining accusation of biblical corruption with claim of biblical attestation, however, is the *Hidāyat al-ḥayāra* of Ibn Qayyim al-Jawziyya. On the one hand, Ibn al-Qayyim asserted textual corruption in the Torah and the Gospel.[93] On the other hand he provided some 100 pages of claims for references to Muhammad in the Bible; and Accad suggests that 'although the authentication of Muhammad's prophethood by means of the Biblical text was not new in itself, Ibn Qayyim was the first to state his case so vehemently'.[94] Ibn al-Qayyim was aware that his accusation of the Bible's corruption contradicted his claim to prove the prophethood of Muhammad from the Bible. 'He resolves this theologically by claiming that God prevented Jews and Christians from altering those particular passages that foretold the advent of Muhammad; the rest of the text was subject to corruption'.[95]

One may well wonder how such an arbitrary treatment of the Bible would affect Muslim interaction with Arab Christianity. Hoover argues that Ibn al-Qayyim's intention was 'apologetic and pastoral' toward ordinary Muslims. 'Ibn al-Qayyim is unfortunately not interested in a dialogue that seeks to

---

90 Adang, *Muslim writers*, p. 225.

91 Adang, *Muslim writers*, pp. 155–6.

92 Goldziher, 'Über muhammedanische Polemik', pp. 369–72. M. El Kaisy-Friemuth, 'Al-ajwiba l-fākhira 'an al-as'ila l-fājira fī l-radd 'alā l-milla l-kāfira', *Christian-Muslim relations. A bibliographical history*, (ed.) D. Thomas, Brill Online, 2013.

93 Hoover, 'The Apologetic and Pastoral Intentions', p. 487. Accad, 'Muḥammad's advent', p. 219.

94 Accad, 'Muḥammad's advent', p. 222.

95 Jon Hoover writes that the *Hidāyat al-ḥayara* contains one of the fullest sets of claims for biblical attestation to Muḥammad, 'if not the fullest.' See Hoover, 'The Apologetic and Pastoral Intentions', p. 487.

understand Jews and Christians in their own terms'.[96] In fact, Ibn al-Qayyim seems to have wanted to supply Muslims with strong arguments in order to turn them away from physical violence toward non-Muslims. In any case, Ibn al-Qayyim's 'theological' resolution of the contradiction between accusation of corruption and claim of attestation points to the overwhelming importance of Muhammad in Ibn al-Qayyim's system. Accad calls it a 'Muḥammado-centric' reading of the Bible.[97] References to the messenger of Islam must be found in the Bible, even if every single other word is judged corrupt.

These many, powerful polemics against Arab Christians, that did not hesitate to combine a claim of biblical attestation to the messenger of Islam with accusations of biblical corruption, produced a number of interesting responses from non-Muslims in the medieval period. Maimonides, for example, considered the Muslim claim that Genesis 17:20, Deuteronomy 33:1 and 18:15 were prophecies of the messenger of Islam, then wrote,

> These arguments have been rehearsed so often that they have become nauseating. It is not enough to declare that they are altogether feeble; nay, to cite as proofs these verses is ridiculous and absurd in the extreme. For these are not matters that can confuse the minds of anyone. Neither the untutored multitude nor the apostates themselves who delude others with them, believe in them or entertain any illusions about them … the Muslims themselves put no faith in their arguments, they neither accept nor cite them, because they are manifestly so fallacious.[98]

Maimonides then proceeded, in his *Epistle to Yemen*, to explain how in his view the verses cited by Muslims could not be understood to refer to Muhammad.[99]

Al-Qirqisānī also provided an interesting response in his *Kitāb al-anwār*. After noting the Muslim claim of biblical attestation, he wrote, 'This is another thing which verifies that [the claim of the messenger of Islam to prophethood is a] lie and falsity, since he ascribed to the Torah and the books of the prophets the mention of him, which is not to be found in them'.[100] Al-Qirqisānī acknowledged that the common Muslim approach to the Jews was to say that they lie when they say that Muhammad is not mentioned in the Torah. However, he suggested that the Muslim 'people of knowledge' have trouble with the

96 Hoover, 'The Apologetic and Pastoral Intentions', pp. 479–80.

97 Accad, 'Muḥammad's advent', p. 225.

98 Maimonides, *Epistle to Yemen*, pp. 40 (Arabic), 40–41 (Hebrew), viii (English).

99 Maimonides, *Epistle to Yemen*, pp. viii–x.

100 Ben-Shammai, 'The Attitude of Some Early Karaites', p. 31. Adang, *Muslim writers*, p. 153.

common view, because it pictures a worldwide Jewish conspiracy over many generations to lie and deny what is written in the Torah even while the Jews continue to recite it. 'From this it would necessarily follow in turn that there is no true transmitted knowledge'.[101]

By the time of Ibn Kammūna, such common-sense arguments were beginning to get a hearing from some Muslims.[102] Ibn Kammūna was able to quote from al-Rāzī's *al-Muḥaṣṣal* to the effect that detailed descriptions of Muhammad could not be found in the Torah and the Gospel, and 'It cannot be said that the Jews and the Christians distorted these two books, because we say that these two books were well-known east and west'.[103]

Conclusion

It is quite true that there is a contradiction between the Muslim accusation of the Bible's corruption or falsification on the one hand, and the Muslim claim of references to Muhammad in the Bible on the other. As McAuliffe writes, scorn for the Bible and a search for proof texts in the Bible have continued along parallel tracks.[104] However, 'scorn' and 'search' have often been united by a need to claim attestation for Muhammad in the earlier scriptures. That need is related to the sense that the earlier scriptures form the authoritative backdrop to the emergence of Islam, and thus need to be dealt with in one way or another.

A number of scholars have attempted to describe that sense of authority, whether found in the Qur'an or in the lore that was available from the scriptural communities. Julian Obermann writes, 'The word of God that had been revealed to the 'people of the Book' is forever reflected in [the messenger's] own revelations and referred to as an ultimate source of authority'.[105] Steven Wasserstrom argues that Jewish and Christian traditions were seen to attest to the truth of Islam: 'Isra'iliyyat was an outside witness brought in to testify to the veracity of the new religion. The older religion is called to the witness box to speak on behalf of the new'.[106] Wansbrough writes, 'By its own express

101 Ben-Shammai, 'The Attitude of Some Early Karaites', p. 31.

102 M. Schreiner, "Zur Geschichte der Polemik zwischen Juden und Muhammedanern," *Zeitschrift der Deutschen Morgenländischen Gesellschaft* xlii (1888), pp. 591–675, p. 641.

103 Ibn Kammūna, *Examination of the three faiths*, p. 140.

104 McAuliffe, 'The Qur'ānic Context', p. 144.

105 J. Obermann, 'Koran and Agada: The Events at Mount Sinai', *The American Journal of Semitic Languages* 57 (1941), pp. 23–48, p. 23.

106 S. Wasserstrom, *Between Muslim and Jew: the problem of symbiosis under early Islam*, Princeton, 1995, p. 174.

testimony, the Islamic kerygma was an articulation … of the Biblical dispensation, and can only thus be assessed.'[107]

Rubin understands a change over the course of time: he writes that direct quotations from the Bible eventually became unpopular among the Muslims, and that the same wordings began to be anchored rather to explicitly Islamic sources such as the Qur'an and hadith.[108] This may help explain some of the diversity among Muslim writings from the eighth to tenth centuries. However, it also creates a false impression. Claiming attestation to the messenger of Islam from the previous scriptures never really lost its appeal. As demonstrated above, it was a major component of Muslim apologetic up to the fourteenth century; and it continues into present-day polemic and dialogue.[109]

Regarding the importance of Q 7:157, the results of this exploration are mixed. On the one hand, when the classical exegetes made the accusation of biblical falsification at certain 'verses of tampering', their favorite object of falsification was alleged mention of the messenger of Islam. This suggests a Muslim response to a Christian or Jewish denial of the claim of Q 7:157. On the other hand, at Q 7:157 the exegetes seemed to show no great enthusiasm to claim attestation from biblical passages that became well known in other Muslim genres. Instead, they retailed traditions that for the most part did not transmit authentic biblical wordings. Only with the fifteenth century commentary of al-Biqāʿī do exegetes show a wider knowledge of the Bible and a substantial effort to justify the claim of Q 7:157.[110]

Works of dialogue and polemic point to a greater role for Q 7:157 in motivating both claim of biblical attestation and accusation of biblical falsification, though in contention with Christians many Muslim writers seem to have preferred Q 61:6. Ibn al-Qayyim certainly made a major effort to present biblical passages in an effort to claim attestation. Al-Maqdisī and al-Juwaynī made the accusation of biblical falsification in an effort to account for absence of attestation. At the centre of both arguments was the importance of Muhammad. In the case of Ibn Ḥazm, however, Q 7:157 does not seem to have been a factor either way. He was able to marshal many other ways to accuse the Bible of corruption.

---

107 Wansbrough, *Sectarian milieu*, p. 45.

108 Rubin, *Eye of the Beholder*, pp. 218–19.

109 Rippin, 'Interpreting the Bible', pp. 254–6. K. Zebiri, *Muslims and Christians Face to Face*, Oxford, 1997, p. 50. Al-Azami, *The history of the Qur'ānic text*, p. 262.

110 al-Biqāʿī, *Naẓm al-durar*, vol. 3, pp. 124–133. W. Saleh, '"Sublime in its style, exquisite in its tenderness": The Hebrew Bible quotations in al-Biqāʿī's Qur'ān commentary', in *Adaptations and innovations*, (eds) Y.T. Langermann and J. Stern, Paris, 2007, pp. 331–47.

Works of dialogue and polemic also indicate the influence that a Muslim understanding of Q 7:157 might have had on interaction with Arab Christianity. For the Muslim accusation of falsification, at least, one can sense the impact on al-Kindī, an Arab Christian, in his *Risāla*. Anticipating the Muslim response to his explanation of the life of Jesus from the Bible, al-Kindī wrote, 'You escape the inference on the plea that the text has been corrupted; so you can apply your favorite argument and shelter behind it'. With evident frustration, he continued, 'I do not know that I have found an argument more difficult to dislodge, more desperate to disarm than this which you advance as to the corruption of the sacred text'.[111]

111 A. Tien, trans., 'The Apology of Al-Kindi', p. 498.

CHAPTER 7

With the Qur'an in Mind

David Thomas

The reversal of power in the seventh century Middle East was decisive. At the beginning of the century Roman rule stretched through Egypt towards the lands of the Fertile Crescent, with victories for the Emperor Heraclius that would have given assurance God's favour shone upon him. Then, not more than fifty years later these lands had been seized by Arab armies streaming north from beyond the empire's boundaries, with the great cities of Alexandria, Jerusalem and Damascus under new rulers and the former Roman masters in retreat north of the Taurus mountains. Politically and militarily this was devastating, while theologically it brought down the judgement that was to be repeated for centuries afterwards whenever Muslim armies got the upper hand over Christians, that God was sending the invaders as a punishment on his church and people for their divisions and misdemeanours.

The mainly Christian inhabitants of the former Roman lands and their Muslim rulers had quickly to come to arrangements that acknowledged the new political reality. Taxes were exacted, although many of the existing structures upon which society was based were allowed to remain intact. Thus, for about a century the language of public administration in the Islamic Empire remained Greek, used by public officials who were not Muslim Arabs but the successors of Christian bureaucrats who had worked for Roman governors, the coinage remained unchanged with the cross that Heraclius had restored to Jerusalem in 629 depicted on the obverse, and in the majority of the towns and cities the most prominent buildings remained Christian churches. The urgency with which the more powerful Umayyad caliphs in the early eighth century made Arabic the language of official discourse, struck coins on which the image of the cross was subtly though decisively changed, and erected the Great Mosque in Damascus and the Dome of the Rock in Jerusalem, as it were facing down the Church of the Holy Sepulchre, is understandable.

These items of tangible evidence could be taken as indications of the Muslim rulers' intent to impress their power on their subjects, though they equally show the strength of the continuing social attitudes and practices that paid little heed to the character of the new rule until they were forced to do so, and may even have threatened to stifle it. The question is worth asking: How seriously did Christians take Islam in the early centuries of the Islamic era,

 | DOI 9789004360747_008

and how seriously did they take the Qur'an? There were considerable cultural and intellectual disparities between Christians, who formed the great majority of the client people within the Islamic empire in the early centuries, and Muslims, at least as Christians saw them. Christians regarded themselves as the heirs of the Graeco-Roman culture that had given unity to the world of the eastern Mediterranean for a millennium and had propelled thought forward in the physical and intellectual sciences. Above everything else, they had made use of their received learning to give definition to their Christian doctrines with elegant precision, even where they differed over the matter of the exact relationship between the human and divine natures in Christ. Their schools and academies guaranteed the preservation and continuing development of their doctrinal structures, and presumably instilled in their educated minds that these were reliable accounts of the nature of God and the way he related to the world. Among the Muslims who now ruled them, and who sought to converse with them, they perceived none of this theological exactness. A brief examination of some well-known texts from the early centuries will confirm this.

John of Damascus's *De haeresibus* contains the earliest (and probably the most influential) account of Islam by a Christian that survives. It is difficult to date it precisely, although it is generally thought to have been written in about 740, during the years after John had withdrawn from public life in the service of the caliphate to a monastery outside Jerusalem. It is startling in its opinionated brevity. John starts by calling Islam the 'deceptive superstition of the Ishmaelites', not recognising Muslims as a community in their own right or gracing their belief with a term such as 'religion', though, of course, since he includes his chapter in a work in which he gives accounts of well-known and little-known heretical offshoots of Christianity, this is understandable. After explaining why they are called Hagarenes and Saracens, he goes on briefly to say that these people were originally idolaters and worshippers of the morning star, continuing until the time of Heraclius, when the false prophet 'Mamed' appeared among them.[1] Here John condemns both the Muslims' past by saying they were idolaters, and also their present by calling their prophet, whose name he does not appear to know accurately, false.

What is significant in this brief introduction to the chapter is that John does not seem to think he needs to explain himself at length, nor to produce arguments to establish that Islam is a 'deceptive superstition' or that Muḥammad is 'false'. Whether he is following the same pattern as he does elsewhere in the *De haeresibus* of keeping accounts of errant sects to a minimum, or proceeding from the assumption that since this faith claimed to add new and varied

1 D.J. Sahas, *John of Damascus on Islam, the 'heresy of the Ishmaelites'*, Leiden, 1972, p. 133.

teachings to Christianity derived from a prophet who appeared after Christ and must by definition be wrong, he appears unshakably confident in his judgement and indifferent to any requirement to treat the faith with respect and fairness. He is expressing a view about Islam that is firmly entrenched in his mind and had more than likely become the accepted view among Christians, despite their subjugation under Muslim rule—though since this 'deceptive superstition' is 'the fore-runner of the Antichrist', it would not be expected to prevail for long.

This strong confidence in the nature of the relationship between Christianity and Islam is also evident in a brief theological argument that John uses. It runs as follows: The Muslims accuse the Christians of being associators (*hetairistai*, representing the Arabic *mushrikūn*), obviously because they call the Son and Holy Spirit divine in addition to God the Father. However, Muslims themselves accept that Christ is word and spirit of God (Q 4:171, 'Christ Jesus, son of Mary, was a messenger of God and his word, which he cast into Mary, and a spirit from him'). But Word and Spirit are both inseparable from the being in whom they have their origin, so if the Word is in God it must be God as well. On the other hand, if they are outside God, then God must be without Word or Spirit, making him no more than a stone, a piece of wood or another inanimate object.[2]

John's point here (which anticipates arguments used by other Christians a century later) is that unless God has Word and Spirit as integral parts of his being, he is reduced to a status below that of Deity, or even human or animal. But his very concise argument contains further implications, firstly that Muslims contradict themselves by accusing Christians of associating other beings with God while accepting the teaching of the Qur'ān that God has Word and Spirit, and secondly that Muslims fail to appreciate the necessity in logic of God possessing Word and Spirit if he is to be recognisably divine. John is the Muslims' teacher in this, leading them to see that while they inaccurately call Christians associators (although Christians do not recognise Word and Spirit as outside and therefore other than God), they themselves are mutilators of God (*koptai*, representing *muʿaṭṭila*) because they deprive him of attributes that characterise his very being.

The brevity with which this argument is laid out indicates how obvious all this is to John, as it must in his mind be to everyone else, and so how uninformed are the people who make the accusation. In this whole chapter on the heresy of the Ishmaelites there is a speed and brevity in description and argument that suggests John is going over ground that Christians will know already.

---

2 Sahas, *John of Damascus on Islam*, p. 137.

He appears confident that his views are historically and logically sound and that Muslim opponents have no basis for claiming any validity in their beliefs.

This peremptoriness contrasts with the approach adopted by the Nestorian Patriarch Timothy I in answer to the long series of questions asked him by the ʿAbbasid Caliph al-Mahdī in a meeting held in 782/3, though, of course, the circumstances were entirely different: John was writing in Greek in the knowledge that few, if any, Muslims would be able to follow what he wrote, while Timothy was speaking in Arabic in a public meeting, knowing full well that his answers had to avoid annoying the most powerful man he had met. He speaks at length and, of course, with great courtesy, though it is possible to see through his words a mind that is carefully unravelling deep technical matters for someone who is totally uninitiated and the level of whose questions glaringly reveal this.

It is no longer possible to know exactly what took place at the meeting itself. The account that has come down was written by Timothy himself in a letter to a friend, and there is a real probability that this has been revised and maybe expanded in the course of time. Nevertheless, if the extant form of the letter reproduces anything of the original exchange, it is possible to see a Christian who is hardly ruffled by the questions his Muslim host asks and who has no difficulty in providing full answers that satisfy his own understanding, if not always that of the caliph.

Maybe the most obvious example of the disparity in understanding between the two interlocutors comes in the part of the exchange where al-Mahdī asks about the Trinity. His question is simple and straightforward: 'Do you believe in Father, Son and Holy Spirit?', and Timothy's affirmative answer leads him to say that Timothy must then believe in three gods. Timothy explains that just as al-Mahdī with his word and spirit is one, or the sun, with its light and heat, so is God (the caliph would not be aware that these are age-old Christian metaphorical explanations). Al-Mahdī objects that a human's word vanishes and disappears, rather simple-mindedly comparing a human with God, to which Timothy explains that no such comparison can be made: God exists eternally and so do his Word and his Spirit 'without beginning and without end, as God with God, without any separation'.[3]

Al-Mahdī goes on to ask whether the Word and Spirit are separable from God, and this allows Timothy to give an explanation that closely resembles the point made by John of Damascus half a century earlier: if God's Word and Spirit could be separated from him he would cease to be rational and living.

3 A. Mingana, 'The Apology of Timothy the Patriarch before the Caliph Mahdi', *Bulletin of the John Rylands Library* 12 (1928) pp. 1–162, here pp. 158–9.

'If one, therefore, ventures to say about God that there was a time in which he had no Word and no Spirit, such a one would blaspheme against God, because his saying would be equivalent to asserting that there was a time in which God had no reason and no life.'[4]

The caliph's questions very conveniently allow Timothy to give a full account of the Trinity in language that is as clear and convincing as it is non-technical. This must raise doubts about the accuracy with which Timothy (or later editors) reproduced the original debate and represented the historical figure of the caliph. Nevertheless, al-Mahdī's words could not have been distorted completely, and so there must be at least a flavour of what went on between them on this crucial point of doctrine. This being so, it is difficult to ignore the almost school-masterly way in which Timothy explains his position, bringing out images that Christians in his entourage would have known well and providing full and rounded replies to the caliph's simple questions. He gives no impression of feeling under threat or of being pressed intellectually to find an answer that was not immediately forthcoming. He does not appear to try very hard, as though he knows that al-Mahdī does not possess the intellectual equipment either to follow what he says or to produce challenging responses.

As Christians in the newly-formed Islamic Empire became aware of the religious preoccupations of their rulers, so they must have come to see how relatively unsophisticated were the forms in which these preoccupations were articulated. They must also have seen how little Muslims understood Christian Bible-based doctrines, and how these agreed with reason when they were expressed in terms taken from philosophy and harmonising with it. There may have been exasperation when Christians entered into discussion with Muslims—John of Damascus's neat demonstration that if Muslims call Christians associators, Muslims must see that they are mutilators of God maybe conveys a hint of this—and there was certainly little will to dispel the misunderstanding by recasting Christian doctrines in terms of the strict monotheism they encountered from Muslims. While they insisted that God was one and was entirely distinct from humanity (and thus the Trinity was about the unity of God and the Incarnation about a God who entered into human experience but was not subsumed within it), they continued to insist upon the reality of the three divine Persons and of the act of uniting between the divine and human natures in Christ.

The closest any Christian came to appearing to take seriously the thought-forms that were typical of Muslim theological discourse was when the early ninth-century Nestorian theologian ʿAmmār al-Baṣrī borrowed a version of

4 Mingana, 'The Apology of Timothy', p. 159.

teaching about the attributes of God that was known in Muslim circles, and applied it to explain the Trinity. But even this borrowing is hardly thorough, and it serves to emphasise starkly the lack of interest Christians showed in explaining themselves to Muslims.

ʿAmmār is a mysterious figure, though from the internal evidence in one of his two extant works of the mention on an incident involving a future caliph and the external evidence of a work by the early ninth-century Muʿtazilī master Abū l-Hudhayl al-ʿAllāf being directed against him, it can be assumed he was active in the years before about 850.[5] These two works, which are among the earliest Christian treatises written in Arabic, are forms of systematic theology, setting out Christian thought in methodically structured ways. In the *Kitāb al-burhān*, probably the later of the two, as ʿAmmār embarks on an elaborate explanation of the Trinity, he turns to ideas he would have encountered among the Muslim intellectuals, such as Abū l-Hudhayl, with whom he evidently mixed. The way in which he uses these ideas is a prime example of the extent to which Christians did and did not engage seriously with Muslim ideas.

ʿAmmār begins by rounding on an unnamed believer in divine unity (*al-muʾmin bi-l-wāḥid*),[6] who has affirmed that although God may be living, powerful and so on, these qualities are not derived from any attributes of life, power and so on in his being. ʿAmmār finds this incredible because it denies any reliable description, and therefore understanding, of God. What he does not say is that Abū l-Hudhayl and other Muʿtazilīs of the day favoured exactly this view out of fear of predicating a series of eternal attributes in addition to God's own being, and thus of violating strict monotheism.

Without naming him, ʿAmmār associates his own thoughts about the divine attributes with a Muslim who is hardly better known now than he is, ʿAbd Allāh ibn Kullāb, a contemporary of Abū l-Hudhayl and therefore of himself. Ibn Kullāb taught that the qualities of God derived from attributes that were real and were part of his being. As ʿAmmār expresses this: 'The name "living" can only be made to apply by applying the entity "life", and the name "inanimate" can only be denied by its continuation' (*lā yajibu ism al-ḥayy ilā bi-wajūb maʿnā ḥayāh wa-annahu lā yunfā ism al-mayyit ilā bi-thabātihā*). In Ibn Kullāb's gnomic definition, they were distinct in their existence but not distinguishable from the being of God (*lā hiya huwa wa-lā hiya ghayruhu*).[7]

5 M. Beaumont, 'ʿAmmār al-Baṣrī', in D. Thomas and B. Roggema, (eds), *Christian-Muslim Relations, a Bibliographical History, volume 1 (600–900)*, Leiden, 2009, pp. 604–10.

6 M. Hayek, *ʿAmmār al-Baṣrī: Apologie et Controverses*, Beirut, 1977, p. 46.

7 Abū l-Ḥasan al-Ashʿarī, *Maqālāt al-Islamiyyīn*, ed., H. Ritter, Istanbul, 1930, p. 169.

In this way, ʿAmmār proves that there must logically be attributes within God as part of his being, doing so in polemical terms that Muslim debaters of the time would comprehend and either applaud or deny. Thus far, his account of the being of the Christian God is entirely set within the thought forms of Muslim theology. However, he now launches out on his own. He first argues that God's life and speech must be hypostases, because according to the known categories of being it is the hypostasis that subsists independently without need of another entity to maintain it in existence.[8] This is immediately a departure from the mode of thinking in which God's life and speech were explained as attributes, because within Muslim understanding attributes could not be said to exist autonomously even though they were logically distinguishable from the being of which they were predicated. In fact, it moves into Aristotelian categories as ʿAmmār seeks to show that God's Life and Word have a reality that is unlike that of the attributes.

He then goes on to argue that within the range of attributes with which God must rationally be endowed, life and reason must be hierarchically superior because they are elements in the actual structure of divinity and the other attributes derive from them, thus establishing that as divine Subject, Life and Word, in his essential reality God is Trinitarian. Muslims would not accept this, and for over a century afterwards it was common for polemicists to argue that other attributes, particularly power, were equally essential elements in the being of God.

In making these two points ʿAmmār leaves behind the Muslim idea of the attributes, in his first step showing that the Trinitarian hypostases only resemble attributes in some respects, and in the second arguing that they subsist and function quite differently from attributes. What in effect he does is to show that the reality of the Trinity is much more profound than attributes language could accommodate, because the reality of the Christian God has an accessibility and stability that the Muslim God cannot attain. It turns out that his use of Muslim attributes is only the first step towards presenting an altogether more sophisticated portrayal of the divine reality, and that his reason for doing so must be to show to any Muslim who might want to join in debate that Muslim argumentation only goes part of the way of its Christian counterpart. More than this, he shows in his gradual moves away from the comparison between the Persons of the Trinity and the attributes of non-Muʿtazilī perceptions of God how little he is interested in pursuing it, and thereby how pointless he sees any full engagement with Muslim theology would be. Christians were involved

8 Hayek, *ʿAmmār al-Baṣrī*, p. 51.

in an enterprise that may appear to resemble what Muslims were doing, but was ultimately quite different.

Other examples like these could be given to show similar reluctance or disinterest on the part of Christians to take Muslim theological thought seriously. It is not that they ignored completely the accusations that Muslims levelled at them, but more a matter of realising they were part of something substantially different and actually more profound than what the Muslims who ruled them were attempting. This being so, they could hardly be expected to take the efforts made by Muslims with the seriousness they perhaps deserved.

This observation also applies to Christian regard for the Qur'an. Most writers show some awareness of its contents, or part of them, and a very few show extensive acquaintance with it. But there is no one who values it as a book of teachings, let alone a scripture with universal appeal. This is, of course, to be expected on a priori grounds: the Christian revelation as recorded in the Gospels and other New Testament writings was the climax and also finality of God's communication with his creation, and there could logically be nothing to continue it and practically nothing needed to add to it—as the anonymous fourteenth century author of a letter to Muslim scholars in Damascus disarmingly though devastatingly put it: 'After such perfection there was nothing left to institute, because everything that preceded it necessitated it, and there was no need for what came after it. For nothing can come after perfection and be superior, but it will be inferior or derivative from it, and there is no need of such a thing'.[9] This statement actually sums up the whole attitude of Christians towards Islam and its scripture. No-one flinched from it, though some saw in this 'inferior' and 'derivative' scripture something that was from God, while it never rivalled the scripture they themselves held for all humankind.

Going back to John of Damascus, like his judgement on Islam as a whole, his judgement on the Qur'an is damning: 'A false prophet appeared among them surnamed Mamed, who, having casually been exposed to the Old and New Testament and supposedly encountered an Arian monk, formed a heresy of his own ... He spread rumours that a scripture was brought down to him from heaven. Thus, having drafted some pronouncements in his book, worthy of laughter, he handed it down to them that they may comply with it.'[10] For him, Muhammad is a fraud, the Qur'an is the result of casual and therefore inaccurate borrowing from the Bible under the influence of a heretical monk,

9 R. Ebied and D. Thomas (eds), *Muslim-Christian polemic during the Crusades, the Letter from the People of Cyprus and Ibn Abī Ṭālib al-Dimashqī's response*, Leiden, 2005, p. 145.

10 Sahas, *John of Damascus on Islam*, p. 133.

and its contents are trite, entirely Muhammad's own work. John can economically explain the similarities between it and the Bible as a result of Muhammad glancing through it, and also many dissimilarities as the result of information from a heretic.

This 'heretic' is identified in the Islamic tradition as the monk Baḥīrā, the anchorite who identifies Muhammad as the prophet his books foretold,[11] and thereby symbolically gives Christian recognition to the bearer of a faith that will replace Christianity. The brief and general way in which John refers to him, and to the whole origin of the Qur'an, raises the possibility that here John is not just representing his own opinion but the consensus of his denomination in the century after Muhammad's death about where Islam has come from.

Given the judgement he makes, it is no surprise that John's treatment is partial or lacking in seriousness. He brings together a number of verses referring to Jesus, some of them corresponding to Christian teachings but containing inaccuracies, and he mentions a number of *sūras*, in particular one he calls The Discourse of the Camel of God.[12] He denounces these and other items from the Qur'an as 'absurdities worthy of laughter'[13] and 'idle tales worthy of laughter',[14] all the time substantiating his initial judgement with these illustrations.

One argument shows that John had more than a passing acquaintance with the Qur'an, but that for all he knew about it he set little store by it. He argues that the Qur'an commands Muslims 'not to do anything or receive anything without witnesses'. However, despite the fact that Muslims cannot marry, make a purchase or acquire property without a witness, 'only your faith and your scripture you have without a witness. And this is because the one who handed it down to you does not have any certification from anywhere, nor is there anyone known who testified about him in advance, but he, furthermore, received this while asleep.'[15] There is an open contradiction here, since John is evidently fully aware that, according to the traditional accounts, Muhammad's first revelation was received in isolation in the cave. John's acquaintance with the Qur'an does nothing but increase his distaste for it.

Another attitude towards the Qur'an is demonstrated in an anonymous work that was written not long after John of Damascus, possibly within a

11 Ibn Hishām, *Al-sīrat al-nabawiyya*, ed., F. Wüstenfeld, Gottingen, vol. 1, 1858, pp. 115–17; trans., A Guillaume, *The life of Muhammad*, Karachi, 1978, pp. 79–81.

12 Sahas, *John of Damascus on Islam*, pp. 139–41.

13 Sahas, *John of Damascus on Islam*, p. 135.

14 Sahas, *John of Damascus on Islam*, p. 141.

15 Sahas, *John of Damascus on Islam*, p. 135.

decade after his death.[16] It is known as *Fī tathlīth Allāh al-wāḥid* ('On the triune nature of the one God'), and it is the earliest extant Christian Arabic writing. It is an apology for Christianity, and its significance partly arises from the way in which it employs the Qur'an in its argumentation. It actually incorporates verses into the points it makes in order to show support and endorsement, and it does so without explanation or excuse, as though under the assumption that this is a function of the complementary scripture. Some examples will illustrate this approach.

Not far from the beginning, the apology affirms in the same way as other eighth century Christian writings that God's Word and Spirit are eternal with him. It does not argue this point in the same rational way that John of Damascus or Timothy I do, but instead it adduces verses from scripture, first the Bible and then, surprisingly, the Qur'an:

> God said in the Torah, 'Let us create man in our image and likeness' [Gen 1:26]. God (may his name be blessed) did not say 'I create man' but 'We create man' that man may know that God by his Word and Spirit created all things, and gave life to all things. He is the wise Creator.
>
> You will also find in the Qur'ān [*wa-tajidūnahu fī l-Qur'ān*], 'We created man in misery' [Q 90:4] and 'We opened the gates of heaven with water pouring down' [54:11] and 'And now you have come to us alone as we created you at first' [6:94]. He also said, 'Believe in God and in his Word and also in the Holy Spirit, but the Holy Spirit has brought it down a mercy and guidance from you Lord'. [see 4:171; 16:102][17]

The author has taken the simple step of selecting verses from the Qur'an that show God speaks of himself in the plural, just as in the Bible. (The first three of the chosen verses reproduce the Qur'anic text more or less in full, with the exception of the verb *tātūnā* for *ji'tunānā* in Q 6:94, though the fourth is more of a Christian realisation of verses that refer to the Word and Spirit of God.) In doing so, he appears to ascribe to it a confirmatory status that would be understood as an acknowledgement of some measure of authenticity.

16 See M. Swanson, 'An apology for the Christian faith', in S. Noble and A. Treiger (eds), *The Orthodox Church in the Arab world, 700–1700, an anthology of sources*, DeKalb IL, 2014, pp. 40–2.

17 M.D. Gibson, ed. and trans., *An Arabic version of the Acts of the Apostles ... with a treatise On the triune nature of God with translation, from the same codex*, London, 1899, text p. 77/ trans. p. 5; Swanson, 'Apology', p. 46.

A second, very subtle use of the Qur'an shows the same regard. This occurs in the proof that Christ's attributes and actions all show that he was divine:

> Christ created (*fa-khalaqa al-Masīḥ*) and only God creates. You will find in the Qur'ān (*wa-antum tajidūna fī l-Qur'ān*), he said, 'He created from clay as it were the form of a bird and breathed into it, and behold it was a bird by the help of God'. [Q 3:49; cf. 5:110][18]

The point here is that in the Qur'an the verb *khalaqa* ('to create') always has God as its subject except in this one instance of Christ creating clay shapes of birds. It must follow, therefore, that the Qur'an affirms Christ is God.

The conciseness of this little argument might easily cause it to be overlooked, though probably not by a Muslim who would be alerted by the words 'You will find in the Qur'ān', just as in the earlier quotation, and also at the later point where the author quotes Q 3:55 ('I will take you and raise you to myself and clear you from those who blaspheme; I will make those who follow you superior to those who reject faith') in support of his argument that Christ is truly the Son of God, sent to the whole world. The author does not go into details, but these words clearly show he is addressing Muslims and is telling them to look to their own book for confirmation of what he says.

Two points arise from this. The first is that, although he makes use of the Qur'an as a major part of his argument, the author of this work gives no indication that he attributes to it any higher status than that it is a text accepted by Muslims. He is silent about his own assessment of it, though there is no reason to think that he is doing any more in using it than acknowledging the reality of Muslim claims about it and challenging them to test these claims by showing them that the book they revere confirms the doctrinal teachings that he sets out. This is a recognised polemical strategy, to direct opponents to an authority which they accept while refraining from expressing one's own judgement about it.

The second point is that this author reads the Qur'an from a Christian stance without any sense that this may be inappropriate. On the basis of the relatively few verses he quotes and of his silence about any status the Qur'an may have, it would be too much to say that he Christianises it, but he clearly sees points of agreement between it and the Bible. It may be accurate to say that from his point of view the true meaning of the Qur'an is only brought out when its support for Christian doctrine is made explicit. This is, of course, in defiance of

18 Gibson, *On the triune nature of God*, pp. 84/12; Swanson does not translate this passage.

other parts that directly contradict the divine sonship of Jesus, which he does not mention.

Many later Christian authors followed what appears to be the same approach to the Qur'an, selecting verses that agreed with their arguments and leaving to one side the larger problem of how such verses could be reconciled with others that flatly denied the interpretation that Christians placed on them. Probably the most flagrant instance of this partial approach was the use Christians made of Q 4:171. In its entirety this verse is less than promising, but successive Christian writers (some of them noted above) were undeterred, seeing in it possibilities that suited their purposes and employing it with enthusiastic selectivity. The verse reads:

> People of the Book! Do not commit excesses in your religion, and say only the truth about God. Christ Jesus was only the son of Mary, and a messenger of God, and his word which he cast into Mary, and a spirit from him. So believe in God and his messengers, and do not say 'Three'; desist, it will be better for you. For God is one god.

The title 'messenger' (*rasūl*) here gives warning that as a being sent from God, Jesus was inferior to him and could not therefore be divine, while the injunction 'Do not say "Three"' is as close as a denial of the Trinity, and therefore of the pre-eternity of Jesus, as the Qur'an ever makes. But despite these, and the other indications in the verse, Christians seized on the reference to Jesus being the word and spirit of God and used it either to argue that the Qur'an supported the doctrinal claim that Jesus was identical with the second Person of the Trinity or to say that here was a confirmation of the doctrine of the Trinity itself.

Strangely enough, the verse is attributed by Ibn Isḥāq, Muhammad's biographer in the mid-eighth century, to the group from the first generation of Muslims who sought refuge in Abyssinia from the persecutions of the Quraysh. When the Quraysh representatives who have pursued them confront them in the presence of the ruler and reveal to him that the Muslims actually believe Jesus was a creature, the Muslims reply, 'We say about him that which our prophet brought, saying, he is the slave of God, and his messenger, and his spirit and his word, which he cast into Mary the blessed virgin'. This was sufficient to prompt the ruler to say that Muslims and Christians were separated by no more than a line in the sand, evidently missing the significance of the words 'slave' and 'messenger' which in Qur'anic terms by definition meant that Jesus was created and not divine.

The Patriarch Timothy refers to the verse in a heavily emended form. In the course of continuing arguments about the Trinity on the second day of his meeting with the Caliph al-Mahdī he quotes a series of verses from the Bible to support his arguments, and adds: 'I heard also that it is written in the Qur'ān that Christ is the Word of God and the Spirit of God, and not a servant.'[19] Clearly, the verse itself does not refer to him as a servant (although elsewhere the Qur'an does state this, e.g. Q 43:59), though in its full form it does not allow the inference that Timothy draws from it. But it is evident that he and other Christians had been so enthused by the references to Word and Spirit that they ignored the full meaning of the verse and took these as references that supported their own position.

Christians continued to use Q 4:171 to suit their purposes for centuries after Timothy and other early Christian apologists. It became one of the most popular, possibly the most popular, proof texts, and it was invariably quoted or referred to in edited form. The way in which it was put to use typifies the majority Christian attitude towards the Qur'an, essentially a flawed and suspect text that contained little to inform and inspire, although it could yield an occasional support to Gospel truth as long as it was interpreted properly. If any systematic understanding can be extracted from this kind of use, it is maybe what John of Damascus presents in the mid-eighth century, that the Qur'an is parasitic upon the Bible and will therefore retain occasional elements of true teaching in among the general detritus of misunderstanding and distortion. A corollary of this attitude is that whatever true teachings are to be found in the Qur'an will only come to light when it is read with Christian eyes.

While this remained the majority view throughout the early centuries (and indeed well into the medieval period and beyond the Arabic-speaking world), there was another.[20] This is attested by fewer witnesses, though it maybe shows more insight into the political and religious phenomenon of Islam and the Prophet Muhammad, as well as God's purposes in causing history to turn in the way it did to allow aliens to gain the upper hand over his supposedly chosen people. The tried explanation, that he sent the Muslim Arabs as a punishment for Christian disunity, could only persuade for so long. If God's ways were to be known and the place of Christianity at the centre of his concerns preserved, another explanation was required.

There are traces of this in one of the earliest known dialogues between Christians and Muslims. This is the Syriac-language *Disputation between a*

19 Mingana, 'The Apology of Timothy', p. 219.

20 See R. Hoyland, *Seeing Islam as others saw it*, Princeton NJ, 1997, pp. 535–8.

monk of Bēt Ḥālē and an Arab notable, which may date from as early as the 720s.[21] The fact that the Muslim interlocutor may have been the son of the Umayyad Caliph ʿAbd al-Malik could well have dictated the monk's whole approach to the dialogue, not least the careful framing of his answers.

At one point, the monk claims that the reference to Christ as Word and Spirit of God in Q 4:171 is evidence that Muhammad knew the Gospel of Luke, specifically the words of the angel Gabriel to Mary that the Holy Spirit would come upon her and the power of the Most High overshadow her (1:35, following the interpretation of Ephrem the Syrian that 'power of the Most High' means the Word of God). In reply, the Muslim asks why, if he knew about such things, Muhammad had not taught the full truth, as Christians see it, of the Trinity. To this the monk replies, 'You know, of course, that a child when it is born, because it does not possess the full faculties for receiving solid food, is nourished with milk for two years, and then they feed it with meat. Thus also Muḥammad, because he saw your simpleness and the deficiency of your understanding, he first taught you of the true God.'[22] The monk suggests that Muhammad knew that his followers must move into fuller truth, and the simple monotheism of the Qur'an was a stage towards the Trinitarian fulfilment.

The implications of this perception are that the Bible, and the Gospel in particular, remains the climax of God's revelation, that Muhammad knew this and appreciated the merits of the Gospel over the Qur'an, that the Qur'an contains the same truth as the Bible but in an incomplete and less profound form, and that the author of the Qur'an was Muhammad. The positive value it contains is that the Qur'an is now placed in an organic relationship with the Bible, as a preparation for it intended for a particular group of people, rather than a patchwork of borrowings from it made without true understanding.

Others also favoured this more benign view, and it is expressed and demonstrated at greatest length as late as about 1200 by the monk Paul of Antioch, who became Melkite Bishop of Sidon. As with so many others, little is known about him apart from the fact of his vocation and ordination. But he was certainly a native Arabic speaker, and he put this to use in a work that reveals as much knowledge about the Qur'an as most Muslims themselves would be likely to possess.

21 See B. Roggema, 'The Disputation between a monk of Bēt Ḥālē and an Arab notable', in Thomas and Roggema, (eds), *Christian-Muslim Relations, a Bibliographical History, volume 1 (600–900)*, pp. 268–73.

22 Trans. Hoyland, *Seeing Islam as others saw it*, p. 538.

This work is entitled *Risāla ilā baʿḍ aṣdiqāʾihi bi-Ṣaydā min al-Muslimīn* ('Letter to one of his Muslim friends in Sidon').[23] Nothing is known about the circumstances in which it was written nor its precise date, though from the fact that it was known to be in circulation in the thirteenth century it can probably be dated to about 1200. Although the actual circumstances of writing may be unknown, Paul himself provides an explanation of what caused him to write. He had been on a journey to Constantinople, Amalfi, parts of Europe and Rome, and had met there leading scholars and he was now writing for his Muslim friend what he had learned about their views on Muhammad.[24] It appeared that when these scholars had found out that Muhammad claimed to be a messenger of God and to have brought a revealed scripture, they obtained a copy of this book. But they did not then become followers of Muhammad or his religion, for reasons they go on to give.

These European scholars show a remarkably intimate knowledge of the Arabic Qur'an as well as unrivalled dexterity in manipulating its verses for their own purposes. For these reasons, they are much less likely to be historical figures who have learnt Arabic and made thorough studies of the Qur'an than to be convenient fabrications whom Paul uses to express his own views about the Qur'an without causing personal offence between his Muslim friend (or whoever his real readership was) and himself.

The scholars' first reason for not converting to Islam and following Muhammad is that they note a number of verses in the Qur'an which say that it is specifically an Arabic Qur'an and that it was sent as a warning to the people of Arabia. Thus, it was not sent to the scholars themselves, who anyway have their own messengers. This being so, when the Qur'an says, 'Whoever seeks a religion other than Islam, it will not be accepted from him, and on the last day he will be among the lost' [Q 3:85], this must mean, in all fairness, the people to whom Muhammad came and not others to whom he did not come.[25] Here is given a first indication of the approach adopted throughout the Letter. There is no hesitation to offer subversive interpretations of verses in the Qur'an.

---

23 See D. Thomas, 'Paul of Antioch's *Letter to a Muslim Friend* and *The Letter from Cyprus*', in Thomas, (ed.), *Syrian Christians under Islam, the first thousand years*, Leiden, 2001, pp. 203–21; Ebied and Thomas (eds), *Muslim-Christian polemic during the Crusades*, pp. 1–5; S.H. Griffith, 'Paul of Antioch', in Noble and Treiger (eds), *The Orthodox Church in the Arab world, 700–1700*, p. 216–19.

24 P. Khoury, *Paul d'Antioche, évêque melkite de Sidon* (*xii*[e] s.), Beirut, 1964, pp. 59–60 (Arabic text)/169–70 (French trans.); Griffith, 'Paul of Antioch', in Noble and Treiger (eds), *The Orthodox Church in the Arab world, 700–1700*, p. 220 (English trans.).

25 Khoury, pp. 61/170–1; Griffith, pp. 220–1.

The scholars go on to say that they see in the Qur'an great praise for Jesus and the Virgin Mary, verses about Christ being conceived without intercourse, his performing miracles, being called the Spirit and Word of God (a passing reference to Q 4:171 with no mention of any of the less exalted titles given to him there), and being elevated to the presence of God. Furthermore, there is praise for the Gospel, hermitages and churches, and the Apostles, and approval of Christians over Jews, as well as for their religious observances.[26] All this is the result of selective quotations of verses and the occasional slight alteration of wording to suit the argument. Paul effectively turns the Qur'an into a text that supports and endorses the teachings of the Gospel and Christianity.

This approach is sustained throughout the remainder of the short work, where the scholars explain that Muslims are wrong to deny the doctrine of the Trinity because they do not understand what it means,[27] that the divine sonship of Christ has no carnal connotations and the Incarnation was the supreme instance of God addressing humankind from behind a veil (as is witnessed in Q 42:51),[28] that Muslims are guilty of anthropomorphism if they accept what the Qur'an teaches and so cannot accuse Christians of this mistake,[29] and that the idea of God as substance must be understood in the terms in which it is intended: We have heard that these [Muslims] are people of merit, culture and learning. Someone whose representation this is and who has read even a little of the books of the philosophers and of logic, will not deny this',[30] and he goes on to show that according to the reasoning that is based on these principles God can be and is substance.

If Paul has not so far shown by implication that the Qur'an supports Christianity and effectively renders the institutional framework of Islam unnecessary, he makes this point in his conclusion. The European experts express amazement that, for all their learning, the Muslims do not appreciate that laws are of two kinds, justice and grace. Moses brought the law of justice, though the law of grace could only be imparted by God's own Word 'because there is nothing more perfect than it',[31] who had to assume the most noble of the

26 Khoury, pp. 62–8/172–6; Griffith, pp. 221–5.

27 Khoury, pp. 69–71/177–8; Griffith, pp. 225–7.

28 Khoury, pp. 71–3/178–80; Griffith, pp. 227–8.

29 Khoury, pp. 77–80/182–5; Griffith, pp. 228–31.

30 Khoury, p. 80/185; Griffith, p. 232.

31 Khoury, p. 82/186; Griffith, pp. 233.

created essences in order to communicate his law. 'After this perfection there was nothing left to establish'.[32]

It goes without saying that this is a bold work, in places astonishing and unlike other Christian appraisals of the Qur'an. Most strikingly, it appears to accept that Muhammad was a messenger sent from God. As the experts say near the beginning: 'We knew that he was not sent to us (*lam yursal ilaynā*), but to those Arabs who were in ignorance',[33] and they go on to argue that other messengers had been sent to them earlier (*atānā rusul min qablihi*). Here Paul more or less acknowledges that Muhammad was divinely sent. By the same token he accepts the Qur'an as a revelation, containing truth of a form. There is nothing demonic or derivative about it—Paul says nothing about it being taken from the Bible or from a heretical Christian monk—but it is from God, just like the Old and New Testaments.

The one great qualification in all this is that the Qur'an has a partial and by implication temporal authority. It is partial because it is intended specifically for the *jāhilī* Arabs and no-one else, and it is temporary because as its teachings are progressively understood so their value is reduced through the process of recognising the far fuller truths they point to in the books of the Bible. The Qur'an is effectively a provisional version of the Bible, simplified down to give only glimpses of the full truth for minds that were particularly resistant.

Uniquely among early Christian authors on the Qur'an who judge that it has some worth, Paul confronts the problem of its relationship with Christian scripture in a short passage that arises from the scholars' use of its verses to support their arguments:

> I said: If we use what is in their book as arguments, the Muslims will say: If you use part of it as argument, you must accept all of it. [The experts] said: The matter does not have this form. If a man has a note of debt against another for a hundred dinars and in the note it says that he has paid, and if the creditor shows the note and seeks the hundred dinars from the debtor, then if the debtor points to the evidence in the note that it is paid, can the creditor say to him: As you accept this, accept the hundred dinars as well and pay them? By no means! He will deny responsibility for the hundred dinars in the note by what is also in the note about

32 Khoury, p. 82/186; Griffith, pp. 233. The more or less identical declaration quoted above from a fourteenth century Christian (see n. 10) is from a letter that reworks Paul's text, and tones down most of its acerbities.

33 Khoury, p. 61/170; Griffith, pp. 221.

> it being paid. In the same way, whatever is acknowledged about us and argued against us from this book we will rebut it on the basis of the book as well, from the arguments we find in it in our favour.[34]

Despite the rather tortuous logic here, Paul evidently means that the Qur'an has been cancelled by the Gospel and can no longer be adduced as valid, although parts have some form of validity because they resemble the Gospel. They are there in the Qur'an, and they cannot be affected or replaced by whatever else it may contain. Here, Paul's lack of seriousness about the Qur'an becomes evident. He has appeared to accept it as revelation, and Muhammad as a messenger from God. But he implies now that it cannot be accorded its own integrity in which the various parts all exert influence on one another and together determine the meaning of any individual passage. It has effectively been superseded, and its true meaning can only be derived from reading it in relation to Christian scripture. Just as the Christian message corrects the partial message of Muhammad to the pagan Arabs, so the Gospel corrects the partial truths of the Qur'an.

Paul of Antioch is one of the few Arabic-speaking Christians who showed extensive knowledge of the Qur'an (another is the author of a ninth century reply to an invitation to convert to Islam that is attributed to a certain ʿAbd al-Masīḥ al-Kindī, who knows both the text of the Qur'an and the history of its origins as a written text), and appeared to be interested in its status as scripture. In his estimation of it as an inspired scripture of sorts he contrasts utterly with John of Damascus and those who agreed with him that the book was Muhammad's fraudulent production intended to mislead and deceive. But at the end of the day, he can only accord it subsidiary status as an elementary preparation for the fullness of the truth of the Gospel.

Paul's Letter confirms the general attitude among Arabic-speaking Christians that the believers who ruled their world were far inferior to themselves. The point he contends through what he writes is that by comparison with the insights offered through Christian scripture and its interpretation, the Qur'an gives no more than a rough and general overview. The implication is that if it is worth studying at all, its value only lies in the confirmation it offers to Christianity. But in truth, as he says at the end of his Letter, 'After this perfection [in the revelation of Jesus Christ] nothing remained to institute'. The Qur'an is a second-rate version of truth at best.

It can be seen, then, that in their differing approaches to the Qur'an and the various uses they made of it, Arabic-speaking Christians in the early centuries

34 Khoury, p. 76/181–2; Griffith, p. 230.

of the Islamic era persisted in their attitude that they were superior to their counterparts. This will have served an obvious psychological purpose, and helped them in part to continue believing that they were still part of God's purpose even in the face of his apparent abandonment of them. But it also made it difficult for them to approach Muslims with respect and a measure of regard.

Such sentiments are maybe as rare today as they were then, though in circumstances where the atrocities that have become the mark of persistent hostilities are so often directly linked to religious claims, they should no longer remain the stock behind the currency of discourse.

CHAPTER 8

Early Islamic Perspectives of the Apostle Paul as a Narrative Framework for Taḥrīf

Michael F. Kuhn

Introduction: The Evolution of Taḥrīf

The Qur'an expresses a high view of the precedent Scriptures known as the Tawrāt, the Zabūr and the Injīl (the Torah, Psalms and the Gospel): 'Say (O Muslims): We believe in Allah and that which is revealed unto us and that which was revealed unto Abraham, and Ishmael, and Isaac, and Jacob, and the tribes, and that which Moses and Jesus received, and that which the prophets received from their Lord. We make no distinction between any of them, and unto Him we have surrendered' (Q 2:136 Pickthall). Therefore it is somewhat surprising that Muslims of subsequent generations accused Christians and Jews of *taḥrīf*—corruption of their Scriptures. The main culprit in this allegation of altering the original texts sent down by God became Paul the apostle. Around four centuries after Muhammad's death, Ibn Ḥazm (d. 1064) wrote:

> Their rabbis on whose authority they have adopted their religion—the Tawrāt as well as the Books of the Prophets (peace be upon them!)—agreed to bribe Paul the Benjaminite (may God curse him!). They ordered him to profess outwardly the religion of Jesus (peace be upon him) and to deceive his followers and to induce them to follow the doctrine of his divinity. They told him: we shall take upon ourselves your sin. He was extremely successful, as is generally known.[1]

Not all Muslim writers were so censorious regarding Paul;[2] nevertheless the Christian apostle emerges in much early Islamic thought as a villain. The

1 P.S. van Koningsveld, 'The Islamic image of Paul and the origin of the Gospel of Barnabas,' *Jerusalem Studies in Arabic and Islam* 20, 1996, pp. 200–28. Quoted from: Ibn Ḥazm al-Andalusī. *Kitāb al-fiṣal fī al-milal wa-al-ahwāʾ wa-al-niḥal* (Cairo 1317–21) (5 vols.), vol. 2, pp. 221–22.

2 Ya'qūbī referred to Paul's experiences in the Acts of the Apostles to provide a straightforward, historical account of the events. See G.S. Reynolds, *A Muslim Theologian in the Sectarian*

 | DOI 9789004360747_009

purpose of this chapter is to examine the role of the Islamic narrative of the Apostle Paul in the crystallization of the charge of *taḥrīf.* Over time, Paul came to be seen as the corruptor of the laws or practices of the true religion, the corruptor of the doctrine of *tawḥīd*, and the corruptor of the preceding Scriptures.

Corruption of Meaning

A brief overview of the development of the doctrine in the early centuries of Islam (seventh–ninth) may provide helpful background. Early Muslim apologists were content to argue that the Christians had misunderstood their Scriptures, corrupting its meaning. This concept is normally described as *taḥrīf al-maʿnā* (corruption of meaning) which is different from changing the words of the Bible (*taḥrīf al-lafẓ*). This confidence was grounded in the view that the Qur'an was the same revelation given by Allāh in the Arabic tongue which had been given in earlier times to other peoples in their language. ʿAlī ibn Rabbān al-Ṭabarī (d. 855) was a convert from Christianity to Islām. In his *Radd ʿalā al-Naṣārā* (Refutation of the Christians) he proposes to show how Christians have misinterpreted their texts: 'with the help of God Most High, I will interpret the words—which [the Christians] have explained in a way contrary to their meanings—as I describe their *taḥrīf*.'[3] By following the plain meaning of their Gospel, al-Ṭabarī believed that Christians would certainly arrive at Islam.[4]

Abū Bakr Muḥammad al-Bāqillānī (d. 1013) was another renowned Muslim polemicist known for his trenchant criticism of Christianity. His incisive responses earned him the title *sayf al-sunna wa-lisān al-umma* (sword of the Sunna and tongue of the milla). Yet, al-Bāqillānī reasoned from the Biblical texts implying Christians had misunderstood them. He invokes Christ's prayer before raising Lazarus as well as the Gethsemane prayer of Jesus that this cup (of his passion) might pass from him. Al-Bāqillānī may be following al-Maturidī in suggesting that this prayer is representative of a prophet, not of

---

Milieu, Leiden, 2004, p. 171. See also al-Yaʿqūbī, Abū al-Abbās Aḥmad. *Tarīkh*, 2 vols. Beirut: Dār al-kutub al-ʿilmiyya, 1419/1999.

3 ʿAlī ibn Rabbān al-Ṭabarī, 'Radd ʿalā al-Naṣārā', eds, I.-A. Khalife and W. Kutsch, *Mélanges de L'université Saint Joseph* 36, 1959, pp. 113–48, p114.
G.S. Reynolds, 'A medieval Islamic polemic against certain practices and doctrines of the East Syrian Church: Introduction, Excerpts and Commentary', David Thomas ed., *Christians at the heart of Islamic rule*, 2003, pp. 215–30.

4 Another renowned Muslim apologist who accused Christians of *taḥrīf al-maʿnā* was Abū al-Ḥasan ʿAli ibn Ismāʿil ibn Isḥāq al-Ashʿarī (d. 935).

divinity—an argument that had become widely known due to its incorporation in the *tafsīr* of Abū Ja'far al-Ṭabarī.[5] He also uses Christian Scripture to suggest that Christ's references to himself as God (e.g. John 14:9) should not carry the implication that Christ is divine.[6]

Islamic Reformulation of Biblical Texts

Other Islamic writers reformulated Biblical texts to conform to Qur'anic standards. One example can be seen in al-Qāsim ibn Ibrāhīm al-Ḥasanī al-Rassī (d. 860). Al-Qāsim's confidence in the inherent superiority of the Qur'an over precedent scriptures is fuelled by his observation that Christians had embraced heretical doctrines in violation of *tawḥīd* (oneness of Allāh). He proposes an alternative methodology of Biblical referencing. The third step of his methodology is built on deriving Biblical truth from five sources: God, the angels, Jesus himself, Mary and the disciples.[7] By virtue of this method, al-Qāsim permits himself to excise and amend certain passages to conform the Biblical witness to Islamic expectations.[8] The absolute confidence of Muslim apologists in unmitigated *tawḥīd* derived from the Qur'an provided a hermeneutical horizon in which Muslim scholars felt at liberty to reformulate Biblical texts. From here, it was a short step to the view that the texts were completely unreliable. Although the categories 'corruption of meaning' and 'corruption of the text' have been used as an analytical tool, in practice the two are closely related. Muslim writers accepted Biblical texts that affirmed their Islamic notions and repudiated those which contradicted them.[9] The writings of Ibn Ḥazm (cited previously) and 'Abd al-Jabbār represent the crystallisation of a view which was rapidly gaining traction in the early centuries of Muslim-Christian relations—the complete unreliability of the Christian Scriptures.

---

5 W.Z. Haddad, *Christian-Muslim encounters*. Gainesville, FL: University Press of Florida, 1995, p. 154 and Reynolds, 'A medieval Islamic polemic', p. 91.

6 Reynolds, 'A medieval Islamic polemic', p. 156.

7 D. Thomas, 'The Bible in early Muslim anti-Christian polemic', *Islam and Muslim Christian relations* 7, 1996, p. 34.

8 See Thomas, *The Bible in early Muslim anti-Christian polemic*, p. 36 and Reynolds, *A Muslim theologian in the sectarian milieu*, p 199–200.

9 See M. Whittingham, 'The value of tahrif (corrupt interpretation) as a category for analysing Muslim views of the Bible: evidence from *al-radd al-jamil* and Ibn Khaldun.' *Islam and Muslim-Christian relations* 22, 2011, pp. 209–222.

Proposing a Framework

Van Koningsveld suggests criteria for grouping the various narratives into two streams of Muslim Pauline tradition. One stream (group a) presents Paul as a Jewish deceiver—a pseudo-convert to Christianity whose sole intention is to deceive Christians and corrupt their faith. A second stream (group b) presents him as a genuine convert to Christianity seeking Roman protection and revenge on the Jews by Rome (not merely defiling the Christian faith as in 'group a').[10] Ostensibly, this second group is most fully represented in 'Abd al-Jabbār while Sayf ibn 'Umar al-Tamīmī (d. 796–7) represents a fusion of the two streams.[11] In fact, the categorization is slightly forced although the distinctions are noteworthy. Paul is only portrayed as a Christian convert in 'Abd al-Jabbār and there his motivation is political power and revenge on the Jews. Even when Paul's conversion is granted, his base character has great affinities with the other accounts. Problems also ensue when considering which stream has chronological priority. The identification of two narrative streams highlights some distinctions between various narrators, however the categories overlap and should not be considered water-tight.

An alternative approach is to examine the narrative purpose: For what purpose is the narrator telling his story? Van Koningsveld pointed out two narrative purposes for Sayf's account which can also be discerned in other accounts.[12] Although the purposes overlap, one can identify three objectives stated clearly in the narratives. 1) Paul corrupted the laws of Islam ('Islam' as monotheism predating Christianity; e.g. abrogating circumcision, permitting unclean foods, intermarriage, etc.) 2) Paul corrupted the doctrine of *tawḥīd*.

---

10 P.S. van Koningsveld, 'The Islamic image of Paul', pp. 207–8.

11 Van Koningsveld discusses the first stream referring to accounts by ibn al-Jawzī, al-Qarafī and al-Damirī. Furthermore he makes the helpful suggestion that Paul's character may have been conflated with Paul of Samosata (Būlus al-Shimshāṭī) who served as Patriarch of Antioch from 260 CE. This Paul of Samosata was dismissed from clerical duties as a result of heretical beliefs. Muslims accused him of interjecting into the Christian faith the doctrine of Christ's union of divinity and humanity. This is precisely the accusation made of Paul in Sayf's account. Van Koningsveld, 'The Islamic image of Paul', pp. 200–228.

12 Concerning Sayf's account, Van Koningsveld noted that Paul's corruption of the faith took on two forms: 1) Paul corrupted some important sacred rules of the faith 2) Paul corrupted the kernel of the faith (i.e. the doctrine of God's oneness was corrupted by the Trinity and Christ's divinity). Our identification of a three-fold narrative purpose of the Pauline narrative is an elaboration on Van Koningsveld's work. See Van Koningsveld, 'The Islamic Image of Paul', p. 203.

(In place of the unity of God, he fabricated doctrines of Trinity and Christ's divinity). This objective includes Paul's inculcation of sectarian tensions among various Christian confessions as this becomes the means of corrupting *tawḥīd*. 3) Paul corrupted the text of the Bible. We suggest that rather than seeing the Islamic narrative of Paul as separate streams of tradition, we should examine each narrative in view of its narrative purpose—what the narrator was hoping to accomplish. The objective in view gives adequate justification for the author's selection of material for the individual narratives.

Islamic Narratives of the Apostle Paul

Many Muslim writers make reference to Paul's role in the origins of the Christian faith, including Abū al-Faraj ibn al-Jawzī (d. 1200), a Ḥanbalī jurisprudent from Baghdad,[13] Shihāb al-Dīn al-Qarāfī[14] (d. 1285), a Malikī scholar from Cairo,[15] Ibn Abī Ṭālib al-Dimashqī (1256–1327),[16] Ibn Taymiyya (d. 1328) and al-Qurṭubī (d. 1273). Limitations of time and space allow us to overview only three contributors to the Islamic narrative of Paul. The following authors are selected due to their antiquity and because they represent the various narrative purposes mentioned above.

Sayf ibn 'Umar al-Tamīmī

Little is known of Sayf ibn 'Umar al-Tamīmī. He was associated with southern Iraq and lived in Kufa.[17] His *Kitāb al-futūḥ wa al-ridda* (*Book of conquest and*

13 Ibn Al-Jawzī, Abū al-Faraj 'Abd al-Rahmān bin 'Alī bin Muḥammad, *al-muntazam fī tarīkh al-umam wa al-mulūk*, Beirut, 1992.

14 Al-Qarāfī's *al-ajwiba al-fākhira* is considered one of the greatest apologetic works of Islam. It is an extensive and ambitious polemic work written as a response to a letter by Paul of Antioch (Būlus al-Rāhib), a monk who later became a Melkite bishop. S.A. Jackson, 'Shihāb al-Dīn al-Ḳarāfī', *Encyclopaedia of Islam, second edition*, Brill Online, 2013.

15 Al-Qarafī, Ahmad ibn Idris, *al-ajwiba al-fākhira 'an al-as'ila al fājira*, sharika sa'id r'fat littba', Cairo, 1987.

16 See R.Y. Ebied and D. Thomas, *Muslim-Christian polemic during the Crusades: the letter from the people of Cyprus and Ibn Abī Ṭālib al-Dimashqī's response*, Leiden, Boston, 2005.

17 F.M. Donner, 'Sayf b. 'Umar,' *The Encyclopaedia of Islam*, C.E. Bosworth, E. van Donzel, W.P. Heinrichs and G. Lecocmte, eds, 1997, p. 102.

apostasy) was the primary source of the historian Abū Jaʿfar Muḥammad ibn Jarīr al-Ṭabarī (d. 923) concerning the Wars of Apostasy and the early conquests of Islam, despite the fact that the veracity of Sayf's account has been disputed.[18]

Van Koningsveld has helpfully summarized his contribution to the Islamic narrative of Paul from Sayf's *Kitāb al-futūḥ wa al-ridda*. The discussion of Paul falls in the context of the assassination of the Caliph ʿUthmān—the third 'rightly-guided Caliph.' The story is related as a parallel account of ʿAbd Allāh b. Saba' a Jewish son of a black mother (for this reason he is referred to as Ibn al-Sawdāʾ) who converted to Islam only to sow discord and disunity amongst Muslims. This ʿAbd Allāh traveled extensively and began to promulgate the idea that, though Muhammad was the seal of the prophets, ʿAlī was the seal of the regents, there being a regent for each of the one thousand prophets. Thus ʿAbd Allāh b. Saba' was depicted as the instigator of the Sunnī-Shiʾīte conflict, similar to Paul who is portrayed as the instigator of sectarian conflict among Christians. Sayf's narration, then, presents a moral paradigm to the Muslim *umma* exhorting Muslims to overcome the sectarianism which had so manifestly divided the Christian community.[19]

Précis

The précis provides a summary of the narrative from the primary source in Arabic.[20] A brief analysis of the narrative purpose of the account follows the

18 The disputation of Sayf's reliability stems primarily from the accusation in medieval times that his transmission of the *ḥadīth* was not reliable. Later Wellhausen suggested that Sayf's historical accounts represented a less reliable *Kufan* stream than those originating from the *ḥijāz*. That binary theory has been largely displaced as Sayf came to be viewed as a compiler whose historical records were an early pillar of the Islamic historical record even if his transmission of *ḥadīth* was not to be accepted uncritically. Nevertheless, Sayf continues to be criticized for his compilations and handling of sources, many of whom cannot be identified with precision. S.W. Anthony, 'The Composition of Sayf b. ʿUmar's account of King Paul and his corruption of ancient Christianity', *Der Islam: Seitschrift fur Geschichte und Kultur des Islamischen Orients* 85, 2008, pp. 164–202.

19 S.W. Anthony, 'The Composition of Sayf b. ʿUmar's Account of King Paul and His Corruption of Ancient Christianity,' *Der Islam: Seitschrift fur Geschichte und Kultur des Islamischen Orients* 85, 2008, pp. 164–202.

20 Sayf ibn ʿUmar al-Tamīmī, *Kitab al-ridda wa al-futuh and kitab al-jamal wa masir ʿA'isha wa ʿAli*, Leiden, 1995.

précis. Sayf cites his version of the apostle Paul on the authority of Yazīd al-Faq'asī from Ibn 'Abbas.[21] The story is also cited by al-Qarāfī (d. 1285).[22]

> After Jesus' assumption, the number of his followers rose to seven hundred. Paul was the king of the Jews at that time and was also known as 'Abū Sha'ūl (as cited by al-Qarāfī 'Qawlas'). Christians were able to escape Paul's command that the *banī Isrā'īl* (sons of Israel) kill Jesus' followers. Paul warned the Jews that these Christians would secure the good graces of the enemies of the Jews and ultimately turn them against the Jews. Paul devised a plan with the Jews' agreement to dress as a Christian in order to infiltrate the Christian camp and accomplish his ploy. Paul was captured upon entering the camp and requested to be taken to the leaders of the Christians in order to present his proofs. He related a tale of conversion in which he encountered Jesus who deprived him of his senses of sight and hearing as well as the faculty of reason. When Jesus later restored these to him, he vowed to enter among the Christians and use his gifts to teach Jesus' followers the Torah.[23]
>
> The credulous Christians were deceived by Paul's trick. Paul ordered that a house be built where he would worship while the Christians circumambulated the house. The Christians were apprehensive that he would see a fearful vision so when he opened his door, they asked him what he had seen and he related his vision to them. Paul had three visions. In the first, he was shown the sun, moon, stars and constellations all coming from one place and proceeding to another. Upon relating the story, Christians recognized that their *qibla* (direction of prayer) was now reoriented [presumably from Jerusalem (*bayt al-maqdis*) to the east]. Paul returned to his house where he remained enclosed for two days provoking great anxiety among the Christians. When he opened the door he relayed an opinion to them in the form of a riddle, saying 'if someone offers a gift to honor you and you return it, you grieve him. God has put all things in heaven and earth at your service and He is the more deserving that his gift of honor be not returned to him.' The Christians replied 'you

21 The attribution to Ibn 'Abbas is noteworthy as he was the paternal cousin of Muḥammad whose mother claimed to have been the second convert to Islam after Khadīja, the wife of the prophet. Thus, at least by Sayf's account, this narrative is from a trusted source whose origin dates to the time of the apostle himself.

22 Ahmad ibn Idris al-Qarāfī, *al-Ajwiba al-fākhira 'an al-as'ila a- fājira*: sharika sa'id r'fat littba', 1987, pp. 323–327.

23 Sayf ibn 'Umar al-Tamīmī, *Kitāb al-ridda*, pp. 132–33.

> have spoken aright.' The effect of the second vision was to render all food—'from the bedbug to the elephant'—ceremonially pure (*ḥalāl*) given that it was all created by God. Paul again closes himself in for three days much to the consternation of the Christians. The content of this vision is to forbid Christians to wage violence or seek revenge.[24] Paul states: 'I see that one should not be harmed or requited. For whoever exposes you to evil, do not retaliate against him. If he strikes your cheek, grant to him the other cheek. And if he takes some of your clothing, provide him with the remainder of it. The Christians accepted Paul's exhortation and forsook *jihād*.'

Paul now remains in his house for an even longer period increasing the dismay of the Christians. Upon his exit, he stipulated that all leave him except four individuals: Ya'qūb, Nasṭūr, Malkūn[25] (in al-Qarāfī's version 'Malaqūt') and a fourth person referred to as 'the Believer.' Paul then interrogates these four concerning whether a human being had ever created a being (*nafs*) out of clay, to which they replied negatively. He questioned them if they knew of a human being who had healed the blind, the leper and given life to the dead. Again, they responded negatively. Paul then asks 'have you known a human being that could inform people of what they eat and store in their homes.'[26] Paul then claims that God almighty manifested himself (*tajallā*) and then was veiled (*iḥtajaba*). 'Some of them replied 'you have spoken correctly.' The other said, 'He is God and 'Īsā (Jesus) is his son.' The other said, 'no, but he [God] is third of three:[27] Jesus a son (*ibn*) and his Father (*abūhu*) and his mother (*umuhu*).'[28]

'The Believer' was angered and said 'may Allāh curse you!' 'The Believer' proceeds to curse Paul and the other disciples of Paul saying that they heard Jesus' teaching firsthand before Paul. He forsakes Paul, urging the others to do the same, but to no avail. The four disciples took a group of followers with them, but 'the Believer' garnered fewer followers than the others. Paul proceeds to

24 This vision is not included in al-Qarāfī's version of the events. It is the only instance of non-violence in the Pauline narratives. The statement reflects Christ's teaching in Matthew 5:39–40. Al-Qarāfī, *al-Ajwiba al-fākhira 'an al-as'ila al-fājira*, 1987, p.325.

25 Although the account names a founder of the Melkites, the name is not derived from a founder as was the case with the Nestorians and the Jacobites. Rather the name derives from *malak* (king) as the Melkites were loyal to the Byzantine Empire.

26 See Q 3:49 and 5:110.

27 'Third of three' is a reference to Q 5:73: 'They surely disbelieve who say: Lo! Allah is the third of three.' (Pickthall).

28 Al-Qarāfī uses the terms *walad* (son) *wālid* (father) and *rūḥ qudus* (a holy spirit). Al-Qarāfī, *al-Ajwiba al-fākhira 'an al-as'ila al-fājira*, 1987, p. 325.

incite the other three to pursue 'the Believer' and make war upon him despite the fact that he has just informed them not to take revenge or act violently. Some of 'the Believer's' followers escaped to Syria where they were captured by the Jews and requested to live in solitude in caves, mountain tops and cells as depicted in Q 57:27.[29] Other believers (*al-mu'minūn*, followers of *al-mu'min*—'the Believer') fled to the Arabian Peninsula. Thirty of them lived there as monks and eventually embraced the message of the prophet Muhammad.

Narrative Purpose

In this early narrative of the Apostle Paul, the first two purposes (corruption of Islamic law and *tawḥīd*) are readily apparent. First Paul succeeds to abrogate some religious laws through his first three visions (prayer direction, kosher laws and jihad). Secondly, he instigates sectarian factions among Christians based on the supposition of Christ's divinity (the fourth vision). The flight to Arabia where the believers live an ascetic life has Qur'ānic precedent. Sayf's narrative purpose is clear—the Believer preserved the true religion of Christ, which was in fact a nascent version of Islam, while Paul deterred Christians from righteous acts while sowing discord among various sects. Thus the narrative is an apologetic for the identification of Islam with the early 'believers' as well as the rejection of Islam by the Christian sects. Furthermore, the whole account is a moral exhortation to Muslims urging them to avert the sectarianism of ibn Saba' who serves as an Islamic parallel to Paul.

Paul's asceticism and visionary revelations reappear throughout the narrative history. They take on an ominous tone as Paul's visions redirect the Christian faith away from its monotheistic roots in the Torah. Additionally, his successful inculcation of sectarian strife into the Christian faith is a repeated feature, producing divisions among the three known Christian sects of the time: the Jacobites from Ya'qūb; the Nestorians from Nastūr and the Melkites from the fictitious 'Malkūn' (or Malaqūt). The believer's pristine monotheism and resistance to Paul's deception reflect Islamic *tawḥīd* and stand in stark contrast to the malevolent Paul who is so brazen as to call his deceived disciples to make war on the Believer.

Finally, Sayf makes only passing reference to Christian Scriptures which originate from Christ's Sermon on the Mount rather than Pauline writings. The content of the Pauline visions is thoroughly Qur'anic with the addition of motifs originating from the *tafsīr* literature surrounding the Qur'anic narratives of

29 Al-Tamimī, *Kitāb al-ridda*, pp. 134–135.

Christ. Thus the narrative is an Islamic interpolation of Paul's character with virtually no consideration of New Testament Pauline sources.

Abū Isḥāq Aḥmad ibn Muḥammad ibn Ibrāhīm al-Thaʿlabī (d. 1035)

Al-Thaʿlabī was a Qur'anic commentator from Nishapur. He included a narrative passage on the Apostle Paul in his commentary on Q 9:31: 'And the Christians say Christ is the son of God, that is what they say with their mouths.'[30] Stern treats al-Damīrī's (d. 1405) version of this narrative found in his work titled *ḥayat al-ḥayawān*.[31] Al-Damīrī's attribution of the narrative to al-Kalbī (d. 763) is of particular interest. If accurate it indicates a very early origin of the narrative.

Précis

In this version of events, Christians were firmly following Islam, praying towards the *qibla* and fasting during Ramadan (al-Damirī adds for a period of 81 years) after Christ's ascension. At that time hostilities broke out between Jews and Christians. A courageous man named *Yūnus* (presumably, Paul)[32] mused that the Christians might in fact be right which would consign him and his Jewish coreligionists to hell. For that reason, he conceived a ploy in which he deceived the Christians by feigning repentance and interjecting confusion into their faith such that they would enter Hell as well. After his pseudo repentance was demonstrated by slaying and hamstringing his steed (previously used to make war against Christians) and putting dirt on his head, he proceeded to enter a church in which he lived for one year, never departing from it, while studying the Gospel. A vision given to Paul and related by him to the Christians confirmed that his repentance was accepted by God. Before traveling to Rome, he taught Nasṭūr that the three members of the Trinity were Christ, his mother

30 al-Thaʿlabi, *al-Kashf wa al-bayyan ʿan tafsir al-Qur'an*. Vol. 5, Beirut, 2002, pp. 33.

31 S. Stern, 'Abd al-Jabbar's account of how Christ's religion was falsified by the adoption of Roman customs', *Journal of theological studies* 18, April 1968, pp. 128–85.

32 The fact that al-Thaʿlabī recorded Paul's name as *Yūnus* raises the question as to whether or not this is indeed Paul. The Arabic name equates to 'Jonah.' Gabriel Reynolds has supplied the reading *Būlus* for *Yūnis* based on an alternate manuscript. Given that al-Isfarāʾīnī and al-Damīrī record the same narrative using Paul's name suggests that it is the same person.

and God. He went to Rome where he taught Yaʿkūb that 'Jesus was no man but became man, was not a body but became a body and was the Son of God.' (al-Damīrī says that Ya'kūb was taught about divine nature and human nature.) Later he taught one 'Malkān' that 'Jesus was and is God.' After imparting this confused doctrine to these disciples, Paul then confides to each of the three men separately that they will be his successor (*khalīfatī*) after his death, thus creating three rival successors to Paul. He proceeds to inform them that he will slay himself (Isfarā'īnī adds 'as a sacrifice') so they should invite the people to the altar. Paul does sacrifice himself and after this profound act of piety, the three men recruit followers to the particular version of Christology which Paul imparted to them. Thus the three disciples of Paul, adhering to three conflicting Christologies which Paul imparted to them, were the source of the three major Christian sects.[33] These sects (*ṭa'ifa* pl. *ṭawā'if*) continue to kill one another and disagree until today.[34]

Furthermore, al-Thaʿlabī also depicts a war which took place between the Jews and the followers of Christ. Reynolds suggests that this dissension between the Christian groups draws inspiration from Q 5:14. 'Abd al-Jabbār also references this war using the less intense word: 'conflict' (*khilāf*).[35] Thus Paul becomes the source of the Christian sects and instigator of theological disunity.[36]

Narrative Purpose

Although the broad lines of this account are found in other accounts, here, Paul's motives are portrayed as exceedingly base. He is moved to such deception by his consideration that Christians may indeed be right resulting in his determination to consign them to hell. The purpose of the narrative is to document Paul's instigation of theological disunity among the various sects of Christianity. Thus, al-Thaʿlabī's account depicts Paul as the corrupter of *tawḥīd*. We note that this version contains no reference to Muslim followers of Jesus who preserved the monotheistic faith of Christ (e.g. the 'Believer' in Sayf's version).

33 S.G. Reynolds, 'A medieval Islamic polemic', p. 165.

34 P.S. van Koningsveld, 'The Islamic Image of Paul', p. 205 and Stern, 'Abd al-Jabbār's account', p. 178.

35 Reynolds, 'A medieval Islamic polemic', p. 165.

36 Al-Thaʿlabī, *al-Kashf*, pp. 188–9.

Stern notes that aspects of the story are parallel to certain versions of a Jewish account of the life of Jesus titled *Toldoth Jeshu* and its appendices (parallels with Sayf's account can also be discerned). In the Jewish version, Jewish leaders are disgruntled with Christians who have desecrated their Sabbaths and festivals and yet insisted on remaining within the Jewish community. The Jewish scholar Elijah conceived a plan. He called himself Paul and deceived the Christians by his miracles. He proceeded to exchange the Sabbath for Sunday, established alternate feast days, permitted eating unclean foods and abolished circumcision.[37] Where al-Thaʿlabī's narrative diverges from *Toldoth Jeshu*, Stern finds the particular motives of a Muslim writer. In *Toldoth*, Paul is a Jew seeking to purge his religion of its impurities. In Thaʿlabī's version, Paul seeks to divert sincere Christians from the true faith rendering him an even more vile character.[38] Al-Thaʿlabī's version shows virtually no influence from the Christian Scriptures other than the idea of Paul's self-sacrifice. (e.g. Phil 1:23, 2:17; 2 Cor 5:8) While *Toldoth* may well have served as an inspiration for the account, in our view, the narrative derives from Qur'anic and *tafsīr* sources primarily.

ʿAbd al-Jabbār (d. 1025)

ʿAbd al-Jabbār was a renowned Mu'tazilī judge who lived in Buyid Rayy, but also moved in and out of Baghdad. He studied jurisprudence and theology (*kalām*) in Iranian cities before moving to Baṣra by 948 and eventually on to Baghdad. There he studied under the leading Mu'tazilī scholar of the time Abū ʿAbdallāh al-Baṣrī. From this point, al-Jabbār devotes himself to *kalām*. Abū ʿAbdallāh al-Baṣrī's sponsorship acquired his appointment as chief judge (*qāḍī al-quḍāt*) of Rayy (near contemporary Teheran), the capital of the province of Jibāl in 977. While in Rayy, al-Jabbār drew disciples from many distant lands and ensured his notoriety as a Mu'tazilī theologian and jurisprudent of the Shāfi'ī *madhab*.[39]

37 *Toldoth Jeshu* is a Jewish version of the life of Jesus of uncertain origin, possibly composed between the sixth and eleventh centuries. The Nazarenes (Christians) had grown to outnumber the Jews of Jerusalem and were preventing the observance of Jewish feast days. Simon Kepha, a Rabbi, agrees to deceive the Nazarenes through his miracles, persuading Christians to observe different feast days than the Jews commanding them not to practice violence. Thus the account bears resemblance to the Muslim accounts we have observed. G. Foote, and J.M. Wheeler, *Jewish life of Christ: being the sepher toldoth Jeshu*, London, 1885.

38 Stern, 'Abd al-Jabbār's account', pp. 179–80.

39 D. Thomas and A. Mallett. *Christian-Muslim relations. A bibliographical history (900–1050)*, D. Thomas ed., Vol. 2, 2010, p. 595 and Reynolds 'A medieval Islamic polemic', p. 50–51.

His work titled *Tathbīt dalāʾil al-nubuwwa* (The Confirmation of the Proofs of Prophethood) written in the year 995 is of particular interest to our topic. The purpose of the *Tathbīt* is to establish the prophethood of Muhammad using sources outside the Qur'an and Ḥadīth.[40] In doing this, 'Abd al-Jabbār also presents his most seasoned critique of Christianity. He does not aim to demonstrate that Christianity is false, but to demonstrate that Christians 'deviated from the religion of Christ' and that 'Muḥammad's knowledge of this is from God'[41] It is this thesis that Gabriel Said Reynolds refers to as 'Abd al-Jabbār's 'critique of Christian origins.' It is an Islamic version of Christian origins incorporating an explanation of how the Bible was corrupted and how Christian leaders, notably the Apostle Paul and Constantine, diverted the faith from its original sources. 'Abd al-Jabbār's writing is unique among Muslims until his time period in that it provides detail as to when, how and why *taḥrīf* (corruption) took place. In effect, 'Abd al-Jabbār seeks to undermine the *tawātur*[42] of the Christian Scriptures.

Précis

What follows is the narrative provided by 'Abd al-Jabbār concerning events of the early development of Christianity.[43] Citing a book titled *Afrāskis* (Syriac for the Acts of the Apostles), 'Abd al-Jabbār relates how a group of Christians went from *bayt al-maqdis* (Jerusalem) to Antioch seeking to call Christians to the true faith and the *sunna* (practice or imitation) of the Torah. Their aim was to prohibit sacrifices of those who were not the people of the Torah—the circumcised. Because this was grievous to the Gentiles (*al-umam*), the Christians gathered in Jerusalem to determine what would be required of the Gentiles. The result was that the Christian leaders decided to allow the Gentiles to follow their desires, legitimizing their practices. [The account is an Islamic reading of the Jerusalem council of Acts 15.]

40 See Reynolds, *A Muslim theologian*, p. 184.

41 G.S. Reynolds and S.K. Samir, *Abd al-Jabbār: Critique of Christian Origins*, Provo, Utah, 2010, p. 161.

42 The term '*tawātur*' is used in reference to the historical reliability of a ḥadīth. It refers to a ḥadīth which is narrated by a large number of narrators such that its authenticity cannot be doubted. 'Abd al-Jabbār's argument, similar to Jāḥiẓ in his *Ḥujaj al-nubuwwa*, is that Christians do not have a valid transmission of their Scriptures from Jesus. Reynolds, *A Muslim theologian*, pp. 167–8.

43 Al-Jabbār, *Tathbīt dalāʾil al-nubuwa*. Abd al-Karim 'Uthman ed., Vol. 1, Beirut, pp. 150–68.

ʿAbd al-Jabbār then provides a commentary on the apostle Paul, citing a book titled *al-salīḥ*,[44] he states that Paul was a Jew when with the Jews, a Roman when with the Romans and *armāʾī* (Aramaic) when with the Aramaic people. Furthermore, among Christians, Paul is more highly honoured than Moses, Aaron, David and all the prophets. His books are more honoured than the Torah which is described as what the Messiah wrote to Moses who divided the sea and whose staff turned to a serpent. Paul's books, in the view of Christians, surpass the gospels which contain the words of Christ.

To one, Paul says the Torah is a 'good *sunna*' and to another that it is *muhīja* (seditionary). [Paul is portrayed as a chameleon, changing his opinion in respect to present company.] He has lifted the obligations of the Torah (*waḍaʿ ʿan al-nās*) and completed the righteousness and favor of God. Paul is the fulfillment of Q 9:34: 'O ye who believe! Lo! many of the (Jewish) rabbis and the (Christian) monks devour the wealth of mankind wantonly and debar (men) from the way of Allah. They who hoard up gold and silver and spend it not in the way of Allah, unto them give tidings (O Muhammad) of a painful doom' (Pickthall). ʿAbd al-Jabbār warns his Muslim readership of the dire consequences of neglecting the *sunna* of Muḥammad and the prophetic word he brought as did the Christians.

In the following paragraphs, a group of Jews in collusion with pagan Romans conspired to corrupt the *Injīl* (gospel) due to a lust for political power. As ʿAbd al-Jabbār relates the story, a Christian delegation went to the Romans to complain about certain Jews with whom they were worshipping (despite their disagreement about Christ). Although the Romans had a pact with the Jews that they would not require them to forsake their religion, they proffered a deal with the delegation. The Romans asked the Christians to come out from their religion and pray to the East as the Romans do, eat what the Romans eat and permit what they permit. On this condition, the Romans would support and strengthen the Christians allowing them to resist the Jews. The Christian delegation agreed whereupon the Romans asked them to go back to their companions and then return to Rome, bringing their Scriptures with them. The delegation returned but the companions would not relinquish their holy books to Rome provoking a schism as the companions accused the delegation of abandoning their religion. The delegation then returned to Rome imploring Roman assistance to overpower the companions and obtain their Scripture. Rome obliged, killing and burning some of the companions who nevertheless

44 This is from the Syriac term '*shlīḥā*' (apostle)—Paul's self-designation in the Peshitta. The Peshitta is the book of the Epistles used for liturgical readings. Reynolds, *A Muslim Theologian*, p. 198.

refused to relinquish their Scripture. These Christians were pursued by the Romans who sent letters to their agents in Mawṣil (Mosul) and the Arabian Peninsula. ʿAbd al-Jabbār states that these were burned and killed [although the possibility that some escaped with their lives is not excluded].

Those who complied with Rome (the delegation) consulted together as to how to replace the Gospel. They composed a gospel relying on their memory of the prophets and their sayings but most of what was in the original Gospel was lost. ʿAbd al-Jabbār specifically mentions that neither the cross nor the crucifix was referenced in the original Gospel. Initially, eighty gospels were produced. Later, they were condensed to four, written by four different individuals in four different periods. These new gospels were no longer in Hebrew, according to ʿAbd al-Jabbār, the language of Christ and Abraham. The Christians, motivated by power and prestige, wrote the gospel in many languages (Roman, Syriac, Persian, Hindi, Aramaic) although not the language in which Christ received it. ʿAbd al-Jabbār adds that the three Christian sects (*tawāʾif*) do not believe that Allāh sent the gospel down to Christ but that Christ made the prophets and sent their books down to them. The gospels in current use contain contradictions and vanity. Out of ignorance Christians claim that Matthew, Mark, Luke and John were the companions of Christ. ʿAbd al-Jabbār states that each one came after the other and wrote his gospel due to deficiencies in the precedent version. Luke is adduced as evidence that the gospel-writers do not know Jesus. A quote from Luke's gospel as he addresses the one for whom he writes, settles the matter: 'I knew your desire for goodness, knowledge and politeness so I have made this gospel from my knowledge and because I was near to those who served the word and saw it.'

The account of Paul's conversion, much of which corresponds to various events in the book of Acts, is introduced by the clear statement that Paul is despicable and evil, a helper of evil ones, a deviser of sectarian rivalries. He absents himself from Jerusalem for a time and returns giving help to the Christians against the Jews. As Paul explains to the Jews, he saw a great light on the road to Damascus and was deprived of sight until a Jewish priest named Ḥayyīm healed him as scales fell from his eyes. Then he was taken up to heaven for fourteen days where he was told things about the Jews too pernicious to repeat.

The Jews deliver Paul to a friend of Caesar where he takes advantage of his Roman citizenship to avoid being beaten and claims that he is an adherent of Caesar's religion and is innocent of Judaism. The friend of Caesar offers to send Paul to Caesar aboard ship and Paul accepts. While in Rome (referred to by ʿAbd al-Jabbār as Constantinople), Paul reminds the Romans of their enmity towards the Jews and urges them against the Jews. Paul is portrayed as a sycophant who accepts the Roman position of monogamy hypocritically as well as the prohibition of divorce whereas the prophets of Israel permitted divorce. He gains the hearing of the emperor's wife who urges Caesar to listen to Paul who now takes a Roman name—Būlus. When interrogated about circumcision, Paul states that it only applies to the Israelites because 'their foreskins are in their heart.' Paul also accepts eating pork—yet another concession to Rome—claiming that lies that come out of the heart are the source of impurity, not the eating of foods.[45] He also permits the eating of meat sacrificed to idols and intermarriage of ethnicities. He permits a believing female to marry an unbelieving male as the believer renders the offspring pure. In summary, Paul Romanized the religion of Christ claiming to have completed or fulfilled the righteousness of God and his favor.

An excursus on Pilate and his wife Helena who bore Constantine follows after which ʿAbd al-Jabbār circles back to Paul describing him as one who impressed the masses of Rome with his trickery and deception. However Paul's deceit did not go unnoticed by the Roman kings, some of whom became wise to Paul and began to ask him about circumcision. Paul vilified the practice but admitted that Christ and the apostles were circumcised as they were Jews. The king then uncovered (*kashafa*) Paul to show that he was circumcised. The event is depicted as the unveiling of Paul's hypocrisy by the Roman rulers. The mention of Paul's being stricken with Elephantiasis is perhaps an indication of retribution for his ruse. Finally, a king gave orders to have Paul slapped, his beard shaved and to be crucified. Paul requested that he not be crucified vertically as had been Jesus.[46] Immediately after this description, ʿAbd al-Jabbār launches into a narrative of Constantine, portrayed as the son of Pilate (*bīlāṭus*) and Helena who inculcates her son with the love of the cross.[47]

ʿAbd al-Jabbār's Narrative Purpose

Abd al-Jabbār's critique of Christianity is certainly a Qur'anic critique of Christian scriptures. However, unlike Sayf and al-Thaʿlabī, he also makes ample use of the Bible. Reynolds finds precedents for these references among numerous other Muslim writers and Christian apologists. Whether ʿAbd al-Jabbār

45 Possibly a reference to Matthew 15:17–20—a teaching of Christ.

46 A similar Christian tradition holds that Peter requested that he not be crucified in the same way as Christ.

47 Thus it seems that in ʿAbd al-Jabbār's understanding, Paul is a contemporary of Constantine's father.

was working from an Arabic text of the Bible (as he surely may have)[48] or not, is somewhat beside the point. He is clearly interacting extensively with Christian texts and oral narratives to which he has been privy in *Rayy* and supplying his own Islamic hermeneutic frame of reference. 'The twists and turns of these stories, even the apparently insignificant details, are all products of 'Abd al-Jabbār's *Weltanschauung*, of his theological, historical and sociological thinking.'[49] In some cases, 'Abd al-Jabbār supplies a non-canonical text ascribing it to the gospel or reformulates a gospel pericope to conform to Qur'anic expectations.[50]

The 'Believer' of Sayf's account finds a fuller elaboration in 'Abd al-Jabbār. Proto Christianity divides into two groups—the first represented by the delegation to Rome which is ultimately responsible for the corruption of the Christian texts and the second represented by the companions who refuse to hand over their texts to the Romans. The entire narrative concords nicely with the Quranic picture presented in Q 61:14 stating that one group (*ṭa'ifa*) believed while the other group did not (*kafarat*).[51] Figures such as Baḥīrā, (See Q 5:82b–83) Waraqa 'ibn Nawfal and Salmān al-Fārisī are identifiable heirs of the companions.[52]

The Christian delegation proceeded to write a false *Injīl*, in fact several false *Injīls*, causing the Christian gospel to exist in multiple forms, each one progressively further from the true *Injīl* of Christ. 'Abd al-Jabbār contends that each of the four gospel writers wrote because the preceding gospel was inadequate and therefore needed to be corrected. While admitting that one finds some of Jesus' sayings in the four gospels, he asserts that they are nonetheless riddled with contradictions throughout. The authentic gospel contained no mention of the cross or crucifixion. 'Abd al-Jabbār's account records that John was the first to write, followed by Matthew, then Mark and finally Luke. The essential defect in this process was the Christians' abandonment of Hebrew—presumably the language of Christ.[53] The absence of the original language of a

48 Reynolds points out the likelihood that Arabic Bibles had reached *Rayy* by the time of 'Abd al-Jabbār. *A Muslim theologian*, p. 197.

49 Ibid., pp. 85–89.

50 Reynolds, *A medieval Islamic polemic*, p. 199.

51 Reynolds, *A Muslim theologian*, pp. 85–89.

52 Reynolds also mentions an elusive 'Nastūr' referred to by Ibn Sa'd in his account of Muḥammad's journey into Syria. Ibid., p. 89.

53 Both Reynolds and Sidney Griffith have noted that the idea that the original gospel was in Hebrew concords well with what Muslims would have known based on the Qur'an. S. Griffith, 'The Gospel in Arabic: an inquiry into its appearance in the first Abbasid century,' *Oriens Christiannus* 69, p. 138 and Ibid., p. 93.

Scripture was perceived to be a sign of its invalidity. The Qur'an, contrariwise, is preserved in the language in which it was given.[54]

The figure of Paul looms large in 'Abd al-Jabbār's account of the Romanization of Christianity and the corruption of its texts. Although 'Abd al-Jabbār does not explicitly include Paul in the delegation to Rome, the narrative implicates Paul in this corruption of Christianity. As the delegation sought Rome's protection, so Paul sought Roman political clout. It was Paul's appeal to Rome that corrupted Christian rules of righteous living (circumcision, dietary restrictions, marriage). It was Paul, abetted by the emperor's wife, who corrupted the *sunna* (practice) of Christ's gospel in order to win the support of Rome. The evil schemes of Paul, who failed to follow the example of Christ, produced a despicable result. Rome did not convert to Christianity, but the Christian gospel was transformed (i.e. corrupted) into a Roman version thereof.[55]

'Abd al-Jabbār melds together a growing consensus around *taḥrīf* (corruption) of the Christian Scriptures with a novel narrative as to how this corrupting influence found a foothold among Christians. The entire narrative supplies a rebuttal of the likes of Ḥunayn 'ibn Isḥāq[56] (d. 873) who argued that Christianity is validated because it was not established by coercion. 'Abd al-Jabbār's argument depicts a scenario in which coercion and lust for political power were motivating factors in establishing a religion fundamentally altered from its origin.[57] Indeed this is the narrative purpose of 'Abd al-Jabbār's critique of Christian origins. Through his narrative of the Apostle Paul and the corruption of the Christian Scriptures, he provides a theological argument demonstrating that Christians no longer follow the religion of Christ which was preserved only in the prophetic message of Muhammad.

The Narrative of Paul in Medieval Muslim-Christian Discourse

The three narrative purposes that we have discussed above are consistent with the major themes of Muslim-Christian discourse of the period. The narrative of the Apostle Paul developed within the Islamic hermeneutical horizon, conditioned by the superiority that Muslims enjoyed during the period

54 Bukhari 3:344 reports the concern of the Muslims over this state of affairs.

55 Reynolds, *A Muslim theologian*, pp. 108–113.

56 Ḥunayn ibn Isḥaq is mentioned five times in the *Tathbīt*. Reynolds, *A Muslim theologian*, p. 197.

57 Reynolds, *A Muslim theologian*, pp. 85–89.

in relation to the unassailability of *tawḥīd*, the excellences of the *sunna* (the prophetic traditions) and the perfection of the Qur'an.

Paul could not be a *rasūl* (apostle) because Muhammad had said there had been none between him and 'Isā.[58] The Christian reverence of his writings in addition to his claimed status as 'the apostle to the Gentiles' rankled Islamic understanding of the prophetic call. Furthermore, as Muslims perceived that Christians were not abandoning their texts (despite the conversion of Christians to Islam), Paul, with his unequivocal writings on Christ's divinity, became a necessary culprit for the corruption of the precedent Scriptures.

Concerning the first narrative purpose—Paul's corruption of laws of righteousness—before Paul took Christianity captive to Rome (as per 'Abd al-Jabbār), he had seriously diverted it from its Jewish, monotheistic roots. Permission to eat unclean foods was a clear indicator of this fact. Circumcision, another law of monotheism, was abolished by the apostle. The direction of prayer was changed from Jerusalem. Christians had, in fact, broken away from the *sunna* of their prophet. Christ had been circumcised, eaten kosher food and prayed toward Jerusalem. The evidence of Paul's diversion of the faith was found in his own writings which declared all foods clean and clearly stated that circumcision was of no benefit. Sayf's account of Paul setting aside *jihād*, permission to intermarry and the worship of images[59] also come under this heading.

A more serious charge was the corruption of the Islamic doctrine of *tawḥīd*—the second narrative purpose identified. The debate between Christians and Muslims had been raging for centuries. The likes of Timothy I (d. 823), Theodore Abū Qurra (c. 785–829), Ḥabīb ibn Khidma Abū Rā'iṭa (fl. 810–830), 'Ammār al-Baṣrī (early ninth c.) and Yaḥyā ibn 'Adī (d. 974) had demonstrated that Trinitarian thought was not confined to a particular sect of Christianity nor would it go away. Islam's *mutakallimūn* (theologians) had built a watertight case for God's unity such that any claim of its mitigation was summarily dismissed from the arena of serious intellectual discourse. Trinitarian thought was increasingly seen as inimical to *tawḥīd*—'exhibit A' of those who had compromised its purity and a sparring partner for Muslim polemicists, Ash'āris and Mu'tazilīs alike. Again, blame was laid at the feet of the Apostle Paul for this clear violation of God's unity.

58 'I am the most rightful person to honor 'Īsa (Jesus) son of Mary, because there will be no prophet between my time and his …' (Collected by Ahmad, hadith no, 9349 and the grade is *ṣaḥīḥ* according to al-Albani).

59 Ibn Abī Ṭālib al-Dimashqī developed the idea that Paul instigated the worship of images. Ebied and Thomas, *Muslim Christian polemic*, p. 400.

Concerning the third narrative purpose, as *taḥrīf* (corruption of Christian Scriptures) proliferated and gained force prior to the eleventh century, the conceptual underpinning of the charge formed accordingly. Increasingly, Muslims were confronted with the sectarian divisions of Christianity and the reality of doctrines that were inimical to *tawḥīd* (e.g. Trinity and Christ's divine nature). Accordingly, the concept of *taḥrīf* expanded in the hermeneutical horizon of Muslim intellectuals. Although the initial charge of *taḥrīf* in the Qur'an was largely directed at the Jews, the medieval narrative of the Apostle Paul is a demolition of any Christian claim of *tawātur* (faithful transmission) of its texts. In the version of ʿAbd al-Jabbār, the original gospel was lost and reconstructed based on the memories of the delegation to Rome. It is hardly surprising that this narrative underpinning of *taḥrīf* would become apparent. Martin Accad argues that:

> Muslims were driven to a similar exercise as early Christians had been, namely the legitimisation of their religion on the basis of the holy texts of the 'older' religions of the land, Judaism and Christianity. But a new realisation was gradually to sink in after the initial enthusiasm of Muslim thinkers. Though the Qur'ān highly commended the Bible, asserting that it confirmed Muḥammad's prophetic mission, when they came to Christians for the hard evidence they were sent back empty-handed. A conclusion was beginning to form: there was something wrong with the Scriptures that Christians and Jews presently had in their hands.[60]

In ʿAbd al-Jabbār, we observe the crystallization of the Pauline narrative. Ibn Ḥazm and others assumed this narrative, even without direct reference to ʿAbd al-Jabbār, in their polemical attacks on Christianity. The fact that two unrelated authors of the eleventh century representing the western and eastern flanks of Islam—ʿAbd al-Jabbār and Ibn Ḥazm—began to ascribe much of the corruption of Christianity to the Apostle Paul suggests that the narrative, in its varied forms, was becoming the plausible explanation for Christianity's

60 Martin Accad has pointed out that the eleventh century represents a point in the development of *taḥrīf* when the exchange became particularly acrimonious and the move from corruption of meaning to textual corruption was obvious. 'Ibn Ḥazm of Andalusia and al-Juwaynî are the two figures of the century that seem to have furthered the accusation to a point of no return. The blow that these two men delivered to the Bible sapped the very root of a long tradition of Muslim-Christian dialogue which had so far been largely centered on the Scriptures.' M. Accad, *The Gospels in the Muslim and Christian exegetical discourse from the eighth to the fourteenth century*, PhD Dissertation, Oxford, 2001, pp. 379–80.

departure from the prophetic message which Muhammad was thought to have confirmed. Paul's deviation nullified *tawātur*. Undoubtedly, the narrative commended itself in an increasingly Islamic religious milieu where Islam held forth the standard of *tawḥīd* by which all deviant religious beliefs were measured.[61]

Muslim Reading of Biblical Material

It is conceivable that Paul's representation in Jewish literature informed the Islamic perception that we have observed.[62] Both the *Talmūd* and the apocryphal *Toldoth Jeshu* (Life of Jesus) bear similarities to Islamic views of the apostle (e.g. al-Thaʿlabī), treating him as a contemptible and power-seeking individual.[63] Reynolds has also pointed out affinities between ʿAbd al-Jabbār and the Jewish *Muqammiṣ* (d. mid 9th c.) of whom we have only a brief citation in the work of Qirqisānī (d. 10th c.).[64] However, it is striking that much of ʿAbd al-Jabbār's Pauline narrative is derived from the Christian scriptures, notably the Acts of the Apostles and the Pauline epistles, both of which are mentioned in the *Tathbīt*.[65] A brief overview will give the reader a sense of ʿAbd al-Jabbār's reliance on Biblical content for the contours of the Pauline narrative whether the source was the Bible, Christian apologists or Islamic writers.

- 'When with the Jew, I was a Jew; with the Romans, a Roman and with the Armāʾī, Armāʾī.'[66] (See 1 Cor 9:20–23)
- 'He says to Jews, "The *Tawrāt* is a good *sunna* to those who practice it;" and he says to Romans and other enemies of Moses, "the *Tawrāt* is seditionary (*muhīja*) to humanity" and as he removed the judgments and precepts of the *Tawrāt* from people, he completed the righteousness of God.'[67] (See Rom 7:12, 16; 8:1–4)

61 D. Thomas, *Christian doctrines in Islamic theology*, Leiden, Boston, 2008, p. 11.

62 Ibn Ḥazm claims that the Jews admit the conspiracy to persuade Paul to deceive the Christians. C. Adang, *Muslim writers on Judaism and the Hebrew Bible*, Leiden, 1996, p. 105.

63 See H. Hirschberg, 'Allusions to the Apostle Paul in the Talmud', *Journal of Biblical literature* 62(2). See G.W. Foote and J.M. Wheeler, *Jewish life of Christ: being the sepher toldoth Jeshu*, 1885.

64 Reynolds, *A Muslim theologian*, p. 237.

65 Reynolds treats ʿAbd al-Jabbār's scriptural references noting seven methods underlying his quotation of Biblical material. Also, the mentions of Acts and the epistles are derived from Syriac—not unpredictable given that Rayy was a significant centre of the Church of the East. Ibid., pp. 97–107.

66 Abd al-Jabbār, *Tathbīt*, pp. 170–171.

67 Ibid., p. 171.

- 'Luke mentioned in his gospel that he did not see Christ. He (Luke) addressed the one for whom he produced his gospel, and he was the last of the four to write, "I know your desire for goodness, knowledge and politeness so I composed the gospel from my knowledge and because I was close to those who were servants of the word."'[68] (See Luke 1:1–4)[69]
- '[Paul] used to be called Saul as a Jew, and he opposed the Christians. Then he left Jerusalem for a long time. Then he returned to Jerusalem and began to help the Christians against the Jews.'[70] (See Acts 8:3; 9:1; 26:10; Gal 1:17–18)
- 'My story is I left from Jerusalem for Damascus. I was overtaken by the darkness of night and a great wind began to blow and my vision was taken from me. And the Lord called to me "Oh Saul, do you strike the brothers and harm the friends of my son?" I said "O Lord, I have repented." And he said to me, "if it is as you say, then go to *Ḥayyim* the Jewish Priest who will return your sight to you." So I went to him and informed him. He wiped (*masaḥa*) his hand on/over my sight and something like egg shells and fish scales fell from it (my sight) and I saw as before.'[71] (See Acts 19:1–19; 22:6–16)
- '... and that God called me to himself in heaven and I resided in heaven with him fourteen days.[72] He commanded me many things and said "in you are many revolting things of which I cannot speak."'[73] (See 2 Cor 12:1–4)
- 'The Roman became angered at him and gave orders concerning him and he was to be beaten. Then he said "Do you strike a Roman?" He responded "Are you then a Roman?" Paul replied, "yes, I am of the religion of Caesar, king of Rome and innocent of Judaism." And they desisted.'[74] (See Acts 22:24–29)
- Paul's appeal to Rome (mentioned by 'Abd al-Jabbār as 'Constantinople')[75] (See Acts 25:10–12)
- Paul's prohibition of polygamy echoes aspects of the Biblical record.[76] (See Eph 5:25–33, 1 Tim 3:2,12)

68 Ibid., p. 155.

69 Al-Jāḥiẓ and al-Ṭabarī also point out that Luke did not know Christ personally. Reynolds, *A Muslim theologian*, p. 160.

70 Ibid., p. 156.

71 Ibid.

72 The account of 2 Cor 12:1–4 states that this event transpired 'fourteen years ago.' Perhaps 'Abd al-Jabbār's reference to 'fourteen days' suggests reliance on his memory of an oral narrative.

73 Abd al-Jabbār, *Tathbīt*, p. 156.

74 Ibid., p. 157.

75 Ibid.

76 Ibid.

- 'Circumcision is not necessary for you but it is required for *banī Isrāʾīl* as their foreskins are in their hearts.'[77] (See Rom 2:29; Col 2:11)
- Paul's mention of eating meat sacrificed to idols.[78] (See 1 Cor 8)
- 'If a believing female marries an unbeliever (*kāfir*), she purifies him. He does not defile her and their son is pure as well.'[79] (See 1 Cor 7:12–14)

While ʿAbd al-Jabbār's reading of the Biblical text is by no means a careful, contextual reading, it is built substantially upon the events of Paul's life as found in the Biblical narrative. ʿAbd al-Jabbār's selection of material flows from his narrative purpose which was to demonstrate that Christianity of his day was no longer the Christianity of Christ but a Roman religion and that Muhammad's knowledge of this fact was proof of his prophethood. Moreover, ʿAbd al-Jabbār occasionally reformulated texts according to His Islamic understanding.[80] A source of Jewish origin may have served as a catalyst for the Islamic narrative of Paul, but there can be no doubt that the Christian narrative was a primary source while his Islamic worldview served as the interpretive grid. This raises interesting questions concerning how the dominant religion views the other and the other's texts, the necessity of openness to correction by the other and the influence of one's hermeneutical horizon in interpreting the texts of the other. The preceding centuries of Muslim-Christian discourse had prepared the way for the narrative development of *taḥrīf*. The Apostle Paul was the apt candidate. The Biblical material was read in view of an overwhelming weight of existential evidence against the reliability of the Christian Scriptures. That evidence drove the Islamic hermeneutic, resulting in a full-fledged doctrine of *taḥrīf al-lafẓ*, now supplied with a supporting narrative framework.

Conclusion

We have observed three versions of the Pauline narrative in early Islam. Three separate but overlapping accusations have been identified: 1) Paul corrupted the laws or practices of the true religion 2) Paul corrupted the doctrine of *tawḥīd* 3) Paul corrupted the preceding Scriptures. The Islamic narrative of the Apostle Paul became an integral aspect of the doctrine of *taḥrīf* reinforcing the assumption that Christians are heir to an inferior view of God and the

77 Ibid., p. 158.

78 Ibid.

79 Ibid.

80 Reynolds, *A Muslim theologian*, pp. 82, 199.

Christian scriptures cannot be trusted as they have been diverted from their origins, faithfully represented in the Qur'an. Although a more objective and constructive assessment of Paul amongst Muslim scholars is rare, there are some attempts to re-examine the Christian apostle through an examination of the Biblical record.[81]

81 Dr. Shabbir Akhtar is a contemporary counter-example of the ancient scholars presented in this paper as he studies the apostle Paul in his Biblical context. He is currently working on a commentary on Galatians and has dealt with Paul's relevance to modern Islam in two books: *The Quran and the secular mind* (Routledge, 2008) and *Islam as political religion* (Routledge, 2010).

CHAPTER 9

Būluṣ ibn Rajā' on the History and Integrity of the Qur'an: Copto-Islamic Controversy in Fatimid Cairo

David Bertaina

Introduction

In August 2013, Muslim Brotherhood supporters destroyed a fourth-century monastery church dedicated to the Virgin Mary at Daliya in the Minya region of Upper Egypt.[1] This singular event was not newsworthy so much as the fact that more than seventy other churches along with hundreds of homes and businesses of Coptic Christians were also damaged or destroyed during the political turmoil in Egypt.[2] In the United States, Coptic Christians protested at the White House and at the Washington Post in response to the lack of news coverage about the targeted violence.[3] Public intellectuals such as John Esposito remarked that 'in the modern period, Copts have continued to experience forms of discrimination, hate crimes, attacks on Copts, and attacks on churches'.[4] Historians have noted the parallels between the destruction of 2013 and the attacks on Coptic Christian property in 1321 and the persecutions under the Fatimid caliph al-Ḥākim from 1004–1012. The parallel causal factors in these events is that some common people in Egypt, when they were mobilized by a particular movement under popular religious sentiment, with little or no threat of retribution from the government and its security forces, felt at liberty to attack non-Muslims and their possessions and properties. Given the highly

1 Samuel Tadros, 'A Coptic monument to survival, destroyed', *The Wall Street Journal* (U.S. edition), August 22, 2013, D4. http://online.wsj.com/news/articles/SB10001424127887324108204579022951847863272.

2 As of 25 August 2013, the human rights organization Egyptian Initiative for Personal Rights documented that 47 churches were attacked, included 25 burned, seven looted and destroyed, five partly damaged, and 10 attacked without sustaining heavy damage. http://eipr.org/en/pressrelease/2013/08/25/1791. That number grew to nearly seventy churches by the end of 2013.

3 The word 'Copt' comes from the Arabic *qibṭ*, which originally stems from the Coptic self-defining name 'Gyptios', meaning someone of Egyptian descent.

4 https://www.pbs.org/newshour/amp/show/world-july-dec13-coptic_09-20.

© KONINKLIJKE BRILL NV, LEIDEN, 2018 | DOI 9789004360747_010 documented evidence of physical and emotional violence perpetrated against Christian minorities living in Islamic-majority countries, academics are often tempted to look back into history for more positive examples of Copto-Islamic cooperation as an antidote to political and religious conflicts.

The life of Būluṣ (Paul) ibn Rajāʾ (c. 950/60–c. 1020) confirms and challenges the historical narrative of violence against Christians in Egypt. He was one of the most famous Copto-Arabic writers of his time, but he was also a Muslim apostate and Coptic Christian convert. On the one hand, Ibn Rajāʾ lived through the persecutions of al-Ḥākim, was put on trial for apostasy by his father, personally experienced the death of his son and the theft of his property, and a mob attempted to murder him at the end of his life. From this perspective, Ibn Rajāʾ might be considered a passive victim due to the tragedies of his life. On the other hand, he freely converted from Islam to Christianity, he publically proclaimed his conversion, he was set free after his apostasy case, and he was able to write a critique of Islam and the Qur'an that was well-known in Egypt. From this view, Ibn Rajāʾ was an active agent who determined his own destiny and contributed to the formation of Qur'an interpretation in Fatimid Egypt.

During the early eleventh century, the Coptic monk and priest Būluṣ ibn Rajāʾ composed *Kitāb al-Wāḍiḥ bi-l-Ḥaqq* ('The book of that which is clear by means of the truth', henceforth *Clarity in Truth*) as a critique of Islamic origins, especially with regard to the Qur'an.[5] Ibn Rajāʾ interpreted the Qur'an based upon the assumption that it was a source of beautiful phrases, but also filled with haphazard repetitions, inconsistencies, contradictory verses, and a convoluted editorial process that marred its integrity. For Ibn Rajāʾ, the fact that his former Muslim compatriots were no longer able to articulate a unified voice regarding its laws and proper interpretation confirmed his analysis. The influence of Ibn Rajāʾ's work and other Christian Arabic analyses of the Qur'an suggest that Christians played a role in the formation of Islamic thinking about the text's

5 The *Kitāb al-Wāḍiḥ bi-l-Ḥaqq* is preserved in three manuscripts. Two of the manuscripts are incomplete and they are excerpted from different parts of the whole text. Sbath 1004 from Aleppo, Syria contains the introduction and most of chapters 1–3 in 111v–121v. The manuscript Paris BNF Syriac 203 from the Maronite Qannubīn monastery in Lebanon contains chapters 21–26 preserved in Karshūnī (Arabic language written in Syriac characters) in 149v–163r. The third manuscript from a private collection in Cairo contains the complete work from 13v–77r. It may very well be a copy of the lost manuscript from the uncatalogued collection of Būluṣ Sbath or Yuḥannā Balīṭ. See M Swanson, 'Būluṣ ibn Rajāʾ', in David Thomas and Alex Mallett, eds, *Christian-Muslim relations: a bibliographical history volume 2 (900–1050)*, Leiden, 2010, pp. 541–46.

interpretation, legal prescriptions, and the relationship between Scripture and tradition.[6]

Dating the Activity of Ibn Rajāʾ

A short description of Būluṣ ibn Rajāʾ's life will help to contextualize his view of the Qurʾan and its impact upon Coptic and Islamic thought. Būluṣ Ibn Rajāʾ's biography is preserved in the *History of the Patriarchs of Alexandria*.[7] Michael al-Damrāwī, the Bishop of Tinnīs, composed the section from 880–1046 in 1051, only a couple of decades after Ibn Rajāʾ's death.[8] While some of the events concerning Ibn Rajāʾ in the account are clearly hagiographic, it would be a mistake to judge the narrative as mostly invented. This assumption would fail to account for Michael al-Damrāwī's view that historical events should be interpreted retrospectively according to divine action in history. It would also fail to account for the fact that Michael al-Damrāwī cites Theodore ibn Mīnā, a synodal secretary for the Patriarchate who knew Ibn Rajāʾ personally. Most convincingly, al-Damrāwī appeared to be using a source for his material and he quotes directly from Ibn Rajāʾ's writings.

Around 973–975 as a youth, Ibn Rajāʾ witnessed the martyrdom of a Muslim convert to Christianity along the Nile River. His father Ibn Rajāʾ al-Shahīd was a jurist in Cairo who had connections with the elite in the city, sitting on the judges' council. Ibn Rajāʾ, whose given name was Yūsuf (Joseph), had the kind of family and education which would make him likely to have been present at the event described above.

Sometime after 980, and more likely in the 990s, he converted to Christianity. After traveling to Mecca for the pilgrimage, he became separated from his

6 For more information on this legacy, see C. Wilde, *Approaches to the Qurʾān in early Christian Arabic texts*, Palo Alto, 2014. For the historic and contemporary relevance of Christians using the Qurʾan, see J.S. Bridger, *Christian exegesis of the Qurʾān: a critical analysis of the apologetic use of the Qurʾān in select medieval and contemporary Arabic texts*, Eugene, 2015, especially pp. 65–104.

7 A.S. Atiya, Y. ʿAbd al-Masīḥ and O.H.E. KHS-Burmester, eds, *History of the Patriarchs of the Egyptian Church: known as the history of the Holy Church, Vol. II. Part 1, Khaël III—Šenouti II (A.D. 880–1066)*, Cairo, 1948, pp. 101–113 (Arabic), 151–170 (English).

8 For a summary of the text's sources, dating, and redaction, see J. Den Heijer, 'Coptic historiography in the Fāṭimid, Ayyūbid, and early Mamlūk periods', *Medieval Encounters* 2, 1996, pp. 67–98, especially pp. 69–77. Den Heijer notes that Michael al-Damrāwī's section was originally composed in Coptic, but since Ibn Rajāʾwrote in Arabic, we should probably assume that al-Damrāwī quoted his work in Arabic instead of translating it into Coptic.

caravan on the return trip (he references his Meccan pilgrimage in chapters 26 and 28 of *Clarity in Truth*). However, he was miraculously returned to Saint Mercurius Church in Old Cairo (Miṣr). In thanks for his desert salvation and its parallel with the conversion experience of Saint Būluṣ, he took the name Būluṣ and was baptized at the church. Since this location was only restored thanks to the caliph al-ʿAzīz and under the direction of Patriarch Abraham (d. 979), his conversion must have come after its reestablishment. His conversion likely occurred prior to al-Ḥākim's persecutions beginning in 1004.

Ibn Rajāʾ flourished during the reign of Patriarch Philotheus (979–1003), which would place his literary activity during the reign of the Fatimid leader al-Ḥākim (996–1021). His biography is included in the patriarch's section in the *History of the Patriarchs of Alexandria*. Representatives of Philotheus asked Ibn Rajāʾ for a donation when he was ordained a priest, and this probably happened around the end of the patriarch's reign (996–1003) and prior to al-Ḥākim's persecutions.

Ibn Rajāʾ's father petitioned for his apostasy case to be heard before al-Ḥākim and his chief justice, sometime between 996–1004. The judge was possibly Muḥammad al-Nuʿmān (984–999) whose father founded the school of Ismaʿili law and whose family ruled as chief justices for four generations.[9] Since Ibn Rajāʾ's father was an elite member of the judges' council and the chief justice was an Isma'ili Shiʿi, it may be possible that personal conflicts affected the outcome of the ruling that freed him. However, we also know that after the persecutions of 1004–1012, al-Ḥākim became more favorably disposed toward Christians. For instance, the Melkite Christian historian Yaḥyā ibn Saʿīd al-Anṭākī (d. 1066), who himself fled from Egypt to Antioch due to al-Ḥākim's policies, remarked that later the caliph allowed coerced converts to return to Christianity. When some Muslims complained that converts were attending the liturgy and partaking in communion, al-Ḥākim ignored their complaints.[10] If this is true, then it seems reasonable that he could have given explicit sanction to Ibn Rajāʾ's conversion during the apostasy case and permitted his later activities.

Ibn Rajāʾ stayed in Cairo after his apostasy case and began building the Church of the Archangel Michael at Ra's al-Khalīj in the southern part of the city. His biographer states that when he had assembled his building materials, some local Muslims from the Ramādiya neighborhood stole them. When he

9 R. Gottheil, 'A distinguished family of Fatimide cadis (al-Nuʿmān) in the tenth century', *Journal of the American Oriental Society* 27, 1906, pp. 217–96.

10 Al-Anṭākī, *Histoire de Yahyā Ibn Saīd d'Antioche*, ed., I. Kratchovsky, and trans, F. Micheau and G. Troupeau, Turnhout, 1997, p. 432. See also p. 416.

found the group, Ibn Rajāʾ offered them amnesty if they returned the wood, but if they did not, he would appeal to al-Ḥākim. They feared his threat and returned everything. Besides the physical evidence of the church, we also know that al-Ḥākim endorsed the rebuilding of churches later in his life and protected people who reverted to Christianity after coercive conversions to Islam.

> When al-Ḥākim permitted the building of churches, along with their renovation and the return of their pious endowments, he announced that a group of Christians who had converted to Islam during the time of persecution, and had thrown themselves at his mercy and had prepared themselves for death, saying to him: 'That which made us profess the religion of Islam was neither our choice nor our desire, so we ask that you order us to return to our religion, if you see it this way, or order our execution'. He immediately ordered that they wear the sash and black clothing, and carry a cross, and each of them returned to change his clothes and to be presented to the police for their protection, and he restrained everyone from interfering with them. So those who asked him for this increased until they got to the point that they were meeting with him in massive crowds ... and those among them who returned to Christianity were protected from what people warned them about (i.e., the danger of apostasy), and everyone from these parties remained in his former situation.[11]

What is important for our case here is the fact that al-Ḥākim's open policy toward apostasy and conversion from Islam to Christianity, along with his permission for the building of churches to take place, corroborates the events described in the biography of Ibn Rajāʾ. Michael al-Damrāwī notes in his biography that Ibn Rajāʾ collaborated with the well-known Christian Arabic theologian and Coptic bishop Severus ibn al-Muqaffaʿ. Ibn al-Muqaffaʿ composed a record of a debate with a Muslim dialectical theologian, which may have been of interest to Ibn Rajāʾ. Since Ibn al-Muqaffaʿ lived into his eighties and was active as late as 987, they likely worked together during his old age when Būluṣ ibn Rajāʾ was still in his thirties and forties. Ibn Rajāʾ mentions in his work that 'Anba Severus al-Muqaffaʿ—may God have mercy upon him—related a story to me,' (ولقد حدّثني أنبا ساويروس المقفّع—رحمه الله) about another Muslim convert to Christianity.[12] This passage reveals that they knew each other and that Ibn al-Muqaffaʿ died prior to his writing *Clarity in Truth*.

11 Ibid., 438, 440. The English translation quoted from K.J. Werthmuller, *Coptic identity and Ayyubid politics in Egypt, 1218–1250*, Cairo, 2010, p. 36.

12 Būluṣ ibn Rajāʾ, *Kitāb al-Wāḍiḥ bi-l-Ḥaqq*, Cairo 23r.

Based upon these data points, we can surmise that Ibn Rajāʾ was probably born around 950–960, had a conversion experience around 980–995, encountered troubles with his family near the end of this period, and went to trial around 996–1004 at the behest of his father. He probably spent the next few years of his life working and writing in Old Cairo at the Church of the Archangel Gabriel, and later at the Monastery of Benjamin in the Wadī l-Natrūn (Scetis) where he was ordained a priest. He could not have been too old because his father was still alive at this time. His biography states that his father bribed some Bedouin Arabs to murder him while he was in the Wadī l-Natrūn. Ibn Rajāʾ fled to the delta region at Sandafā near al-Maḥallah and lived out his final years there as a steward at the church of Saint Theodore.[13] As he lay deathly ill, Muslim locals heard about the convert and stirred up a mob to seize him. But he died prior to their arrival and his remains were safely hidden in a crypt beneath the church.

Būluṣ ibn Rajāʾ's connection with well-placed leaders is likely why a recorder for the Coptic synod composed his biography for posterity. In the account, Michael al-Damrāwī confirms that the story had been shared with him by a synodal secretary for the Patriarchate, his predecessor Theodore ibn Mīnā.[14] Since Ibn Rajāʾ had gained notoriety at the highest levels among the Coptic, Sunni, and Ismaʿili communities in Fatimid Cairo, it would not be surprising to find that his writings made an impact on the culture of the time.

In Būluṣ ibn Rajāʾ's *Clarity in Truth*, he mentions that it has been four hundred years since the time of Muhammad; however, this should probably be interpreted as a round figure rather than an exact number. Thus he was probably writing ca. 1012–1020. The reasons for this conjecture are because it is early enough for him to have worked with Ibn al-Muqaffaʿ (d. after 987) and late enough to fit in after caliph al-Ḥākim's persecutions from 1004–1012, when he was more amenable to Christian concerns. In *Clarity in Truth*, he mentions two other works that he had already written, so this was the last of his three known publications.[15] Finally, he cites oral traditions (*ḥadīth*) in his work from his teachers who were active around the end of the tenth century, such as Abū al-ʿAbbās Aḥmad al-Naysabūrī (fl. 1000), al-Ḥasan ibn Rashīq al-ʿAskarī (d. 980) and al-Ḥasan ibn Ismāʿīl al-Ḍurrāb (d. 1002).[16] In *Clarity in Truth*, Ibn Rajāʾ made use of the Qurʾan and other Islamic sources to argue for the intelligibility

13 See S. Timm, *Das christlich-koptische Ägypten in arabischer Zeit*, vol. 5 (Q–S), Wiesbaden, 1991, pp. 2278–79.

14 See Atiya, ʿAbd al-Masīḥ, and KHS-Burmester, eds, *History of the Patriarchs of the Egyptian Church*, pp. 112, 168–69.

15 The other two works are now lost. See M. Swanson, 'Būluṣ ibn Rajāʾ', pp. 541–46.

16 See D. Bertaina, 'Ḥadīth in the Christian Arabic Kalām of Būluṣ Ibn Rajāʾ (c. 1000)', *Intellectual History of the Islamicate World* 2, 2014, pp. 267–86.

of Christian truth claims and to critique Muslims' knowledge of their own Scripture. While most Christian Arabic authors preferred the anonymous approach to analyzing the Qur'an, Ibn Rajā' composed his works under his own name. These pieces defended his Biblical and theological claims. But they also provided critical assessments of how Muslims viewed the Qur'an and their Islamic tradition.

Christian Attitudes toward the Qur'an

The emergence of Christian Arabic polemics against the Qur'an suggests Christians and Muslims frequently debated the nature of Scripture and its interpretation. In the seventh century, Christians expressed little awareness of the Qur'an as an Arabic Scripture. In the Umayyad period (661–750), Christians began to recognize its import but largely dismissed the significance of the text. By the Abbasid period (750–1258) and under Fatimid rule in Egypt (969–1171), Christian approaches to the Qur'an reached greater maturity. They composed systematic critiques of its historical origins, its interpretation, and its relation to the Islamic community. Christians adapted Qur'anic verses for apologetic and polemical arguments and created testimonial collections that demonstrated the truth of Christianity. They refuted passages they suspected to be erroneous and concluded that the Qur'an was an unreliable source.

Ibn Rajā' utilized all of these arguments, but he was not unique in his analysis of the Qur'an. Rather, he took up a longstanding tradition among Christian Arabic authors to assess the Qur'an's divine inspiration.[17] In his study of the Qur'an in Christian Arabic texts, Sidney Griffith made the following insights:

> In Arab Christian apologetical texts generally one finds a certain ambivalence about the Qur'an. On the one hand, some authors argue that it cannot possibly be a book of divine revelation, citing in evidence its composite and, as they see the matter, its all too human origins. But on the other hand, given the progressive inculturation of Christianity into the Arabic-speaking world of Islam from the eighth century onward, most Arab Christian writers themselves commonly quoted words and phrases from the Qur'an. Inevitably its language suffused their religious consciousness. Some of them even built their apologetical arguments in behalf of Christianity on a certain interpretation of particular verses

17 See examples in Wilde, *Approaches to the Qur'ān in early Christian Arabic texts*.

> from the Islamic scripture. In short, they nevertheless also often quoted from it as a testimony to the truth.[18]

Historians have identified a spectrum of attitudes toward the Qur'an in Christian Arabic writings. Authors established a set of criteria for the value of the Qur'an's content. They interpreted it to substantiate Christianity and suggested its lack of integrity disproved Islam. We might characterize these approaches from generally negative to somewhat more affirmative of the Qur'an's value. In the apprehensive camp, Christians generally viewed the Qur'an as a defective text. First, we find some Christians critiquing its literary character. In chapter 101 from his work *On Heresies*, John of Damascus explains that the Qur'an's flaws were its lack of a chronological structure, opaque language, and 'tales worthy of laughter' contained within it.[19] The ninth-century Christian Arabic letter (*Risāla*) of ʿAbd al-Masīḥ ibn Isḥāq al-Kindī argues that Muslims are under the false impression that the Qur'an is verified because of its 'clear Arabic speech'. It is impossible for any living language to be 'clear' or 'pure' (i.e. every language is dynamic) and the Qur'an itself contains a number of foreign words. Further, it conforms to Arabic poetic styles of the period.[20] These critiques directly challenged the Qur'an's claim to be inimitable.

Another attitude Christians expressed was that the Qur'an was an arbitrary compilation that could not be definitively attributed to any single figure. In the disputation of the monk of Bēt Ḥālē with a Muslim figure, the monk assumes that the Qur'an was different from surat al-Baqara and explains that its collection was accomplished only after the death of Muhammad.[21] The letter of al-Kindī details the collection of the text and the various insertions, deletions, emendations, and re-arrangements that were made to the Scripture, as well

18 S. Griffith, 'The Qur'ān in Arab Christian texts; the development of an apologetical argument: Abū Qurrah in the mağlis of al-Ma'mūn', *Parole de l'Orient* 24, 1999, pp. 203–33, especially p. 204.

19 See D. Sahas, *John of Damascus on Islam: the "Heresy of the Ishmaelites"*, Leiden, 1972, pp. 132–41.

20 Tien, A. ed., *Risālat ʿAbd Allah ibn Ismāʿīl al-Hashimī ilā ʿAbd al-Masīḥ ibn Isḥāq al-Kindī yadʿūhu bi-hā ilā al-Islām, wa-risālat ʿAbd al-Masīḥ ilā al-Hashimī yaruddu bi-hā ʿalayhi wa-yadʿūhu ilā al-Nasrānīya*, London, 1885, reprint, 1912. The English translation of the relevant passages is located in N.A. Newman, ed., *The early Christian-Muslim dialogue: a collection of documents from the first three Islamic centuries (632–900 A.D.); translations with commentary*, Hatfield, 1993, pp. 460–66.

21 For a summary of the discussion, see G. Reinink, 'Bible and Qur'an in early Syriac Christian-Islamic disputation', in M. Tamcke, ed., *Christians and Muslims in dialogue in the Islamic orient of the middle ages*, Beirut, 2007, pp. 57–72, especially pp. 60–61.

as the suppression of the alternate versions belonging to ʿAlī and Ibn Masʿūd.[22] The different titles and orders of the chapters (*suras*), the fact that some *suras* are absent in collections, and the fact that some verses were omitted or deleted, confirmed for Christian apologists the earthly process by which Muslims compiled the text. These same arguments are leveled against the Qur'an by Būluṣ ibn Rajā'.

Related to the compilation critique is the view that the Qur'an was a derivative work based upon earlier Scriptures. In the *Baḥīrā Legend*, for instance, Christians argued that the Qur'an had a semi-Christian origin thanks to a renegade monk who instructed Muhammad by using the Bible.[23] Likewise John of Damascus argued that an 'Arian' monk (or perhaps a heretical Tritheist monk—as they were called neo-Arians at this time) was responsible for inspiring some of Muhammad's content. Others argued that the Jewish convert Kaʿb al-Aḥbār inserted Scripture stories into the Qur'an when it was edited after Muhammad's death.[24]

For Christian Arabic polemicists, the Qur'an was flawed because of its literary shortcomings, its haphazard assembly as an incoherent text, its plagiarized Biblical content, and its lack of authentication for itself or its prophet. In his dialogue with the caliph al-Mahdī in 781, Patriarch Timothy of the Church of the East recalled:

> And our King said to me: 'Do you not believe that our Book was given by God?' And I replied to him: 'It is not my business to decide whether it is from God or not. But I will say something of which your Majesty is well aware, and that is all the words of God found in the Torah and in the prophets, and those of them found in the Gospel and in the writings of the Apostles, have been confirmed by signs and miracles; as to the words of your Book they have not been corroborated by a single sign or miracle ... Since signs and miracles are proofs of the will of God, the

22 See the relevant section in Newman, ed., *The early Christian-Muslim dialogue*, pp. 455–60. For more detailed information on al-Kindī's approach, see the chapters 3 and 4 in this book by Sandra Toenies Keating and Emilio Platti.

23 See the study by B. Roggema, *The legend of Sergius Bahira: Eastern Christian apologetics and apocalyptic in response to Islam*, Leiden, 2009.

24 See B. Roggema, 'The confession which Kaʿb al-Aḥbār handed down to the Ishmaelites', in David Thomas and Barbara Roggema, eds, *Christian-Muslim relations: a bibliographical history volume 1 (600–900)*, Leiden, 2009, pp. 403–5.

> conclusion drawn from their absence in your Book is well known to your Majesty'.[25]

But not all Christian Arabic authors regarded the Qur'an in a negative light. Some theologians viewed it as a text with limited access to truth. Others were willing to cite the Qur'an as an authority. In this part of the spectrum, writers argued that the Qur'an provided provisional wisdom concerning Biblical revelation. In the anonymous eighth-century Arabic work *On the Triune Nature of God*, the author points out that the Qur'an also contains key teachings about God's Word and Spirit being one with Him.[26] In this sense, the Qur'an was cited as an authority for Christian revelation. For these authors, the Qur'an affirmed the Bible, intertwining the two sources in a coherent divine message.

Nevertheless, they contended that while the Qur'an contains truth, Muslims misinterpreted their Scripture and distorted its intended meaning. This was a counter-argument to the widespread Muslim view that Christians had corrupted the interpretation of the Bible (*taḥrīf maʿnawī*).[27] In the *Debate of Abū Qurra with Muslim mutakallimūn at the court of al-Maʾmūn*, Theodore Abū Qurra only quotes from the Qur'an, given that his opponents rejected the authority of the Bible. At one point Abū Qurra explains: 'If I told the truth, then your book tells the truth. And if you were to reject these words of mine, then it is your prophet you reject and from your religion you depart'.[28] For Abū Qurra, the Qur'an provides sufficient reason to prove the truth of Christianity:

> You insult your book, and belie the saying of your prophet wherein he says, 'Let the people of the Gospel judge by what had been sent down upon them from their Lord';[29] and that 'among them are priests and monks, and they are not arrogant';[30] and that 'they are closest in affection

25 See A. Mingana, 'The apology of Timothy the Patriarch before the Caliph Mahdi', *Bulletin of the John Rylands Library* 12, 1928, pp. 137–226, especially pp. 172–3.

26 See D. Bertaina, 'The development of testimony collections in early Christian apologetics with Islam', in David Thomas, ed., *The Bible in Arab Christianity*, Leiden, 2007, pp. 151–73, especially pp. 162–7.

27 On this Muslim view of the Bible in Fatimid Egypt, see M. Whittingham, 'The value of *taḥrīf maʿnawī* (corrupt interpretation) as a category for analysing Muslim views of the Bible: evidence from *Al-radd al-jamīl* and Ibn Khaldūn', *Islam and Christian–Muslim Relations* 22, 2011, pp. 209–22.

28 W. Nasry, *The caliph and the bishop: a* 9th *century Muslim-Christian debate: al-Maʾmūn and Abū Qurrah*, Beirut, 2008, p. 213.

29 Q 5:47.

30 Q 5:82.

> to those who believed'.[31] Hence, your book calls us believers, and you call us infidels, polytheists and blasphemers. You wish, by this, to fault us with a false charge, and you hope by this to be redeemed of fault. And if you were to know the certain truth, you would have said that your book is the one that has corrupted [the Scripture] … Rather, he said, 'I have sent down the Qur'an, confirming what was before it from the Gospel and the Torah'.[32]

Būluṣ ibn Rajā''s views of the Qur'an cover this spectrum of perspectives. For Ibn Rajā', the Qur'an was a valuable source to use authoritatively. He lauds the parts of the Qur'an that agree with the Bible and that it regards the Bible as an authority. He considers many verses in the Arabic text beautiful. But on the other hand, Ibn Rajā' found the Qur'an a problematic text because of the lack of a consensus over its interpretation, the problematic means of its disclosure, its divergent readings in the seven schools, omissions from earlier versions of the text, its arbitrary canonization process, various word and phrase inconsistencies and repetitions, and outright contradictions. He devotes a chapter of his work to each of these problems demonstrating that ultimately, he found the Qur'an a defective message.

Ibn Rajā' was very comfortable in the linguistic world of the Qur'an. His language is suffused with Islamic nuances. He quotes the Qur'an accurately as a source. He references local Islamic traditions. He quotes oral traditions from his teachers and names them including the transmission line (*isnād*). All of this divulges his familiarity with the Islamic worldview. Since he was a former Muslim who converted to Christianity, it should not be surprising to see him use Qur'anic verses to reaffirm his polemical argument. In the following sections, I will outline his work and analyze relevant passages that exemplify Ibn Rajā''s use of the Qur'an.

Outline of *Clarity in Truth*

Būluṣ ibn Rajā''s work consists of an introduction, thirty chapters, and a conclusion that ranges over a variety of apologetic and polemical topics. Nearly all of the chapters deal with the Qur'an in a significant way. The table summarizes the chapters that are relevant to the Qur'an:

31 Ibid.

32 This is a paraphrase of Q 3:3: 'He has sent down upon you the Book in truth, confirming what was before it. And He revealed the Torah and the Gospel'. The block quotation is an adaptation from Nasry, *The caliph and the bishop*, pp. 240–41.

Chapter	Relevance to the Qur'an (Q)
Introduction	Ibn Rajā''s conversion and education in the Q
1	The lack of interpretive consensus about the Q
2	The reliability of the Bible according to the Q
6	Problems regarding the revelation of the Q
7	7 vocalizations/readings (*qirāʿāt*) of the Q
8	Omissions from the Q
9	Canonization process of the Q
11	Inconsistencies and repetitions of words and phrases in the Q
14	Sexual themes in the Q
15	Repetition of passages in the Q taken from Torah, Psalms, and Gospel
16	The local rather than universal Arabic message of the Q
17	The Bible as a source for the Q
18	Contradictions in the Q
29	Alcohol in the Q
30	Marriage in the Q

Clarity in Truth concentrates on the history of the Islamic Scriptures, their Prophet, and the history of the Islamic community. The Qur'an's verses are ubiquitous in his narrative, even in the chapters on ancillary matters. A few sections concentrate on Christian theological themes in reply to Muslim *kalām* questions. Ibn Rajā' cites the Bible on only sixteen occasions, and in several instances these are allusions rather than direct quotations. He alludes to stories from the Hebrew Bible on three occasions (Gen 3:8–10; Gen 17:1; Exod 3:2–6) and only quotes from it twice (Ps 33:6 and Isa 7:14). From the New Testament, he cites from the Gospels according to Matthew and John exclusively—no other books are mentioned. Further, Ibn Rajā' never quotes the Bible and Qur'an in tandem to prove a point. In contrast, Ibn Rajā' mentions parts of the Qur'an approximately 170 times within his work and quotes from it on more than 125 occasions.

The Qur'an According to Būluṣ ibn Rajā'

In the introduction to *Clarity in Truth*, Būluṣ ibn Rajā' explains that he was an expert in Qur'anic studies and the history of its interpretation. But he viewed his knowledge of Islam's holy text as an obstacle, because 'Satan had hardened my heart, presenting my evil works to me favorably. So I continued to stray in my blindness and my ignorance' (قد طبع الشيطان على قلوبنا، فزين لنا سوء أعمالنا. فظللنا نشطح في عمانا و جهلنا.).[33] For Ibn Rajā', the Qur'an could only act as a conduit to direct Muslims toward God's truth which the 'People of the Book' already possessed:

> When I thought about the bad situation of my previous state, I had to clarify that and not conceal it, in order for anyone who is not sure of his misguidance to know that. Perhaps God will bless him just as He blessed me and will guide him just as He guided me.
>
> لما نظرنا لعتب ما كنا فيه، وجب علينا أن نبين ذلك لا نكتمه، ليعلم ذلك من هو على غير يقين من ضلالته. فعسى أن يمن الله عليه كما من علينا، و يهديه كما هدانا.[34]

In the first chapter, Ibn Rajā' argues that Muslims have subsumed the Qur'an under their own worldly traditions. He points out occasions when the Qur'an suggests a clear reading, but later Muslim commentators and jurists have ignored, misinterpreted, or contradicted the clear intention of the text. He claims that:

> Even if the Qur'an was considered reliable as it is, then that would be the least of their disagreements. But within it are contradictions and trouble-some matters and repetition which are obvious to whoever examines it.
>
> لو كان القرآن في حالته صحيحا، لكان ذلك أقل اختلافهم. غير أن فيه من التناقض و الاضطراب والتكرير ما لا خفاء به على من تدبره.[35]

For Ibn Rajā', the religion of the Qur'an was co-opted by the practice of Islam. He argues that since more than forty men interpreted the Qur'an after Muhammad's death, Muslims were never able to develop a consensus about its interpretation. Instead they relied upon local dialects from the Hudhayl

33 Sbath 1004 112v; Cairo 14r–v. Ibn Rajā' writes about himself using the first-person plural (the 'royal we') although I have translated it in the first-person singular to convey the sense of his work as a personal endeavor.

34 Sbath 1004 113v; Cairo 14v–15r.

35 Sbath 1004 115r; Cairo 16r.

and Quraysh, along with poetic forms and other criteria, to arbitrarily shape the text.[36]

In the first chapter, Ibn Rajāʾ cites Q 2:173, 5:3, and 6:145 as a clear restriction against consuming blood and pork meat. Nevertheless, he argues, in one case an imam permitted his followers to eat pork grease as long as they drained the blood properly and separated it from the meat. They claimed this was a legitimate interpretation since they were not technically eating the meat with the blood. Ibn Rajāʾ found this interpretation violated the spirit of its meaning.

Along with rules governing meals, Ibn Rajāʾ also cites the misuse of the Qurʾan in marriage laws. He cites Q 4:3, 'Marry whoever is pleasing to you among the women, a second and third and fourth'. However, some commentators claimed that the verse's context was meant to be understood in the sense of addition: two plus three plus four (2+3+4=9). Ibn Rajāʾ had heard of legal consent for men marrying up to nine wives and finds this approach twisted the verse's intended meaning.

In the second chapter, Ibn Rajāʾ claims that Muslims misinterpreted the Qurʾan's attitude toward the Jewish and Christian Scriptures. If a Muslim claims that the Torah was changed after Moses' death and the Gospel was altered after Jesus' ascension, then Ibn Rajāʾ says to respond:

> He said in the Qurʾan in sura 'Jonah' (Q 10:94): 'If you are in doubt about what we have revealed to you, then ask those who have been reading the Scripture before you'. If what he says about altering the Torah and the Gospel is true—and they are lies—then he has brought an accusation against God for commanding [Muḥammad] to ask the liars. How can those intellectuals not comprehend this clear impossibility!

> قال في القرآن في سورة يونس: "فإن كنت في شك مما أنزلنا إليك فاسأل الذين يقرءون الكتاب من قبلك." فإن كان ما يقول من تغير التوراة والإنجيل حق—وأنهما كذب—فقد ادعى على الله أنه أمره أن يسأل الكذابين. أفلا يتدبر أولياء العقول هذا المحال البين![37]

The Qurʾan does not claim the Bible is corrupted in meaning or interpretation because that would put it in contradiction with itself, according to Ibn Rajāʾ.

---

36 Sbath 1004, 115v; Cairo 16r–v.

37 Sbath 1004 117r; Cairo 17v.

Verses referring to alteration must be understood in another way in order to adhere to the internal integrity of the Qur'an.

After quoting 'It is we who revealed the recollection and we will indeed be its guardian' (Q 15:9), Ibn Rajā' explains how the context for this verse must mean that God is the guardian of the Bible. In other words, the Qur'an recalls Biblical accounts to remind its audience what they have already learned about God's revelation.[38] The Qur'an recalls the Bible to justify its own authority, but this transitively lends authority to the Bible as well. For Ibn Rajā', the Qur'an authenticates the Jewish and Christian Scriptures (e.g. Q 3:3), but Muslims have not interpreted their own text with the same due diligence. He concludes in his opening sections that the Qur'an is an authoritative source for Muslims, but its followers cannot live up to its standards either through ignorance, misinterpretation, or intentional obfuscation of its rules. Ibn Rajā''s work, on the contrary, is presented as the opposite of obfuscation—it is a clarification (*al-wāḍiḥ*).

In the sixth chapter and following, Ibn Rajā' presents the Qur'an as a text with dubious value due to the process by which it took shape. Ibn Rajā' claims the monk Baḥīrā provided Muhammad with Scriptural material and served as his guide until the monk's untimely death.[39] Afterward, Salman the Persian and 'Abd Allāh ibn Salām (a Jewish convert) read the Scriptures to Muhammad so that he could meditate upon them and develop his own text:

> He summarized [the Scriptures] using the language of the ancient Arabs and eloquence of the Quraysh and other Arabs. He gathered in [the Qur'an] stories and legends of the prophets and others among the ancients.

> ولخصها بكلام العرب المتقدمين من العرب وفصاحة قريش وغيرهم من العرب.
> جمع فيه قصصًا وطرائق طوائف من الأنبياء وغيرهم من المتقدمين.[40]

The seventh chapter includes four sections on the meaning of the Qur'an. Ibn Rajā' recounts many of the basic facts known about the formation of the book. He mentions the seven vocalization traditions (*qirā'āt*) and their historic origins. He argues that there was no single version of the Qur'an, which was memorized differently by 'Abd Allāh ibn Mas'ūd (d. 653), Zayd ibn Thābit

38 See the description of this process in S.H. Griffith, *The Bible in Arabic: the scriptures of the "People of the Book" in the language of Islam*, Princeton, 2013, pp. 54–96.

39 On the Baḥīrā legend, see Roggema, *The legend of Sergius Bahira*.

40 Cairo 28r.

(d. ca. 665), ʿUmar (d. 644) and ʿUthmān ibn ʿAffān (d. 656). However, Ibn Rajāʾ asserts that Ibn Masʿūd's version of the Qurʾan did not include Q 1, Q 113, or Q 114. These were liturgical prayers added by Zayd ibn Thābit. He continues:

> For instance [Ibn] Masʿūd would read (Q 39:6), 'God took you out from the wombs of your women,' while all of the people read: 'God took you out from the wombs of your mothers.' In addition, he read (Q 70:9): 'The mountains were like puffed-up wool [*ṣūf*],' while all of the people read: 'like puffed-up dyed wool [*ʿihn*]'—dyed wool is wool. And Ibn Masʿūd read (Q 12:31): 'She prepared for them citrus fruit,' pronounced without doubling, while all of the people read 'banquet' with doubling. And Ibn Masʿūd read (Q 75:17–19): 'Indeed it is up to us to put it together and to recite it [*qurʾānahu*]. So when you recite it, follow its reading [*qirāʾatahu*]. Then, its exposition lies with us,' while all of the people read: 'Indeed it is up to us to put it together and to explain it [*bayānahu*]. So when we recite it, follow its recitation [*qurʾānahu*]. Then, its exposition lies with us'. In many cases Ibn Masʿūd is unique so that no one follows him on them.

ولم يوافقهم أيضًا في اللفظ، وكان مسعود يقرأ: "والله أخرجكم من بطون إمائكم،" والناس كلهم يقرؤون: "والله أخرجكم من بطون أمهاتكم،" وقرأ أيضًا: "وتكون الجبال كالصوف المنفوش،" والناس كلهم يقرؤوا: "كالعهن المنفوش"—العهن هو الصوف. وقرأ ابن مسعود: "وأعتدت لهن متكًا" مخفف، والناس كلهم يقرؤون: "متكّا" مثقل. وقرأ ابن مسعود: "إن علينا جمعه وقرآنه فإذا قرأته فاتبع قراءته، ثم إن علينا بيانه،" والناس كلهم يقرؤون: "إن علينا جمعه و بيانه فإذا قرأناه فاتبع قرآنه، ثم إن علينا بيانه." مع أشياء كثيرة تفرد بها ابن مسعود لم يتابعه عليها أحد.[41]

In the following sections of chapter seven, Ibn Rajāʾ offers examples of changes made by Zayd ibn Thābit, grammatical mistakes noted by ʿUthmān, and Abū Bakr's alternative readings. It was only under Marwān ibn al-Ḥakam (d. 685), he explains, that the Qurʾan reached its canonical state.

He continues his polemic in the eighth chapter concerning omissions from the original text. He insists that earlier versions contained passages about stoning adulterers as well as other punishments such as whipping. Ibn Rajāʾ notes additional omissions:

---

41 Cairo 29v.

> In addition, they transmit in one of their authentic oral traditions that sura 'Divorce' (Q 65) was considered as long as sura 'The Cow' (Q 2), two hundred and eighty-five verses and more. Today it is twelve verses and its remainder is omitted. In addition, sura 'The Cow' (Q 2) was numbered to a thousand verses and today it is two hundred and eighty-five verses and its remainder is omitted.
>
> و رووا أيضًا في حديثهم الصحيح عندهم أن سورة الطلاق كانت تعادل سورة البقرة، مائتي آية وخمسة وثمانون آية وزاد فيه. وهي اليوم إثني عشر آيةٍ وسقط بقيتها. وأيضا أن سورة البقرة كان عددها ألف آية وهي اليوم مائتي خمسة وثمانون آية وسقط بقيتها.[42]

In the ninth chapter on the canonization process, Ibn Rajāʾ suggests that when various versions of the Qurʾan were destroyed to prevent alternative readings, this only reinforced its human origins. When Marwān ibn al-Ḥakam destroyed Ḥafṣa's version along with the alternative texts of ʿUthmān, ʿAlī, Ibn Masʿūd, and Zayd ibn Thābit, it proved that Muslims had not been careful with their Scripture. If this is the case, he argues, then they have no basis in critiquing the integrity of the Bible.

The eleventh chapter argues that many phrases from the Qurʾan are redundant. For instance, Ibn Rajāʾ quotes Q 11:82: 'We rained stones of baked clay upon it'. Stones cannot be baked clay or this is merely wasteful repetition, he claims.

The fourteenth chapter recounts the story of Zayd's wife and her marriage to Muhammad. After narrating the verses in the Qurʾan and oral tradition, Ibn Rajāʾ argues that sexual matters like this have no proper place in a holy text to be read for prayer. Worship should focus on God or moral lessons rather than recitations of marital intrigues, according to Ibn Rajāʾ.

In the fifteenth chapter, his main argument is that the Qurʾan is comprised primarily of pre-existing materials in the Torah and the Gospel. He explains:

> So what is the point in going to what is in the ancients' Scriptures and the Scriptures of those who came before him among those who prophesied, and then ascribing that to himself? Rather it would have been better if he came up with something by himself which none of those ones had

42 Cairo 32v.

> brought, in order to distinguish his words from their words and he would have a place [among the prophets].
>
> فما الفائدة أن يجيء إلى ما في زبر الأولين وصحف من تقدمه من المتنبين، فينسب ذلك إلى نفسه؟ و إنما كان ينبغي لو جاء بشيء من عنده لم يأتي به أحدا من هولاء كلهم، ليتميز كلامه من كلامهم و يكون له موضع.[43]

Ibn Rajāʾ argues in the sixteenth chapter that the Qurʾan's message could not be universal since Muhammad could only produce it in Arabic. But the Christian Bible was meant to be translated and shared with all peoples. He acknowledges that many passages in the Qurʾan are beautiful, and he provides a few examples (Q 12:80; Q 11:44). But he does not believe the verses are inimitable and many other examples of Arabic poetry counter this claim.

In the seventeenth chapter, Ibn Rajāʾ claims that the Bible was Muhammad's main source of inspiration, which he adapted and ascribed to himself as his own Scripture. Ibn Rajāʾ laments that despite the fact that children learn it from teachers and the faithful read it and recite it in prayers, the clearly derivative nature of its content is lost on people.

The eighteenth chapter is the most extensive analysis in *Clarity in Truth*. Ibn Rajāʾ offers dozens of examples of what he sees as contradictions in the Qurʾan. For instance, he mentions certain passages in the Qurʾan that differ about the order of creation. He also cites Q 54:1 that the moon was split and then cites an oral tradition, concerning the legend that Muhammad literally split the moon. He writes:

> Another proof testifies that it is a lie and impossible and it is what al-Ḥasan ibn Rashīq al-ʿAskarī (d. 980) reported to me (from) Abū Bishr al-Dulābī (d. 923) from Abū ʿAbd al-Raḥmān al-Shaybānī al-Nasāʾī (d. 915) from Qutayba ibn Saʿīd (d. 854), (from) Mālik (d. 795), from Hishām ibn ʿUrwa (d. 763) from his father (ʿUrwa ibn al-Zubayr, d. 712) that he said: 'I asked Ibn ʿAbbās and I said to him: Tell me about this moon and how big it is'. So he said: 'I heard Muhammad say that this moon was eighteen times as big as the entire world'. Think about it, my brother—may God guide you—this impossibility has no truth to it. They allege that the moon was eighteen times as long as the whole world. They allege that it fell between two (mountains)—upon Abū Qabīs Mountain and the Red Mountain, and they are in Mecca. How can these two mountains

43 Cairo 41v.

encompass this great moon which is eighteen times as big as the whole world? If they reflect on this, then [this argument] would be convincing for them. One verse (of the Qur'an) is contradicted by the oral traditions and logic.

ودليل غير هذا يشهد أنّ ذلك كذب ومحال، وهو ما حدثنيه الحسن ابن رشيق العسكري، قد حدثنا ابو بشر الدولابي. قال حدثنا ابو عبد الرحمن الشيباني النسائي، قال حدثنا قتيبة ابن سعيد (عن) مالك، عن هشام ابن عروة، عن ابيه أنّه قال: "سألت ابن عباس فقلت له أخبرني عن هذا القمر وما قدره." فقال: "سمعت محمد يقول أن هذا القمر قدر الدنيا كلها ثمانية عشر مرة." فتدبّر يا أخي—وفقك الله—هذا المحال الذي لا حقًّا به. وهم يزعمون أنّ القمر طول الدنيا كلها ثمانية عشر مرة. و يزعمون أنّه سقط بين اثنين—على جبل أبي قبيس والجبل الأحمر، وهما بمكة. كيف يجوز أنّ هذا الجبلين يسعان هذا القمر العظيم الذي في قدر الدنيا ثمانية عشر مرة؟ ولو تفكّروا في هذا الكان لهم فيه مقنع. آية ينقضها الحديث والقياس.[44]

Despite the eschatological tone of some verses in the Qur'an, Ibn Rajā' points out that it has been four hundred years since Muhammad's lifetime and no judgment seems imminent. His goal in this chapter is to show the Qur'an is not worthy of use for divine worship.

The following chapters of *Clarity in Truth* largely focus on other aspects of Islamic history and practice, as well as Christian apologetics. But the Qur'an is by no means absent from Ibn Rajā''s analysis. In the twenty-ninth chapter, he returns to the topic of Qur'anic contradictions, this time in reference to alcohol (Q 2:219; Q 7:33, Q 5:90; Q 16:67; Q 6:145; Q 4:43) and whether Islamic practice sanctions it.

The thirtieth chapter closes with a critique of divorce practices outlined in the Qur'an as illogical—each subsequent divorce should require a stronger punishment if the text has a divine origin. Finally, he closes with an extensive retelling of the legend of Muhammad's Night Journey, when the Prophet traveled upon the animal al-Burāq to Jerusalem and then with Gabriel up to the seven heavens. The details of the legend, he asserts, don't make sense. Most importantly, Muslims cannot claim the story as sign for Muhammad, since that would invalidate the Qur'an's claims to the contrary, according to Ibn Rajā'.

44 Cairo 49r–v.

Conclusion

Būluṣ Ibn Rajāʾʾs work *Clarity in Truth* is one of the most substantial assessments of the Qurʾan by a medieval Christian Arabic writer. The sophisticated product is a result of his upbringing, his apostasy from Islam and his conversion to Coptic Christianity. Yet he is also one of its most knowledgeable critics, due to his training in traditional Islamic education. Scholars have long recognized that converts are often the ones most likely to write explanations of their new conviction and why they felt that their former religion was insufficient.[45] The story of Ibn Rajāʾʾs approach to the Qurʾan fits into the wider history of Christian responses to Islam. While Muslims reinterpreted the Bible for their own theological concerns, Christians scrutinized the Qurʾan in turn. They responded to Muslim criticisms, gave an account for the legitimacy of the Bible, and examined the Qurʾan for deficiencies. Writers such as Ibn Rajāʾ concluded that the Qurʾan had been corrupted, along with its interpretation, and only the Bible was a reliable Scripture.

Similar to the Qurʾan's use of Biblical recall to authenticate its own authority, Ibn Rajāʾ employed the Qurʾan to certify his arguments and correct perceived mistakes. But ultimately, Ibn Rajāʾ believed the Qurʾan lacked integrity. He modeled his argument on contemporaneous Islamic approaches to the Bible. For instance, the Qurʾan suggests that Christians had confused, obscured, replaced, tampered, twisted, and/or forgot their Scriptures.[46] The Qurʾan and most early Muslims assumed that these changes were incidental and not deliberate fabrications.[47] Nevertheless, they argued that Christians had misinterpreted verses resulting in a corrupted interpretation (*taḥrīf maʿnawī*). Further, they made mistakes in transmission that altered the text itself (*taḥrīf lafẓī*). They were still interested in the Bible's practical value for Muslim doctrine but they wavered between tentative approval and outright dismissal of its content. In a similar fashion, Ibn Rajāʾ sanctioned the Qurʾan's use at some

45 Ibn Rajāʾʾs work is not so different from that of the Christian convert to Islam, ʿAlī b. Rabban al-Ṭabarī (d. 855). He composed apologetic and polemical works that cited Biblical passages as proof of Islam and criticized Christianity. See for instance A. Mingana, *The book of religion and empire: a semi-official defence and exposition of Islam written by order at the court and with the assistance of the caliph Mutawakkil (A.D. 847–861) by ʿAlī al-Ṭabarī*, Manchester, 1922.

46 See G. Nickel, *Narratives of tampering in the earliest commentaries on the Qurʾān*, Leiden, 2011, pp. 52–61.

47 G.S. Reynolds, 'On the Qurʾānic accusation of scriptural falsification (*taḥrīf*) and Christian anti-Jewish polemic', *Journal of the American Oriental Society* 130, 2010, pp. 189–202.

points and disdained its worth at other junctures: its textual history was confirmation of its corruption in both word and interpretation.

For Ibn Rajā', the Qur'an held probative value because its content established a set of criteria by which he could analyze his former Islamic community. By reinterpreting the Arabic Scripture, he argued that Muslims did not remain faithful to its admonitions. He believed its content did not inspire religious devotion once one understood the historical circumstances that led to its final—and heavily-edited—canonical form. He concludes that the internal strife of the Islamic community, coupled with the lack of knowledge about the Qur'an's linguistic and historical contexts, had led to poorly-applied interpretation, unreliable oral traditions, and faulty legal pronouncements. But as part of his former worldview and religious identity, the Qur'an held sentimental value for him. He quotes from the Qur'an faithfully while subjecting it to new hermeneutical possibilities.

The reception of *Clarity in Truth* likely contributed to Muslim defenses of the Qur'an's inimitability and criticisms of the Bible's integrity. At the turn of the twelfth century, the Egyptian work *Al-Radd al-jamīl* (*A fitting reply*) attributed to al-Ghazālī asserts that Christians mistook the Gospels' figurative meanings about Jesus' status for literal truths. The author resolves contradictions between the Qur'an and Bible, such as using Islamic terminology and meanings for Biblical concepts. This work also emphasizes the reliability of passages sympathetic to the Qur'anic message while refuting passages commonly used by Christian Arabic apologists.[48] The author proceeds on a point-by-point analysis of Biblical passages to demonstrate their misreading.[49] In fourteenth-century Cairo, the Muslim apologist al-Ṭūfī (d. 1316) composed a critical exegesis of the Bible in response to a Copto-Arabic polemic against Islam.[50] The Christian critique of the Qur'an was nicknamed *al-Sayf al-murhaf fī'l-radd ʿalā'l-muṣḥaf* (*The whetted sword in refutation of the Book*) and was possibly written by al-Mu'taman Abū Isḥāq Ibrāhīm ibn al-ʿAssāl (d. after 1270) according to his contemporary Ghāzī ibn al-Wāsiṭī. This work was definitely

48 See Whittingham, 'The value of *taḥrīf maʿnawī* (corrupt interpretation) as a category for analysing Muslim views of the Bible', pp. 212–14.

49 M. Beaumont, 'Appropriating Christian scriptures in a Muslim refutation of Christianity: the case of *Al-radd al-jamīl* attributed to al-Ghazālī', *Islam and Christian-Muslim Relations* 22, 2011, pp. 69–84. See also *Al-Radd al-jamīl*—A Fitting Refutation of the Divinity of Jesus, *attributed to Abū Ḥāmid al-Ghazālī*, Arabic edition and English Translation by M. Beaumont and M. El-Kaisy Friemuth, Leiden, 2016.

50 L. Demiri, *Muslim exegesis of the Bible in medieval Cairo: Najm al-Dīn al-Ṭūfī's* (*d. 716/1316*) *Commentary on the Christian Scriptures*, Leiden, 2013.

different than Ibn Rajāʾ's work because it uses quotations from later authorities. But according to al-Ṭūfī's summary of its now-lost contents, it seems possible that the refutation incorporated several of Būluṣ ibn Rajāʾ's arguments into the work.[51] The text covers much of the same ground, including a closing chapter on the permissibility of divorce. However, what details we know indicate there is no evidence for it being a derivative work but rather something that may have been inspired by Ibn Rajāʾ's critiques. This episode indicates that Ibn Rajāʾ was part of a larger conversation taking place between Christians and Muslims concerning the integrity of Scriptures.

Būluṣ Ibn Rajāʾ's *Clarity in Truth* demonstrates that passages from the Qurʾan shaped Coptic Christian identity and their views of Islam. His use of the Qurʾan also reveals how Copts reinterpreted its passages to endorse their confessional identity. He cited the Qurʾan to reinforce his historical, socio-political, and theological claims about Islam. As a former Muslim, Ibn Rajāʾ was comfortable citing Qurʾanic passages to critique its historical origins and to question its perceived manipulation in Islamic society. Given that Copts were active agents and contributors to Fatimid society, Ibn Rajāʾ's writings were a significant contribution to the controversies surrounding the Qurʾan at the turn of the eleventh century.

51 Ibid., pp. 40–41.

Bibliography

ʿAbd al-Jabbār, *tathbīt dalāʾil al-nubuwwa*, ed., ʿAbd al-Karim ʿUthman, Beirut, 1966.

Abdel Haleem, M.A.S., trans., *The Qur'an: A New Translation*, Oxford, 2004.

Abel, A., 'L'apologie d'al-Kindī et sa place dans la polémique islamo-chrétienne', in *L'Oriente cristiano nella storia della civiltà. Atti de Convegno internazionale (Rome 31 marzo–3 aprile—Firenze, 4 aprile 1963)*, coll. Problemi attuali de scienza e di cultura, Quaderno n° 62, Rome, 1964, pp. 501–23.

Abū Qurra, Theodore, *'Maymar fī-l-radd ʿalā man yankaru li-llāh al-tajassud'*, in C. Bacha, ed., *Les oeuvres Arabes de Théodore Aboucarra Évêque d'Harran*, Beyrouth, 1904, pp. 180–86.

Abū Rāʾiṭa, Ḥabīb ibn Khidma, *'al-Risāla al-thānīa li-Abī Rāʾiṭa fī-l-tajassud'* in S.T. Keating, ed. and trans., *Defending the 'People of Truth' in the early Islamic period: The Christian apologies of Abū Rāʾiṭah*, Leiden, 2006, pp. 217–97.

Accad, M., *The Gospels in the Muslim and Christian exegetical discourse from the eighth to the fourteenth century*, PhD dissertation, University of Oxford, 2001.

Accad, M., 'Muḥammad's advent as the final criterion for the authenticity of the Judeo-Christian tradition: Ibn Qayyim al-Jawziyya's *Hidāyat al-ḥayārā fī ajwibat al-yahūd wa-ʾl-naṣārā*', in *The Three Rings: Textual studies in the historical trialogue of Judaism, Christianity and Islam*, eds, B. Roggema, M. Poorthuis, and P. Valkenberg, Leuven, 2005, pp. 217–236.

Adang, C., 'Some Hitherto Neglected Material in the Work of Ibn Ḥazm', *Al-Masāq: Studia Arabo-Islamica Mediterranea* 5, 1992, pp. 17–28.

Adang, C., *Muslim writers on Judaism and the Hebrew Bible from Ibn Rabban to Ibn Hazm*, Leiden, 1996.

Adang, C., 'Medieval Muslim polemics against the Jewish Scriptures', in *Muslim perceptions of other religions. A historical survey*, ed., J. Waardenburg, Oxford, 1999, pp. 143–159.

Adang, C., 'Torah', *Encyclopaedia of the Qurʾān*, ed., J.D. McAuliffe, Leiden, 2006, Vol. 5, p. 304.

Adang, C., 'Polemics (Muslim-Jewish)', *Encyclopedia of Jews in the Islamic World*, ed., N.A. Stillman, Brill Online, 2010.

Akhtar, S., *The Quran and the secular mind*, Oxford, 2008.

Akhtar, S., *Islam as political religion*, Oxford, 2010.

Ali, M.M., *Translation of the Holy Quran*, London, 1955.

d'Alverny, M.-T., 'Deux traductions latines du Coran au Moyen Âge', *Archives d'histoire doctrinale et littéraire du Moyen Âge*, n° 22–23, 1947–1948, pp. 69–131.

ʿAmmār al-Baṣrī, *'Kitāb al-burhān'* in M. Hayek, ed., *ʿAmmār al-Baṣrī. Apologie et controverses*, Beirut, 1977, pp. 21–90.

'Ammār al-Baṣrī, '*Kitāb al-masā'il wa-l-ajwiba*' in M. Hayek, ed., *'Ammār al-Baṣrī. Apologie et controverses*, Beirut, 1977, pp. 91–266.

Amir-Moezzi, M.A., 'Le Coran silencieux et le Coran parlant: histoire et écritures à travers l'étude de quelques texts anciens', in M. Azaiez and S. Mervin, eds, *Le Coran. Nouvelles approches*, Paris, 2013.

Al-Anṭākī, *Histoire de Yahyā Ibn Saīd d'Antioche*, ed., I. Kratchovsky, and trans, F. Micheau and G. Troupeau, Turnhout, 1997.

Anthony, S.W., 'The composition of Sayf b. 'Umar's account of King Paul and his corruption of ancient Christianity', *Der Islam*, 85, 2008, pp. 164–202.

Arberry, A., *The Koran interpreted*, Oxford, 1955.

al-Ash'arī, Abū l-Ḥasan. *Maqālāt al-Islamiyyīn*, ed., H. Ritter, Istanbul, 1930.

Atiya, A.S., Y. 'Abd al-Masīḥ, and O.H.E. KHS-Burmester, eds, *History of the patriarchs of the Egyptian Church: known as the history of the Holy Church, Vol. II. Part 1*, Cairo, 1948.

al-Azami, M.M., *The history of the Qur'ānic text from revelation to compilation*, Leicester, 2003.

al-Bakri, M.Ḥ., 'Risālat al-Hāšimī ilà l-Kindī, wa-radd al-Kindī 'alay-hā', *Bulletin of the Faculty of Arts, Fouad I University of Cairo*, May 1947, pp. 29–49.

Bardy, G., ed., *Eusèbe de Césarée, histoire ecclésiastique*, Paris, 1952, 1955, and 1958.

al-Bayḍāwī, *Anwār al-tanzīl wa-asrār al-ta'wīl*, Beirut, 1988.

Beaumont, M., *Christology in dialogue with Muslims*, Carlisle, 2005.

Beaumont, M., "Ammār al-Baṣrī on the alleged corruption of the gospels', in D. Thomas, ed., *The Bible in Arab Christianity*, Leiden, 2007, pp. 241–56.

Beaumont, M., 'Debating the cross in early Christian dialogues with Muslims', in D.E. Singh, ed., *Jesus and the cross: reflections of Christians from Islamic contexts*, Oxford, 2008, pp. 55–64.

Beaumont, M., "Ammār al-Baṣrī', in D. Thomas and B. Roggema, eds, *Christian-Muslim relations. A bibliographical history volume 1 (600–900)*, Leiden, 2009, pp. 604–10.

Beaumont, M., 'Appropriating Christian scriptures in a Muslim refutation of Christianity: the case of *Al-radd al-jamīl* attributed to al-Ghazālī', *Islam and Christian-Muslim Relations* 22, 2011, pp. 69–84.

Beaumont, M., 'Speaking of the Triune God: Christian defence of the Trinity in the early Islamic period', *Transformation* 29, 2012, pp. 111–27.

Beaumont, M, and M. El-Kaisy Friemuth, eds, *Al-Radd al-jamīl*—A Fitting Refutation of the Divinity of Jesus, *attributed to Abū Ḥāmid al-Ghazālī*, Leiden, 2016.

Bell, R., *The Qur'ān: translated, with a critical re-arrangement of the sūras*, Edinburgh, 1937.

Ben-Shammai, H., 'The Attitude of Some Early Karaites Towards Islam', in *Studies in Medieval Jewish History and Literature, Volume II*, ed., I. Twersky, Cambridge, Mass., 1984, pp. 3 40.

Ben Zvi, E., 'The dialogue between Abraham and Yhwh in Gen. 18.23–32: a historical-critical analysis', *Journal for the Study of the Old Testament* 17, 1992, pp. 27–46.

Bertaina, D., 'The development of testimony collections in early Christian apologetics with Islam', in D. Thomas, ed., *The Bible in Arab Christianity*, Leiden, 2007, pp. 151–73.

Bertaina, D., 'Ḥadīth in the Christian Arabic Kalām of Būluṣ Ibn Rajā' (c. 1000)', *Intellectual History of the Islamicate World* 2, 2014, pp. 267–86.

al-Biqāʿī, *Naẓm al-durar fī tanāsub al-āyāt wa 'l-suwar*, Beirut, 1995.

Blachère, R., *Introduction au Coran I–III*, Paris, 1947.

Bobzin, H., 'A Treasury of Heresies': Christian Polemics against the Koran', in S. Wild, ed., *The Qur'ān as Text*, Leiden, 1996, pp. 157–75.

Bobzin, H., 'Translations of the Qur'ān', in *Encyclopaedia of the Qur'ān, volume 5*, Leiden, 2006, pp. 340–58.

Bottini, L., 'The Apology of al-Kindī', in D. Thomas and B. Roggema, eds, *Christian-Muslim relations. A bibliographical history volume 1 (600–900)*, Leiden, 2009, pp. 587–94.

Böwering, G., 'Chronology and the Qur'ān', in J.D. McAuliffe, ed., *Encyclopaedia of the Qur'ān* 1, Leiden, 2001, pp. 316–335.

Böwering, G., 'Recent research on the construction of the Qur'ān', in G.S. Reynolds, ed., *The Qur'ān in its historical context*, London, 2008, pp. 70–87.

Bridger, J.S., *Christian exegesis of the Qur'ān: a critical analysis of the apologetic use of the Qur'ān in select medieval and contemporary Arabic texts*, Eugene, 2015.

Brown, F., S.R. Driver and C.A. Briggs, *Hebrew and English lexicon of the Old Testament*, Boston, 1906.

Bruns, P., 'Briefwechsel min einem Muslim: Al-Kindis Apologie des Christentums (9. Jh.)', in S.H. Griffith and S. Grebenstein, eds, *Christsein in der islamischen Welt*, pp. 269–81.

al-Bukhārī, *Ṣaḥīḥ*, Cairo, 1955.

Burman, T., 'The Influence of the Apology of Al-Kindi and *Contrarietas alfolica* on Ramon Llull's Late Religious Polemics, 1305–1313', *Mediaeval Studies* 53, 1991, pp. 197–228.

Burman, T., *Reading the Qur'ān in Latin Christendom, 1140–1560*, Philadelphia, 2007.

Calder, N., 'The *ummī* in early Islamic juridic literature', *Der Islam* 67, 1990, pp. 111–123.

Chabot, J.-B., *Chronique de Michel le Syrien: Patriarche Jacobite d'Antioche*, Paris, 1899–1910.

Chaine, M., *Grammaire éthiopienne*, Beirut, 2002.

Ciancaglini, C.A., *Iranian loanwords in Syriac*, Wiesbaden, 2008.

Comerro, V., *Les traditions sur la constitution du muṣḥaf de ʿUthmān*, Beyrouth-Würzburg, 2012.

Corriente, F., 'Some notes on the Qur'ānic *lisānun mubīn* and its loanwords', in J.P. Monferrer-Sala and A. Urbán, eds, *Sacred text: explorations in lexicography*, Frankfurt am Main, 2009, pp. 31–45.

Cyril of Jerusalem, *Catecheses ad illuminandos* x.6, eds, W.C. Reischl and J. Rupp, *Cyrilli Hierosolumorum archiepiscopi opera quae supersunt omnia*, 2 vols, Munich, 1948.

al-Dānī, *al-Muqniʿ fī rasm maṣāḥif al-amṣār*, Istanbul, 1932.

Demiri, L., *Muslim exegesis of the Bible in medieval Cairo: Najm al-Dīn al-Ṭūfī's (d. 716/1316) commentary on the Christian Scriptures*, Leiden, 2013.

Den Heijer, J., 'Coptic historiography in the Fāṭimid, Ayyūbid, and early Mamlūk periods', *Medieval Encounters* 2, 1996, pp. 67–98.

Derenbourg, J., ed., *Œuvres complètes de R. Saadia ben Iosef al-Fayyoûmî. Vol. I. Version arabe du Pentateuque*, Paris, 1893.

Dietrich, F., *Arabisch-deutsches Handwörterbuch zum Koran und Thier und Mensch vor dem König der Genien*, Leipzig, 1894.

Donner, F.M., 'Sayf b. 'Umar,' *Encyclopaedia of Islam* 9, 1997, p. 102.

Ebied, R.Y. and D. Thomas, eds, *Muslim-Christian polemic during the Crusades, the letter from the people of Cyprus and Ibn Abī Ṭālib al-Dimashqī's response*, Leiden, 2005.

Eisenman, R. and M. Wise, *The Dead Sea Scrolls uncovered. The first complete translation and interpretation of 50 key documents withheld for over 35 years*, New York, 1993.

Elias of Nisibis, '*Kitāb al-majālis*', in L. Cheikho, ed., *Trois traits de polémique et de théologie chrétiennes*, Beyrouth, 1923, pp. 26–71.

Elmarsafy, Z., *The Enlightenment Qur'ān: The Politics of Translation and the Construction of Islam*, Oxford, 2009.

Ephrem Syrus, *In Genesim*, ed. and trans., R.-M. Tonneau, CSCO 152–153, Louvain, 1955.

Epp, E.J. and G.D. Fee, *Studies in the theory and method of New Testament textual criticism*, Grand Rapids, 1992.

Epstein, I., ed., and E.W. Kirzner, trans., *Babylonian Talmud; Seder Nizikin*, London, 1935.

Eutychius of Alexandria, *Annals*, ed., L. Cheikho, Beirut, 1906.

Evans, E., ed., *Tertullian adversus Marcionem*, Oxford, 1972.

Firestone, R., 'The Qur'ān and the Bible: some modern studies of their relationship', in J.C. Reeves, ed., *Bible and the Qur'ān: essays in Scriptural intertextuality*, Leiden, 2003, pp. 11–16.

Foote, G. and J.M. Wheeler, *The Jewish life of Christ: being the sepher toldoth Jeshu*, London, 1885.

Frank, R.M., *Beings and their attributes; the teaching of the Basrian school of the Muʿtazila in the classical period*, Albany, 1978.

Freedman, H. and M. Simon, eds, *The Midrash Rabbah*, London, 1977.

Freytag, G.W., *Lexicon arabico-latinum*, Halle, 1830–37.

Gallo, M., trans., *Palestinese anonimo: omelia arabo-cristiana dell'VIII secolo*, Rome, 1994.

Gammie, J.G., 'Paraenetic literature: towards the morphology of a secondary genre', *Semeia* 50, 1990, pp. 41–77.

Gibson, M.D., ed., and trans., *An Arabic version of the Acts of the Apostles; with a treatise on the triune nature of God with translation, from the same codex*, London, 1899.

Ginzberg, L., *The legends of the Jews*, Philadelphia, 1901–1938.

Goldfeld, Y., 'The illiterate prophet (*nabī ummī*): An inquiry into the development of a dogma in Islamic tradition', *Der Islam* 57, 1980, pp. 58–67.

Goldziher, I., 'Über muhammedanische Polemik gegen Ahl al-Kitab', *Zeitschrift der Deutschen Morgenländischen Gesellschaft* 32, 1878, pp. 341–87.

González Muñoz, F., *Exposición y refutación del Islam: la versión latina de las epístolas de al-Hāšimi y al-Kindi.* A Coruña, 2005.

Gottheil, R., 'A distinguished family of Fatimide cadis (al-Nu'mān) in the tenth century', *Journal of the American Oriental Society* 27, 1906, pp. 217–96.

Graf, G., 'Christliche-arabische Texte. Zwei Disputationen zwischen Muslimen und Christen', in F. Bilabel and A. Grohmann, eds, *Griechische, koptische und arabische Texte zur Religion und religiösen Literatur in Ägyptens Spätzeit*, Heidelberg, 1934, pp. 8–23.

Graf, G., *Die Schriften des Jacobiten Ḥabīb ibn Hidma Abū Rāiṭa*, Corpus Scriptorum Christianorum Orientalium 130–131, Louvain, 1951.

Griffith, S.H., 'The concept of *al-uqnūm* in 'Ammār al-Baṣrī's apology for the doctrine of the Trinity', in S.K. Samir, ed., *Actes du premier congrès international d'Études arabes Chrétiennes*, Rome, 1982, pp. 161–91.

Griffith, S.H., "Ammār al-Baṣrī's *Kitāb al-Burhān*: Christian kalām in the first Abbasid century', *Le Museon* 96, 1983, pp. 145–81.

Griffith, S.H., 'The Prophet Muḥammad, his scripture and his message according to Christian apologies in Arabic and Syriac from the first Abbasid century', in *La vie du Prophète Mahomet. Colloque de Strasbourg (octobre 1980)*, (Bibliothèque des Centres d'Études Supérieures spécialisées), Paris, 1983.

Griffith, S.H., 'The Gospel in Arabic: an inquiry into its appearance in the first Abbasid century', *Oriens Christianus* 69, 1985, pp. 126–67.

Griffith, S.H., 'Anastasios of Sinai, the *Hodegos* and the Muslims', *Greek Orthodox Theological Review* 32, 1987, pp. 341–58.

Griffith, S.H., 'The monks of Palestine and the growth of Christian literature in Arabic', *The Muslim World* 78, 1988, pp. 1–28.

Griffith, S.H., 'The Qur'ān in Arab Christian texts; the development of an apologetical argument: Abū Qurrah in the mağlis of al-Ma'mūn', *Parole de l'Orient* 24, 1999, pp. 203–33.

Griffith, S.H., 'Disputing with Muslims in Syriac: The Case of the Monk of Bêt Ḥālê with a Muslim Emir', *Hugoye* 3, 2000, http://syrcom.cua.edu/Hugoye/Vol3No1/HV3N1/Griffith.html.

Griffith, S.H., 'Christians and Christianity', in *Encyclopaedia of the Qur'ān 1*, ed., J.D. McAuliffe, Leiden, 2001, pp. 307–16.

Griffith, S.H., 'Answers for the Shaykh: A 'Melkite' Arabic Text from Sinai and the Doctrines of the Trinity and the Incarnation in 'Arab Orthodox' Apologetics', in

E. Grypeou, M. Swanson and D. Thomas, eds, *The Encounter of Eastern Christianity with Early Islam*, Leiden, 2006, pp. 277–309.

Griffith, S.H., *The church in the shadow of the mosque*, Princeton, 2008.

Griffith, S.H., 'John of Damascus and the Church in Syria in the Umayyad Era: The Intellectual and Cultural Milieu of Orthodox Christians in the World of Islam', *Hugoye* 11, 2008, http://syrcom.cua.edu/Hugoye/Vol11No2/HV11N2/Griffith.html

Griffith, S.H., *The Bible in Arabic: the scriptures of the "People of the Book" in the language of Islam*, Princeton, 2013.

Griffith, S.H., 'Paul of Antioch', in S. Noble and A. Treiger, eds, *The Orthodox Church in the Arab world, 700–1700*, p. 216–19.

Grypeou, E. and H. Spurling, 'Abraham's angels: Jewish and Christian exegesis of Genesis 18–19', in E. Grypeou and H. Spurling, *The exegetical encounter between Jews and Christians in late antiquity*, Leiden, 2009, pp. 181–203.

Guillaume, A., *The life of Muḥammad: a translation of (ibn) Isḥāq's "sīrat rasūl allāh"*, London, 1955.

Guillaume, A., 'New Light on the Life of Muhammad', *Journal of Semitic Studies*, Monograph No. 1, Manchester, n.d.

Haag, H., 'Abraham und Lot in Gen 18–19', in A. Caquot and M. Delcor, eds, *Mélanges bibliques et orientaux. Festschrift M. Henri Cazelles*, Kevelaer, 1981, pp. 173–179.

Haddad, W.Z., 'A tenth-century speculative theologian's refutation of the basic doctrines of Christianity: al-Bāqillānī (d. A.D. 1013)', in Y.Y. Haddad and W.Z. Haddad, eds, *Christian-Muslim encounters*, Gainsville, 1995, pp. 82–94.

ibn Ḥanbal, Aḥmad. *Musnad*, Cairo, 1931.

Halkin, A.S., ed., and B. Cohen, trans., *Moses Maimonides' epistle to Yemen: The Arabic original and the three Hebrew versions*, New York, 1952.

Hayek, M., "Ammār al-Baṣrī. La première somme de théologie chrétienne en langue arabe, ou deux apologies du christianisme', *Islamochristiana* 2, 1976, pp. 69–133.

Ibn Ḥazm al-Andalusī. *Kitāb al-fiṣal fī al-milal wa-al-ahwā' wa-al-niḥal*, Cairo, 1939–44.

Heffening, W., 'mut'a', *Encyclopaedia of Islam* 7, Leiden, 1993, pp. 757–9.

Hirschberg, H., 'Allusions to the Apostle Paul in the Talmud', *Journal of Biblical Literature*, 62, 1943, pp. 73–87.

Hirschfeld, H., *New researches into the composition and exegesis of the Qoran*, London, 1902.

Ibn Hishām, *Al-sīrat al-nabawiyya*, ed., F. Wüstenfeld, Gottingen, 1858.

Hoover, J., 'The Apologetic and Pastoral Intentions of Ibn Qayyim al-Jawziyya's Polemic against Jews and Christians', *Muslim World* 100, 2010, pp. 476–89.

Hoover, J., 'Kitāb hidāyat al-ḥayārā fī ajwibat al-Yahūd wa-l-Naṣārā', *Christian-Muslim relations. A bibliographical history*, ed., D. Thomas, Brill Online, 2013.

Hopkins, J., *Nicholas of Cusa's De Pace Fidei and Cribratio Alkorani: translation and analysis*, 2nd ed., Minneapolis, 1994.
Horowitz, J., 'Tawrāt', *Encyclopaedia of Islam*, eds, M.Th. Houtsma et al., Leiden, 1934, vol. 4, pp. 706–707.
Horovitz, J., "Abd Allāh Ibn Salām', *Encyclopaedia of Islam* 1, Leiden, 1979, p. 52.
Hoyland, R., *Seeing Islam as others saw it*, Princeton, 1997.
Husseini, S.L. *Early Christian-Muslim Debate on the Unity of God*, Leiden, 2014.
Ignatius, *ad Antiochenos*, eds, F.X. Funk and F. Diekamp, in *Patres apostolic*, Tübingen, 1913.
Isho'dad of Merv, *Commentaire d'Iṣo'dad de Merv sur l'Ancient Testament. I. Genèse*, eds, J.-M. Vosté and C. van den Eynde, trans., C. van den Eynde, CSCO 126–156, Louvain, 1950–55.
Jackson, S.A., *Islamic Law and the State: The Constitutional Jurisprudence of Shihāb al-Dīn al-Qarāfī*, Leiden, 1966.
Jackson, S.A., 'S̱hihāb al-Dīn al-Ḳarāfī', *Encyclopaedia of Islam, second edition*, Brill Online, 2013.
James, M.R., ed., *Visio Pauli* 39, *Apocrypha anecdota*, Cambridge, 1893.
Janosik, D.J., 'John of Damascus: first apologist to the Muslims', PhD dissertation, London School of Theology, 2011.
Ibn al-Jawzī, Abū al-Faraj 'Abd al-Rahmān bin 'Alī bin Muḥammad, *al-muntazam fī tarīkh al-umam wa al-mulūk*, Beirut, 1992.
Jeffery, A., *Materials for the history of the text of the Qur'an: the old codices* (*Kitāb al-Maṣāḥif* of Ibn Abī Dāwūd together with a collection of the variant readings), Leiden, 1937.
Jeffery, A., 'Ghevond's text of the correspondence between 'Umar II and Leo III', *Harvard Theological Review* 37, 1944, pp. 269–321.
Josephus, *Jewish Antiquities*, trans. H.St.J. Thackeray, London, 1930.
Josephus, *The Jewish War*, trans. H.St.J. Thackeray, London, 1928.
Julius Africanus, *Chronographiae* (fragmenta), IX ed., M.J. Routh, *Reliquiae sacrae*, Oxford, 1846 [rep. Hildesheim, 1974].
Justin Martyr, Dialog, ed., E.J. Goodspeed, *Die ältesten Apologeten*, Göttingen, 1915.
Juynboll, G.H.A., *Encyclopaedia of Canonical Ḥadīth*, Leiden, 2007.
El Kaisy-Friemuth, M., 'Al-ajwiba l-fākhira 'an al-as'ila l-fājira fī l-radd 'alā l-milla l-kāfira', *Christian-Muslim relations. A bibliographical history*, ed., D. Thomas, Brill Online, 2013.
Ibn Kammūna, *Examination of the Three Faiths*, trans. M. Perlmann, Berkeley, 1971.
ibn Kathīr, Ismā'īl ibn 'Umar, *Tafsīr al-Qur'ān al-'Aẓīm*, ed., Muṣṭafā al-Sayyid Muḥammad, Jīza, 2000.
Ibn Kathīr, *Qiṣaṣ al-anbiyā'*, Cairo, 1918.

Katsh, A.I., *Judaism in Islam. Biblical and Talmudic backgrounds of the Koran and its commentaries*, New York, 1980.

Keating, S.T., *Defending the "People of Truth" in the early Islamic period: the Christian apologies of Abū Rā'iṭah*, Leiden, 2006.

Keating, S.T., 'An early list of the Ṣifāt Allāh in Abū Rā'iṭa al-Takrītī's "First Risāla 'On the Holy Trinity'", *Jerusalem Studies in Arabic and Islam* 36, 2009, pp. 339–355.

Kermani, N., *God is Beautiful: The Aesthetic Experience of the Quran*, Cambridge, 2015.

Khalidi, T., *Arabic historical thought in the classical period*, Cambridge, 1994.

Khoury, A.-T., *Polémique byzantine contre l'Islam (VIIIᵉ–XIIIᵉ S.)*, Leiden, 1972.

Khoury, P., *Paul d'Antioche, évêque melkite de Sidon (xiiᵉ s.)*, Beirut, 1964.

al-Kindī, *Apologia del Cristianesimo*, Traduzione dall'Arabo, Introduzione a cura di Laura Bottini, Patrimonio Culturale Arabo Cristiano 4, Milano, 1998.

al-Kisā'ī, *Qiṣaṣ al-anbiyā'*, ed., I. Eisenberg, Leiden, 1922–23.

Koningsveld, P.S. van, 'The Islamic image of Paul and the origin of the Gospel of Barnabas,' *Jerusalem Studies in Arabic and Islam* 20, 1996, pp. 200–28.

Koningsveld, P.S. van, 'The Apology of Al-Kindî', in T.L. Hettema and A. Van der Kooij, eds, *Religious polemics in context*, Assen, 2004, pp. 69–92.

Kotter, B., *Die Schriften Des Johannes Von Damaskos*, New York, 1981.

Kritzeck, J., *Peter the Venerable and Islam*, Princeton, 1964.

Lagarde, P. de, ed., *Materialien zur Kritik und Geschichte des Pentateuchs*, Leipzig, 1867.

Landron, B., *Chrétiens et Musulmans en Irak: Attitudes Nestoriennes vis-à-vis de l'islam*, Paris, 1994.

Lazarus-Yafeh, H., *Intertwined worlds. Medieval Islam and Bible criticism*, Princeton, 1992.

Lazarus-Yafeh, H., 'Tawrāt', *Encyclopaedia of Islam*, New Edition, P.J. Bearman et al., eds, Leiden, 2000, Vol. X, p. 394.

Lecomte, G., 'Les citations de l'Ancien et du Nouveau Testament dans l'œuvre d'Ibn Qutayba', *Arabica* 5, 1958, pp. 34–46.

Le Coz, R., ed., *Jean Damascène: Écrits sur Islam*, Paris, 1992.

Leemhuis, F., 'Lūṭ and his people in the Koran and its early commentaries', in E. Noort, and E.J.C. Tigchelaar, eds, *Sodom's sin: Genesis 18–19 and its interpretation*, Leiden, 2004, pp. 97–113.

Lenzi, G., et al., *Afraate. Le esposizioni vol. I–II*, Brescia, 2012.

Leslau, W., *Comparative dictionary of Geʿez (Classical Ethiopic)*, Wiesbaden, 1991.

Lowin, S., 'Revision and Alteration', *Encyclopaedia of the Qur'ān*, ed., J.D. McAuliffe, Leiden, 2004, vol. 4, p. 450.

Madelung, W., 'Al-Qāsim ibn Ibrāhīm', in D. Thomas and B. Roggema, eds, *Christian-Muslim relations. A bibliographical history volume 1 (600–900)*, Leiden, 2009, pp. 540–3.

Madigan, D.A., *The Qur'ān's Self-Image: Writing and Authority in Islam's Scripture*, Princeton, 2001.

Marcuzzo, G.B., ed. and trans., *Le Dialogue d'Abraham de Tibériade avec 'Abd al-Raḥmān al-Hāšimī à Jérusalem vers 820*, Rome, 1986.

Margoliouth, D.S., 'On "The book of religion and empire" by 'Ali b. Rabban al-Tabari', *Proceedings of the British Academy* 16, 1930, p. 170.

Maróth, M. *'Ammār al-Baṣrī: Das Buch des Beweises*, Piliscsaba, 2015.

Martinez, F.J., 'La Literatura Apocalíptica y las Primeras Reacciones Cristianas a la conquista islámica en Oriente', in G. Anes and Á. de Castrillón, eds, *Europa y el Islam*, Madrid, 2003, pp. 143–222.

Masson, D., *Le Coran et la révélation judéo-chrétienne. Études comparées*, Paris, 1958.

McAuliffe, J.D., 'The Qur'ānic Context of Muslim Biblical Scholarship', *Islam and Christian-Muslim Relations* 7, 1996, pp. 141–158.

McAuliffe, J.D., 'The prediction and prefiguration of Muḥammad', in *Bible and Qur'ān: Essays in scriptural intertextuality*, ed., J.C. Reeves, Atlanta, 2003, pp. 107–31.

Meyer, D.Y., Simoens, and S. Bencheikh, *Les versets douloureux. Bible, Evangile et Coran*, Bruxelles, 2008.

Michel, T.F., *A Muslim Theologian's Response to Christianity: Ibn Taymiyya's al-Jawab al-Sahih*, Delmar, 1984.

Mikhail, W. 'Ammār al-Baṣrī's *Kitāb al-Burhān*: A Topical and Theological Analysis of Arabic Christian Theology in the Ninth Century, PhD dissertation, University of Birmingham, 2013.

Mingana, A., *The book of religion and empire: a semi-official defence and exposition of Islam written by order at the court and with the assistance of the caliph Mutawakkil (A.D. 847–861) by 'Alī al-Ṭabarī*, Manchester, 1922.

Mingana, A., 'The apology of Timothy the Patriarch before the Caliph Mahdi', *Bulletin of the John Rylands Library* 12, 1928, pp. 137–226.

Monferrer-Sala, J.P., '*Marginalia semitica.* II: entre la tradición y la lingüística', *Aula Orientalis* 25, 2007, pp. 115–17.

Monferrer Sala, J.P., 'Elias of Nisibis', in D. Thomas and A. Mallett, eds, *Christian-Muslim relations: a bibliographical history, volume 2 (900–1050)*, Leiden, 2010, pp. 727–41.

Monferrer-Sala, J.P., '"The Antichrist is coming ..." The making of an apocalyptic *topos* in Arabic (Ps.-Athanasius, Vat. ar. 158 / Par. Ar. 153/32)', in D. Bumazhnov et al. eds, *Bibel, Byzanz und christlicher Orient. Festschrift für Stephen Gerö zum 65. Geburtstag*, Louvain, 2011, pp. 653–78.

Monferrer-Sala, J.P., '"Texto", "subtexto" e "hipotexto" en el "Apocalipsis del Pseudo Atanasio" copto-árabe', in R.G. Khoury, J.P. Monferrer-Sala and M.J. Viguera Molins, eds, *Legendaria Medievalia en honor de Concepción Castillo Castillo*, Córdoba, 2011, pp. 403–21.

Monferrer-Sala, J.P., 'Maimonides under the messianic turmoil: Standardized apocalyptic *topoi* on Muḥammad's prophecy in *al-Risālah al-yamaniyyah*', in *Judæo-Arabic culture in al-Andalus: Proceedings of the 13th Conference of the society for Judæo-Arabic studies, Cordoba 2007*, ed., A. Ashur, Cordoba, 2013, pp. 173–196.

Monferrer Sala, J.P., 'Ibn Ḥazm', *Christian-Muslim relations. A bibliographical history*, ed., D. Thomas, Brill Online, 2013.

Motzki, H., 'The collection of the Qur'ān', *Der Islam* 78, 2001, pp. 1–34.

Motzki, H., 'Alternative accounts of the Qur'ān's formation', in J.D. McAuliffe, ed., *The Cambridge Companion to the Qur'ān*, New York, 2006, pp. 59–75.

Muir, W., *The apology of al Kindy written at the court of al-Mâmûn (circa A.H. 215; A.D. 830) in defence of Christianity against Islam*, London, Second Edition, 1887.

Muñoz, F.G., ed., *Exposición y refutación del Islam: la versión de las epistolas de al-Hāšimī y al-Kindī*, La Coruña, 2005.

Muqātil ibn Sulaymān, *Tafsīr Muqātil ibn Sulaymān*, ed., ʿA.M. Shihāta, Beirut, 2002.

Ibn Muṭarrif al-Ṭarafī, *Qiṣaṣ al-anbiyā'*, ed., R. Tottoli, Berlin, 2003.

al-Nadīm, *Al-Fihrist li-bn al-Nadīm*, ed., G. Flügel, Beyrouth, 1964.

al-Nadīm, *The Fihrist of Al-Nadīm*, ed., A.F. Sayyid, London, 2009.

Nasry, W., *The caliph and the bishop: a* 9th *century Muslim-Christian debate: al-Ma'mūn and Abū Qurrah*, Beirut, 2008.

Neuwirth, A., *Studien zur Komposition der mekkanischen Suren*, Berlin, 1996.

Neuwirth, A., 'Vom Rezitationstext über die Liturgie zum Kanon', in S. Wild, ed., *The Qur'ān as Text*, Leiden, 1996, pp. 69–105.

Neuwirth, A., 'Myths and legends in the Qur'ān', in J.D. McAuliffe, ed., *Encyclopaedia of the Qur'ān* 3, Leiden, 2003, pp. 477–497.

Neuwirth, A., 'Meccan text—Medinan additions? Politics and the re-reading of liturgical communications', in *Words, texts and concepts cruising the Mediterranean Sea*, eds, R. Arnzen and J. Thielmann, Leuven, 2004, pp. 71–93.

Newman, N.A., ed., *The early Christian-Muslim dialogue: a collection of documents from the first three Islamic centuries (632–900 A.D.); translations with commentary*, Hatfield, 1993.

Nickel, G., *Narratives of tampering in the earliest commentaries on the Qur'ān*, Leiden, 2011.

Nickel, G., 'Erzälungen über zuverlässige Texte—vergnügliches Lesen, bei dem der islamische Fälschungsvorwurf geprüft wird', In *Der Islam als historische, politische und theologische Herausforderung*, eds, C. Schirrmacher and T. Schirrmacher, Bonn, 2013, pp. 23–34.

Nickel, G., *The gentle answer to the Muslim accusation of scriptural falsification*, Calgary, 2015.

Nöldeke, T. and Schwally, F., *Geschichte des Qorâns*, Leipzig, 1909.

Noort, E., 'For the sake of righteousness. Abraham's negotiations with YHWH as prologue to the Sodom narrative: Genesis 18:16–33', in E. Noort and E.J.C. Tigchelaar, eds, *Sodom's sin: Genesis 18–19 and its interpretation*, Leiden, 2004, pp. 3–15.

Obermann, J., 'Koran and Agada: The events at Mount Sinai', *The American Journal of Semitic Languages* 57, 1941, pp. 23–48.

Origène, *Contre Celse*, ed., M. Borret, Paris, 1967–9.

Payne Smith, R., *Thesaurus syriacus*, Oxford, 1879 and 1901.

Perlmann, M., 'The medieval polemics between Islam and Judaism', in *Religion in a Religious Age*, ed., S.D. Goitein, Cambridge, Mass., 1974, pp. 103–138.

Peters, F.E., *The children of Abraham: Judaism, Christianity, Islam*, Princeton, 2004.

Pietruschka, U., 'Die Verwendung und Funktion von Koranzitaten in christlichen Apologien der frühen Abbasidenzeit (Mitte 8. Jahrhundert—Anfang 10. Jahrhundert)', in W. Beltz and J. Tubach, eds, *Religiöser Text und soziale Struktur*, Halle, 2001, pp. 271–88.

Platti, E., 'Il contesto teologico dell'apprezzamento dell'Islam di S. Tommaso', in D. Lorenz and S. Serafini, eds, *Studi 1995*, Roma, 1995, pp. 294–307.

Platti, E., 'Des Arabes chrétiens et le Coran: Pérennité d'une polémique', in D. De Smet, G. de Callataÿ, and J.M.F. Van Reeth, eds, *Al-Kitāb: La sacralité du texte dans le monde de l'Islam*, Bruxelles, Louvain-la-Neuve, Leuven, 2004, pp. 333–45.

Platti, E., 'L'image de l'islam chez le Dominicain Vincent de Beauvais (m. 1264)', *Mélanges de l'Institut Dominicain d'Etudes Orientales* 25–26 (2004) pp. 65–140.

Platti, E., *Islam, friend or foe?* Louvain, 2008.

Platti, E., 'Criteria for authenticity of prophecy in 'Abd al-Masīḥ al-Kindī's risāla', in A. Rippin and R. Tottoli, eds, *Books and written culture of the Islamic world. Studies presented to Claude Gilliot on the occasion of his 75th birthday*, Leiden, 2015, pp. 3–25.

de Prémare, A.-L., *Aux origines du Coran*, Paris, 2004.

Pulcini, T., *Exegesis as polemical discourse: Ibn Ḥazm on Jewish and Christian scriptures*, Atlanta, 1998.

Putman, H., *L'Église et l'Islam sous Timothée I (780–823)*, Beirut, 1975.

al-Qarafī, Ahmad ibn Idris, *al-ajwiba al-fākhira 'an al-as'ila al fājira*, Cairo, 1987.

al-Qāsim ibn Ibrāhīm, 'Al-radd 'alā al-Naṣārā', in I. Di Matteo, ed., 'Confutazione contro i Christiani dello Zaydati al-Qāsim b. Ibrāhīm, *Revista degli Studi Orientali* 9, 1921–2, pp. 301–31.

al-Qurtubī, Muḥammad ibn Aḥmad, *Al-Jāmi' al-aḥkām al-qur'ān*, Beirut, 2006.

al-Rāzī, *Al-Tafsīr al-kabīr li-imām al-Fakhr al-Rāzī*, Beirut, 1973.

Reinink, G.J., 'Bible and Qur'an in early Syriac Christian-Islamic Disputation', in Martin Tamcke, ed., *Christians and Muslims in dialogue in the Islamic orient of the middle ages*, Beirut, 2007, pp. 57–72.

Reynolds, G.S., 'A medieval Islamic polemic against certain practices and doctrines of the East Syrian Church: introduction, excerpts and commentary', in D. Thomas, ed., *Christians at the heart of Islamic rule*, Leiden, 2003, pp. 215–30.

Reynolds, G.S., *A Muslim theologian in the sectarian milieu: 'Abd al-Jabbār and the critique of Christian origins*, Leiden, 2004.

Reynolds, G.S., *The Qur'ān and Its Biblical subtext*, Oxford, 2010.

Reynolds, G.S., "Abd al-Jabbār', in D. Thomas and A. Mallett, eds, *Christian-Muslim relations. a bibliographical history volume 2 (900–1050)*, Leiden, 2010, pp. 594–609.

Reynolds, G.S., 'On the Qur'ānic accusation of scriptural falsification (*taḥrīf*) and Christian anti-Jewish polemic', *Journal of the American Oriental Society* 130, 2010, pp. 189–202.

Reynolds, G.S., 'Le problème de la chronologie du Coran', *Arabica* 58, 2011, pp. 477–502.

Reynolds, G.S. and S.K. Samir, eds, and trans, *'Abd al-Jabbār: critique of Christian origins*, Provo, 2010.

Rippin, A., 'Interpreting the Bible through the Qur'ān', in *Approaches to the Qur'an*, eds, G.R. Hawting and A.A. Shareef, London, 1993, pp. 249–259.

Rippin, A., 'al-sidjistānī', *Encyclopaedia of Islam* 9, Leiden, 1997, pp. 546–7.

Rissanen, S., *Theological encounters of Oriental Christians with Islam during early Abbasid rule*, Åbo, 1993.

Roggema, B., 'A Christian Reading of the Qur'ān: The Legend of Sergius-Baḥīrā and Its Use of Qur'ān and Sīrā', in D. Thomas, ed., *Syrian Christians under Islam; the First Thousand Years*, Leiden, 2001, pp. 57–73.

Roggema, B., *The legend of Sergius Bahira: Eastern Christian apologetics and apocalyptic in response to Islam*, Leiden, 2009.

Roggema, B., 'The confession which Kaʿb al-Aḥbār handed down to the Ishmaelites', in D. Thomas and B. Roggema, eds, *Christian-Muslim relations. a bibliographical history volume 1 (600–900)*, Leiden, 2009, pp. 403–5.

Roggema, B., 'The disputation between a monk of Bēt Ḥālē and an Arab notable', in D. Thomas and B. Roggema, eds, *Christian-Muslim relations. a bibliographical history volume 1 (600–900)*, Leiden, 2009, pp. 268–73.

Roggema, B., 'Risālat Abī l-Rabīʿ Muḥammad ibn al-Layth allatī katabahā li-l-Rashīd ilā Qusṭanṭīn malik al-Rūm', *Christian-Muslim relations. A bibliographical history*, ed., David Thomas, Brill Online, 2013.

Rousseau, A. and L. Doutreleau, *Irénée de Lyon. Contre les heresies*, Paris, 1974.

Rubin, U., *The Eye of the beholder: The life of Muḥammad as viewed by the early Muslims: a textual analysis*, Princeton, 1995.

Saʿd, 'A., ed., *Al-Sīrat an-nabawwiyyah l'ibn Hishām*, 4 vols, Beirut, 1975.

Ibn Saʿd, *Kitāb al-ṭabaqāt al-kubrā*, Beirut, 1937.

Sadeghi, B., 'The chronology of the Qur'ān: a stylometric research program, *Arabica* 58, 2011, pp. 210–299.

Sahas, D.J., *John of Damascus on Islam: the "Heresy of the Ishmaelites"*, Leiden, 1972.

Sahas, D.J., 'The Formation of Later Islamic Doctrines as a Response to Byzantine Polemics: The miracles of Muhammad', *Greek Orthodox Theological Review* 27, 1982, pp. 307–324.

Saleh, W., '"Sublime in its style, exquisite in its tenderness": The Hebrew Bible quotations in al-Biqāʿī's Qur'ān commentary', in *Adaptations and innovations*, eds, Y.T. Langermann and J. Stern, Paris, 2007, pp. 331–47.

Samir, S.K., 'Notes sur la 'lettre à un musulman de Sidon' de Paul d'Antioche', *Orientalia Lovaniensia Periodica* 24, 1993, pp. 179–95.

Samir, S.K., 'The earliest Arab apology for Christianity (c. 750)' in S.K. Samir and J.S. Nielsen, eds, *Christian Arabic apologetics during the Abbasid period (750–1258)*, Leiden, 1994, pp. 57–116.

Samir, S.K., *Foi et culture en Irak au XIe siècle*, Aldershot, 1996.

Samir, S.K., 'La version latine de l'Apologie d'al-Kindi (vers 830 ap. J.-C.) et son original arabe', in M. Penelas, P. Roisse and C. Aillet, eds, *¿Existe una identidad mozárabe? Historia, lengua y cultura de los cristianos de al-Andalus (siglos IX–XII)*, Madrid, 2007, pp. 33–82.

Sarrió Cucarella, D.R., *Muslim-Christian Polemics across the Mediterranean: The Splendid Replies of Shihāb al-Dīn al-Qarāfī (d.684/1285)*, Leiden, 2014.

Sayf, ibn 'Umar al-Tamīmī. *kitab al-ridda wa al-futuh and kitab al-jamal wa masir 'A'isha wa 'Ali*, Leiden, 1995.

Schmid, N.K., 'Quantitative text analysis and its application to the Qur'ān: some preliminary considerations', in A. Neuwirth, N. Sinai and M. Marx, eds, *The Qur'ān in context: historical and literary investigations into the Qur'ānic milieu*, Leiden, 2010, pp. 441–460.

Schmidtke, S., 'The Muslim Reception of Biblical Materials: Ibn Qutayba and his *Āʿlam al-nubuwwa*', *Islam and Christian-Muslim Relations* 22, 2011, pp. 249–274.

Schmidtke, S., 'The Muslim reception of the Bible: al-Māwardī and his *Kitāb aʿlām an-nubbuwwa*', in *Le Sacre Scritture e le loro interpretazioni*, eds, C. Baffioni, R.B. Finazzi, A.P. Dell'Acqua and E. Vergani, Milan/Rome, 2015, pp. 71–97.

Schmitz, M., 'Kaʿb al-Aḥbār', *Encyclopaedia of Islam* 4, Leiden, 1978, pp. 316–17.

Sĕʿadyah, Ibn Danān., *Libro de las raíces*, ed., and trans., M. Jiménez Sánchez, Granada, 2004.

Sefer Pirqê Rabî 'Elîʿezer, Warsaw, 1870.

Sendino, J.M., 'Al-Kindi, Apologia del Christianismo', *Miscelanea Comillas* 11 and 12, 1949, pp. 339–460.

al-Sharfī, ʿA. M., ʿAl-Fikr al-islāmī fī l-radd ʿalā l-naṣārā ilā nihāyat al-qarn al-rābīʿ al-ʿāshirʾ, in *Kulliyyat al-ādāb wa-l-ʿulūm al-insāniyya, Tūnis, al-silsila al-sādisa* 29, Tūnis, 1986.

Sinai, N., 'Qurʾānic self-referentiality as a strategy of self-authorization', in S. Wild, ed., *Self-Referentiality in the Qurʾān*, Wiesbaden, 2006, pp. 103–134.

Sinai, N., 'The Qurʾān as a process', in A. Neuwirth, N. Sinai and M. Marx, eds, *The Qurʾān in context: historical and literary investigations into the Qurʾānic milieu*, Leiden, 2010, pp. 407–439.

Sozomen, *Historia ecclesiastica* II.4, eds, J. Bidez and G.C. Hansen, Sozomenus, *Kirchengeschichte*, Berlin, 1960.

Stern, S., "Abd al-Jabbār's account of how Christ's religion was falsified by the adoption of Roman customs', *Journal of Theological Studies* 18, 1968, pp. 128–85.

Stol, M., 'Blindness and night-blindness in Akkadian', *Journal of Near Eastern Studies* 45, 1986, pp. 295–9.

al-Suyūṭī, Jalāl al-Dīn. *al-Itqān fī ʿulūm al-Qurʾan*, Cairo, 1967.

Swanson, M., 'Some considerations for the dating of *fī tatlīt allāh wāḥid* (Sinai Ar. 154) and *al-gāmiʿ wugūh al-īmān* (London, British Library op. 4950)' *Parole de L'Orient* 18, 1993, pp. 118–141.

Swanson, M.N., 'Abū Nūḥ al-Anbārī', in D. Thomas and B. Roggema, eds, *Christian-Muslim relations: a bibliographical history volume I (600–900)*, Leiden, 2009, pp. 397–400.

Swanson, M., 'Būluṣ ibn Rajā", in D. Thomas and A. Mallett, eds, *Christian-Muslim relations. a bibliographical history volume 2 (900–1050)*, Leiden, 2010, pp. 541–46.

Swanson, M., 'An apology for the Christian faith', in S. Noble and A. Treiger eds, *The Orthodox Church in the Arab world, 700–1700, an anthology of sources*, DeKalb, 2014, pp. 40–59.

Szilágyi, K., 'Muḥammad and the Monk: The Making of the Christian Baḥīrā Legend', *Jerusalem Studies in Arabic and Islam* 34, 2008, pp. 169–214.

Szilágyi, K., 'Christian Learning about Islam in the Early Abbāsid Caliphate: The Muslim Sources of the *Disputation of the Monk Abraham of Tiberias*', in J. Scheiner and D. Janos, eds, *The Place to Go: Contexts of Learning in Baghdād, 750–1000 C.E.*, Princeton, 2014, pp. 267–342.

al-Ṭabarī, Abu Jaʿfar., *The History of Ṭabarī XVI. The Community divided*, trans., A. Brockett, Albany, 1985.

al-Ṭabarī, Abu Jaʿfar., *Jāmiʿ al-bayān fī taʾwīl al-qurʾān*, Beirut, 2005.

al-Ṭabarī, ʿAlī ibn Rabbān., 'Radd ʿalā al-Naṣārā', eds, I.-A. Khalife and W. Kutsch, *Mélanges de L'université Saint Joseph* 36, 1959, pp. 113–48.

Ibn aṭ-Ṭaiyib, *Commentaire sur la Genèse*, edité et traduit par J.C.J. Sanders, 2 vol., CSCO 274–275, Louvain, 1967.

Tartar, G., *Dialogue islamo-chrétien sous le calife al-Ma'mūn. Les épîtres d'al-Hāshimī et d'al-Kindī*. Thèse pour le Doctorat de 3e cycle, Strasbourg, 1977.

Tartar, G., 'L'authenticité des épîtres d'al-Hāsimī et d'al-Kindī sous le calife al-Ma'mūn (813–834)' in K. Samir, ed. *Actes du Ier Congrès international d'ètudes arabes chrétiennes (Goslar, septembre 1980)*, coll. Orientalia Christiana Analecta, 118, Rome, 1982, pp. 207–21.

Tartar, G., *Dialogue islamo-chrétien sous le calife al-Ma'mūn. Les épîtres d'al-Hāshimī et d'al-Kindī*, Paris, 1985.

Taylor, D.G.K. 'The Disputation between a Muslim and a Monk of Bēt Ḥālē: Syriac Text and Annotated English Translation', in S.H. Griffith and S. Grebenstein, eds, *Christsein in der islamischen Welt: Festschrift für Martin Tamcke zum 60. Geburtstag*, Wiesbaden, 2015, pp. 187–242.

Ibn Taymiyyah, Taqī al-Dīn Aḥmad, *Al-jawāb al-ṣaḥīḥ liman baddala dīn al-masīḥ*, ed., M. Ismā'īl, 2 vols, Cairo, 2003.

al-Tha'labī, *al-kashf wa al-bayyan 'an tafsīr al-Qur'ān*, (online version ar.islamway.net/book/16994/الكشف-والبيان-تفسير-الثعلبي).

al-Tha'labī, *Qiṣaṣ al-anbiyā' al-musammā 'arā'is al-majālis*, Beirut, 2000.

Theodor, J. and C. Albeck, eds, *Midrasch Bereschit Rabbah*, Berlin, 1936.

Thomas, D., 'The Bible in early Muslim anti-Christian polemic', *Islam and Christian-Muslim Relations* 7, 1996, pp. 29–38.

Thomas, D., 'Paul of Antioch's *Letter to a Muslim friend* and *The letter from Cyprus*', in D. Thomas, ed., *Syrian Christians under Islam, the first thousand years*, Leiden, 2001, pp. 203–21.

Thomas, D., 'The Bible and the *kalām*', in *The Bible in Arab Christianity*, ed., D. Thomas, Leiden, 2007, pp. 176–91.

Thomas, D., *Christian doctrines in Islamic theology*, Leiden, 2008.

Thomas, D., 'Dalā'il al-nubuwwa', *Christian-Muslim relations. A bibliographical history*, ed., D. Thomas, Brill Online, 2013.

Thomas, D., 'Shifā' al-ghalīl fī bayān mā waqa'a fī l-Tawrāt wa-l-Injīl min al-tabdīl', *Christian-Muslim relations. A bibliographical history*, ed., D. Thomas, Brill Online, 2013.

Tien, A., *The apology of El-Kindi. A work of the ninth century, written in defence of Christianity by an Arab*, London, 1880, repr. London 1885; Cairo, 1895; Cairo, 1912; Damascus, 2005.

Tien, A., ed., *Risālat 'Abd Allah ibn Ismā'īl al-Hashimī ilā 'Abd al-Masīḥ ibn Isḥāq al-Kindī yad'ūhu bi-hā ilā al-Islām, wa-risālat 'Abd al-Masīḥ ilā al-Hashimī yaruddu bi-hā 'alayhi wa-yad'ūhu ilā al-Nasrānīya*, London, 1885, reprint, 1912.

Timm, S., *Das christlich-koptische Ägypten in arabischer Zeit*, Wiesbaden, 1991.

Tov, E., *Textual criticism of the Hebrew Bible*, Assen, 1992.

Tränkle, H., ed., *Tertulliani Aduersus Iudaeos*, Wiesbaden, 1964.

VanderKam, J.C., ed., and trans., *The Book of Jubilees*, CSCO 510–511, Louvain, 1989.

Van Rompay, L., ed., and trans., *Le Commentaire sur Genèse-Exode 9,32 du manuscrit (olim) Diyarbakir 22*, CSCO 483–484, Louvain, 1986.

al-Wāḥidī, *Asbāb al-nuzūl*, Beirut, 2006.

Wansbrough, J., *Quranic studies: Sources and methods of scriptural interpretation*, Oxford, 1977.

Wansbrough, J., *The Sectarian milieu: Content and composition of Islamic salvation history*, Oxford, 1978.

Wasserstrom, S., *Between Muslim and Jew: the problem of symbiosis under early Islam*, Princeton, 1995.

Watt, W.M., 'The early development of the Muslim attitude to the Bible', *Transactions of the Glasgow University Oriental Society* 16, 1955–6, pp. 50–62.

Watt, W.M., 'The dating of the Qur'ān: a review of Richard Bell's theories', *Journal of the Royal Asiatic Society* 89, 1957, pp. 46–56.

Watt, W.M., *Bell's Introduction to the Quran, completely revised and enlarged by W. Montgomery Watt*, Edinburgh, 1970.

Watt, W.M., *Muslim-Christian encounters: Perceptions and misperceptions*, London, 1991.

Wensinck, A.J., 'qunūt', *Encyclopaedia of Islam* 5, Leiden, 1986, p. 395.

Wensinck, A.J., 'witr', *Encyclopaedia of Islam* 11, Leiden, 2002, p. 213.

Werthmuller, K.J., *Coptic identity and Ayyubid politics in Egypt, 1218–1250*, Cairo, 2010.

Whittingham, M., 'The value of *taḥrīf maʿnawī* (corrupt interpretation) as a category for analysing Muslim views of the Bible: evidence from *Al-radd al-jamīl* and Ibn Khaldūn', *Islam and Christian–Muslim Relations* 22, 2011, pp. 209–22.

Whybray, R.N., 'Genesis', in J. Barton and J. Muddiman, eds, *The Oxford Bible Commentary*, Oxford, 2007, pp. 52–53.

Wilde, C., *Approaches to the Qur'ān in early Christian Arabic texts*, Palo Alto, 2014.

De Young, J.B., 'The meaning of "nature" in Romans 1 and its implications for biblical proscriptions of homosexual behavior', *Journal of the Evangelical Theological Society* 31, 1988, pp. 429–441.

Zammit, M.R., *A comparative lexical study of Qur'ānic Arabic*, Leiden, 2002.

Zebiri, K., *Muslims and Christians Face to Face*, Oxford, 1997.

Index

Aaron 163
ʿAbd al-Jabbār al-Hamadhānī 152–153, 160–172
ʿAbd al-Malik, caliph 144
Abraham 18, 20, 27–28, 32, 40, 45, 62, 91, 96, 102, 106, 150, 164
Abū ʿAbdallāh al-Baṣrī 161
Abū Bakr al-Ṣiddīq, caliph 59–60, 71–72, 79, 115, 189
Abū al-Hudhayl al-ʿAllāf 90–91, 136
Abū Mūsā al-Ashʿarī 74
Abū Nūḥ al-Anbārī 9
Abū Qurra, Theodore 2–3, 98, 116, 168, 181n, 183
Abū Rāʾiṭa, Ḥabīb ibn Khidma 52–54, 98–99, 168
Acts of the Apostles 150n, 162, 164, 170–171
Adam 62, 97, 108
Afterlife 103–105
ʿĀʾisha 79
ʿAlī ibn Abī Ṭālib, caliph 59–61, 71–74, 79, 81, 155, 182, 190
ʿAmmār al-Baṣrī 5, 83–105, 135–137, 168
ʿAmr ibn al-ʿĀṣ 111
Angels 17, 20n, 27n, 29, 40–41, 45n, 96, 104–105, 144, 152, 192
ʿAnastasios of Sinai 1
al-Anṭākī, Yaḥyā ibn Saʿīd 177
Antichrist 40, 133
Apology of al-Kindī 2, 50, 52–76, 78–82, 119n, 130, 181
Apology of Timothy I 116, 134–135, 143, 182–183
al-ʿAskarī, al-Ḥasan ibn Rashīq 179, 191
al-Ashʿarī, Abū al-Ḥasan 136n, 151n, 168
Aquinas 66
ʿAṭāʾ ibn Yasār 110–111, 113, 115
al-ʿAzīz, Abū Manṣūr Nizār, caliph 177
Baḥīrā, Serguis 14–18, 56, 58–59, 64, 68n, 70, 139, 166, 182, 188
al-Bāqillānī, Abū Bakr Muḥammad ibn al-Ṭayyib 11, 151
al-Bayḍāwī 36n
al-Biqāʿī, Burhān al-Dīn 115, 129
Book of conquest and apostasy 154–159
Book of Jubilees 21, 32n, 38–39n
Book of the Proof concerning the Course of the Divine Economy 83–87, 89–91, 93–98, 100–104, 136
Book of Questions and Answers 83, 88–91

Clarity in Truth 175, 177–179, 184–195
Confirmation of the Proofs of Prophethood 162–167
Constantine, emperor 162, 165
Contra Gentiles 66
Copts, Coptic 174–176, 178–179, 193, 195
Corruption of the Bible 17, 54, 64, 83, 87–90, 103–104, 106–107, 113, 116–127, 129–130, 150–152, 154, 162, 166–169, 172, 183, 187, 190, 193
Corruption of the Qurʾan 54, 56–64, 71, 77, 79, 81–82, 90, 104, 127, 138–139, 143–144, 147–148, 175, 180–191, 193
Cribratio Alcorani 51
Cross 17, 83, 88, 98–102, 105, 164–166, 178

al-Damirī 153n, 159–160
al-Damrāwī, Michael 176, 178–179
David 86, 163
Debate of Abū Qurra with Muslim mutakallimūn at the court of al-Maʾmūn 183–184
Deuteronomy 57, 115–116, 126–127
al-Dimashqī, Muḥammad ibn Abī Ṭālib 13, 138n, 154, 168n
Disputation of the Monk Abraham of Tiberias in Jerusalem 10
Disputation between a Muslim and a Monk of Bēt Ḥālē 1, 143–144, 181
al-Dulābī, Abū Bishr 191
al-Ḍurrāb, al-Ḥasan ibn Ismāʿīl 179

East Syrian 94, 105, 151n, 170n, 182
Elias of Nisibis 10
Ephrem the Syrian 144
Eutychius of Alexandria 32
Eve 96–97
Exodus 45n, 57, 185

al-Faq'asī, Yazīd 156
al-Fārisī, Salmān 166

Genesis 18n, 20–21, 25, 27–30, 32–33, 35–39, 41–43, 45–46n, 118, 126–127, 140, 185
al-Ghazālī, Abū Ḥāmid 194
God the Father 16, 18, 83, 89, 93, 95, 105, 134
Gospel 3, 6–7, 17, 57, 69, 87–88, 90, 103, 106–110, 112–113, 115–120, 128, 144, 146, 148, 150–151, 159, 163–164, 166, 169, 182–185, 187, 190
Gospel of John 103, 115, 117, 122, 164, 166, 185
Gospel of Luke 85, 103, 144, 164, 166, 171
Gospel of Mark 164, 166
Gospel of Matthew 57, 85, 89, 103, 117, 157n, 164, 166, 185
Gospel of Barnabas 150n

Ḥadīth 71–73, 78–79, 129, 155n, 162, 168n, 179
Ḥafṣa 75, 77, 190
Hagar 102
al-Ḥākim, Abū ʿAlī Manṣūr, caliph 174–175, 177–179
al-Hāshimī, ʿAbd Allāh ibn Ismāʿīl 55, 57–58, 63, 66, 69
Heraclius, emperor 131–132
Holy Spirit 7–8, 16, 18, 59, 83, 89, 91–94, 105, 133–135, 140, 143–144, 146, 157n, 183

Ibn al-ʿAbbās, ʿAbd 74, 76, 79, 123n, 156, 191
Ibn Abī Dāwūd al-Sijistānī 71–73, 76, 81–82
Ibn ʿAdī, Yaḥyā 168
Ibn al-ʿĀṣ, Saʿīd 75–76, 113
Ibn al-ʿAssāl, al-Mu'taman Abū Isḥāq Ibrāhīm 194
Ibn Diʿāmah, Qatādah 11
Ibn Ḥanbal, Aḥmad 60n, 73
Ibn Ḥazm, Abū Muḥammad ʿAlī 117, 120, 123–124, 129, 150, 152, 169, 170n
Ibn Hishām, ʿAbd al-Raḥmān Ibn al-Ḥārith 75, 139
Ibn Isḥāq, Abū ʿAbdallāh 70, 78, 114, 122, 139, 142
Ibn Isḥāq, Ḥunayn 167
Ibn Jabr, Mujāhid 11
Ibn al-Jawzī, Abū al-Faraj 153n–154
Ibn Kaʿb, Ubayy 73, 77, 80
Ibn Kammūna 119, 128
Ibn Kathīr, Ismāʿīl ibn ʿUmar 29–30n, 36n, 41, 45n, 60n, 114–115, 120, 123n
Ibn Khaldun, ʿAbd al-Raḥmān 152n, 183n
Ibn al-Layth, Abū al-Rabīʿ Muḥammad 125
Ibn Masʿūd, ʿAbdallāh 60–61, 73–74, 78, 81, 182, 188, 190
Ibn al-Munabbih, Wahb 70
Ibn al-Muqaffaʿ, Severus 178–179
Ibn Muṭarrif al-Ṭarafī 30n, 40n–41, 45n
Ibn al-Nadīm, Abū al-Faraj 80
Ibn Qayyim al-Jawziyya 107n, 124n, 126–127, 129
Ibn Kullāb, ʿAbdallāh 136
Ibn Qutayba, Abū Muḥammad 117
Ibn Rajā', Būluṣ 174–180, 182, 184–195
Ibn Sabaʿ, ʿAbdallāh 155n, 158
Ibn Saʿd 70, 111n, 166n
Ibn Saʿīd, Qutayba 191
Ibn Sallām, ʿAbdallāh 70, 72, 188
Ibn Taymiyya, Taqī al-Dīn Aḥmad 13, 154
Ibn al-Ṭayyib, Abū al-Khayr 27n, 38–39, 45–46n
Ibn ʿUrwa, Hishām 191
Ibn al-Wāsiṭī, Ghāzī 194
Ibn al-Yamān, Hudhayfa 75
Ibn Yūsuf, al-Ḥallāj 71, 81
Ibn al-Zubayr, ʿAbdallāh 75
Ibn al-Zubayr, ʿUrwa 191
Ignatius 38n
Incarnation 7–8, 52, 54n, 83, 92n, 94–95, 98, 105, 135, 146
Irenaeus 29n
Isaac 150
Isaiah 93, 111, 116–117, 122, 125, 185
al-Isfarā'īni 159n–160
Ishmael 150
Ishmaelites 1, 18, 91, 101, 132–133
Ishoʿdad of Merv 45n
Ismā'īlī 179

Jacob 150
Jacobite 54, 99, 157n–158, 160
al-Jāḥiẓ, Abū ʿUthmān 162n, 171n
the Jalālayn 123n
Jesus 6, 17–18, 40–41, 55, 57–58, 67, 83, 85, 86–89, 91, 93–94, 98–99, 101–104, 106–107, 116, 125, 130, 132, 139, 141–143, 150, 144, 146, 148, 151–154, 156–160,

162–163, 165–166, 168–169, 171–172, 187
Job 93
John of Damascus 1–2, 91–92, 101–102, 105, 132–135, 138–139, 143, 148, 181–182
John the Baptist 101, 105
Josephus 27n, 41n, 45–46
Joshua 58
Jews, Judaism 4, 15, 17, 19, 27n, 32, 40n–42n, 45–46, 48–49, 54, 59, 62, 64–65, 67, 69–70, 72, 85–88, 100, 107n–108, 112–115, 117–129, 146, 150, 153, 155–156, 158–161, 163, 165, 168–172, 182, 187–188, 193n
Justin Martyr 29n, 38n
al-Juwaynī, Abū al-Maʿālī 118, 124, 129, 169n

Kaʿb al-Aḥbār 15, 70, 72, 111, 113–114, 182
al-Kalbī 159
Khadīja 156n
al-Kindī, ʿAbd al-Masīḥ 52–63, 65–66, 68–69, 71–75, 79–82, 148, 181
al-Kisāʾī 30n, 39n, 45n–46n
Kitāb al-majālis 10
Kitāb al-Maṣāḥif 71–72
Kitāb al-ṭabaqāt al-kabīr 70

Leo III, emperor 107n, 116
Lot 20–21, 29, 32, 35, 43–44, 47

al-Mahdī, caliph 94–95, 100, 116, 134–135, 143, 182
Maimonides, Moses 107n, 118–119, 127
al-Maʾmūn, caliph 54, 63, 66–67, 181n, 183
al-Maqdisī 117, 126, 129
Marwān ibn al-Ḥakam, caliph 189–190
Mary 6, 8, 91, 95, 142, 144, 146, 152, 159
al-Maturidī, Abū Manṣūr 151
al-Māwardī 118
Melkite 8n–9n, 11, 144, 154n, 157n–158, 160, 177
Messiah 6, 17, 41, 83, 85, 88, 91, 99, 116, 163
Monotheism 10–11, 136, 144, 153, 158, 160, 168
Moses 57–58, 67, 85, 106, 108, 110, 113, 146, 150, 163, 187
Muḥammad 2, 4, 11, 15–18, 24n–25, 29, 47, 54–62, 64–71, 78, 80–81, 84–85, 89, 101, 104, 106–129, 132–133, 138–139, 143–145, 147–148, 150, 155, 158, 162–163, 166n, 168–170, 172, 179, 181–183, 185–186, 188, 190–192
al-Muʿtaṣīm, caliph 86
al-Mutawakkil, caliph 193n
Muqātil ibn Sulaymān 109–110, 114, 123
Muʿtazili 67, 90, 136–137, 161, 168

al-Nasāʾī, Abū ʿAbd al-Raḥmān al-Shaybānī 191
al-Naysabūrī, Abū al-ʿAbbās Aḥmad 179
Nestorian 9, 38, 45, 58, 94, 134–135, 157n–158
Nicholas of Cusa 51
Noah 106

On the Triune Nature of God 5, 7–8, 92, 140–142, 183
Origen 45n

Paul, apostle 103, 150–151, 153–173, 177
Paul's letter to the Colossians 172
Paul's first letter to the Corinthians 170, 172
Paul's second letter to the Corinthians 161, 171
Paul's letter to the Ephesians 171
Paul's letter to the Galatians 171
Paul's letter to the Philippians 161
Paul's letter to the Romans 32n, 103, 170, 172
Paul's first letter to Timothy 171
Paul of Antioch 11–14, 144–148, 154n
Paul of Samosata 153n
Peter, apostle 165n
Peter the Venerable 51
Polytheism 4, 11, 17, 102–103
Prophet/s 55, 57, 61, 63, 65–68, 70, 71–73, 78–79, 84–86, 100–101, 107, 112–120, 122–123, 125–126, 132–133, 138–139, 143, 145, 147–148, 150–151, 155, 158, 162–163, 165, 168–170, 172, 182–183, 185, 188, 191
Proud Answers to Impudent Questions 12
Psalms 6–7, 86, 93, 106, 117, 150, 185

al-Qarafī, Aḥmad ibn Idrīs 12, 126, 153n–154, 156
al-Qāsim ibn Ibrāhīm 99, 152
Al-Qirqisānī 119, 127, 170
al-Qurtubī, Muḥammad ibn Aḥmad 60n, 113–114, 123n, 154

al-radd al-jamil 152n, 183n, 194
al-Rāzī, Fakhr al-Dīn 111, 128
Resurrection 83, 97–98
Risāla on the Holy Trinity 52–54n
Risāla on the Incarnation 53–54n, 99
Robert of Ketton 51

Saʿadyah 38–39, 45n
Ṣaḥīḥ Bukhārī 60n, 71n–75, 77, 82, 111n, 113, 115, 167n
Ṣaḥīḥ Muslim 60n
Salman the Persian 188
Samson 86
Sarah 27
Satan 55, 57–58, 96–97, 102, 185
Sayf ibn ʿUmar al-Tamīmī 153–159, 161, 165–166, 168
Sīra nabawiyya 70, 78
Solomon 86
Son of God 8, 16, 18, 83, 89, 91, 93–95, 98, 100–101, 105, 133–134, 141–142, 146, 157, 159–160
al-Suyūṭī, Jalāl al-Dīn 78
Syrian Orthodox 54, 99

al-Ṭabarī, ʿAlī ibn Rabban 117, 125, 151, 193n
al-Ṭabarī, Abū Jaʿfar Muḥammad 11, 30n, 36n, 45n, 71, 79, 82, 109–111, 113, 115, 123n, 152, 155, 171n
Talmud 32n, 40, 170
Tertullian 39
al-Thaʿlabī, Abū Isḥāq Aḥmad ibn Muḥammad ibn Ibrāhīm 30n, 36, 38, 41, 45n, 159–161, 165, 170
Timothy I, patriarch 94–95, 100, 105, 116, 134–135, 143, 168, 182
Toldoth Jeshu 161, 170
Torah 3, 6–7, 57–59, 69, 85–86, 106–110, 112–120, 123, 125–126, 128, 150, 156, 158, 182, 184–185, 187, 190
Trinity 7, 18, 52–55, 67, 83, 90, 92–94, 105, 134–137, 140, 142–144, 146, 153n–154, 157, 159, 162–163, 168–169
al-Ṭūfī, Najm al-Dīn 194–195

ʿUmar ibn al-Khaṭṭāb, caliph 72, 78, 115, 189
ʿUmar II, caliph 107n, 116
Unity of God 10, 55, 67, 83, 90–91, 93–94, 135–136, 142, 151–154, 158, 160, 168–170, 172
ʿUthmān ibn ʿAffān, caliph 60–61, 71, 73–77, 80, 155, 189–190

al-Wāḥidī 123
Waraqaʿ ibn Nawfal 166

al-Yaʿqūbī, Abū al-Abbās Aḥmad 150n–151n

al-Zamakhsharī 123n
Zayd ibn Thābit 72, 74–77, 188–190
Zephaniah 118